Can psychoanalysis ever be part of modern university curricula in ways other academic disciplines take for granted? According to Max Cavitch, psychoanalysis is inseparable from all university activities, even when not recognized as a distinct discipline. Neither activity, psychoanalysis nor higher education, is merely about transmitting facts; both rely upon the power of relationships to impart knowledge to students and teachers alike. So what, to paraphrase D. W. Winnicott, might a "pedagogical holding environment" look like? After presenting a detailed history of psychoanalytic pedagogy since Freud, *Psychoanalysis and the University* offers educators and psychoanalytically-oriented clinicians some thoughtful suggestions to answer that question.

Jack Drescher, *M.D., training and supervising analyst, William Alanson White Institute*

Must we now have a psychoanalysis "in ruins" for a university "in ruins"? Max Cavitch makes a compelling argument that now is the moment to rethink what has long been a conflict about where and who should be involved in the training of psychoanalysts and how such training can begin to reshape the very notion of an academic pedagogy within professional as well as liberal arts settings. The right book for the right moment.

Sander L. Gilman, *distinguished professor emeritus of the Liberal Arts and Sciences and professor of psychiatry emeritus, Emory University*

Max Cavitch is the champion psychoanalysis needs to break down barriers between psychoanalytic institutes and the university. Critiquing the utilitarian trend of knowledge acquisition in the contemporary neoliberal university, Cavitch argues that the university's disavowal of the unconscious is one clear key to its impoverished state. His psychoanalytic sensibility widens our very understandings of what knowledge is and what it is for. Cavitch makes a compelling case for how, in his words, teaching *with* rather than *about* psychoanalysis can powerfully transform any classroom, no matter the discipline.

Lynne Layton, *pychoanalyst; assistant clinical professor of psychology, Harvard Medical School; author of* Toward a Social Psychoanalysis: Culture, Character, and Normative Unconscious Processes

This book will be essential for anyone invested in the histories and futures of both education and psychoanalysis (which, to my mind, should be all of us). Fluidly weaving historical and contemporary sources on the complex, fraught, and fertile relationship between psychoanalysis and teaching, Cavitch's account not only provides a lucid overview of the inter-implication of the two fields, but also offers an intervention on current thinking about the production and uses of knowledge. As the twenty-first century university finds itself in crisis; as new generations of students work to change our cultural relationship to questions of authority, identity, responsibility, and truth; and as psychoanalysis has reemerged on the contemporary scene in conversation with these shifts, this book should serve as an orienting point as we re-think what it means to learn how to live.

Emma Lieber, *psychoanalyst; part-time assistant professor of literary studies,*
Eugene Lang College, The New School; author of The Writing
Cure *and editor of* The Queerness of Childhood: Essays
from the Other Side of the Looking Glass

In an era when psychoanalysis has been systematically devalued, Max Cavitch's book comes as a revelation: that psychoanalysis is a tool not only for understanding the inner lives of individual subjects, but also for understanding our relationship to the outside world and its nuances. Within universities, psychoanalysis has been attacked as too obscure usefully to inform teaching, criticism, humanism. Yet this apparent uselessness is the very point: that insight has inherent value even when it does not have implications, and that in losing track of that notion, we lose track of education itself. Written from the standpoint of profound knowledge, deep experience, and meticulous research, this book stands as a persuasive defense of psychoanalysis in pedagogy, and establishes that the stripping away of psychoanalytic principles from university curricula has been a regressive step reflective of our yearning for simplicity in the face of an ever more complex reality. Cavitch ultimately proves that this represents not an escalation into clarity, but a descent into sophistry and chaos, a failure of education to understand or prepare students for the intricate convolutions of the world they constitute or the one they will inhabit.

Andrew Solomon, *professor of clinical psychology, Columbia University*
Medical Center; lecturer in psychiatry, Yale School of Medicine;
author of Far from the Tree: Parents, Children, and the Search for
Identity *and* The Noonday Demon: An Atlas of Depression

In its early years, psychoanalysis benefited from being excluded from a restrictive and conservative university culture. Today, the university has become open to many forms of thought, but at the same time it is in a crisis of its own. Max Cavitch brings these two histories together, with unexpected and illuminating consequences.

Eli Zaretsky, *professor of history, New School for Social Research, author of*
Secrets of the Soul: A Social and Cultural history of Psychoanalysis

Psychoanalysis and the University

This book charts the past and present vicissitudes of psychoanalysis's relation to education and emphasizes the necessity of its increased presence in university settings.

Why can fewer and fewer people afford either time-intensive psychoanalytic psychotherapy or a three- to four-year college education? Why have psychoanalytic teaching and research become so marginalized? Where and how does psychoanalysis retain a foothold in academia? In an era when the futures of both psychoanalysis and higher education seem evermore uncertain, *Psychoanalysis and the University* argues for the need to overcome existing precarities and mutual resistances and suggests ways in which their prospects for survival could be reciprocally enhanced. Each chapter surveys and interprets present conditions, while arguing the necessity of supporting and expanding psychoanalytic teaching and research at both the undergraduate and graduate levels

Drawing on Cavitch's deep understanding of both psychoanalysis and university settings, this is essential reading for psychoanalysts, university teachers and administrators, and all students interested in how augmented psychoanalytic education could enhance their understanding of the world.

Max Cavitch is Associate Professor of English and Co-director of Psychoanalytic Studies at the University of Pennsylvania, where he also edits the APsA-award-winning blog, *Psyche on Campus*. His books include *American Elegy: The Poetry of Mourning from the Puritans to Whitman* and the forthcoming *Ashes: A History of Thought and Substance*.

PSYCHOANALYSIS IN A NEW KEY BOOK SERIES

DONNEL STERN

Series Editor

When music is played in a new key, the melody does not change, but the notes that make up the composition do: change in the context of continuity, continuity that perseveres through change. Psychoanalysis in a New Key publishes books that share the aims psychoanalysts have always had, but that approach them differently. The books in the series are not expected to advance any particular theoretical agenda, although to this date most have been written by analysts from the Interpersonal and Relational orientations.

The most important contribution of a psychoanalytic book is the communication of something that nudges the reader's grasp of clinical theory and practice in an unexpected direction. Psychoanalysis in a New Key creates a deliberate focus on innovative and unsettling clinical thinking. Because that kind of thinking is encouraged by exploration of the sometimes surprising contributions to psychoanalysis of ideas and findings from other fields, Psychoanalysis in a New Key particularly encourages interdisciplinary studies. Books in the series have married psychoanalysis with dissociation, trauma theory, sociology, and criminology. The series is open to the consideration of studies examining the relationship between psychoanalysis and any other field—for instance, biology, literary and art criticism, philosophy, systems theory, anthropology, and political theory.

But innovation also takes place within the boundaries of psychoanalysis, and Psychoanalysis in a New Key therefore also presents work that reformulates thought and practice without leaving the precincts of the field. Books in the series focus, for example, on the significance of personal values in psychoanalytic practice, on the complex interrelationship between the analyst's clinical work and personal life, on the consequences for the clinical situation when patient and analyst are from different cultures, and on the need for psychoanalysts to accept the degree to which they knowingly satisfy their own wishes during treatment hours, often to the patient's detriment.

A full list of all titles in this series is available at: https://www.routledge.com/Psychoanalysis-in-a-New-Key-Book-Series/book-series/LEAPNKBS

Psychoanalysis and the University

Resistance and Renewal from
Freud to the Present

Max Cavitch

Routledge
Taylor & Francis Group

LONDON AND NEW YORK

Designed cover image: © "Unwrapping of Oscar Nemon's sculpture
of Sigmund Freud at the campus of the Medical University of Vienna.
Stephan Doering, chair of the Department of Psychoanalysis and
Psychotherapy, carefully removes the protective sheet. Freud's sculpture
returned to his former workplace exactly 80 years after he was forced to
leave the country in 1938."

First published 2025
by Routledge
4 Park Square, Milton Park, Abingdon, Oxon OX14 4RN

and by Routledge
605 Third Avenue, New York, NY 10158

Routledge is an imprint of the Taylor & Francis Group, an informa business

© 2025 Max Cavitch

British Library Cataloguing-in-Publication Data
A catalogue record for this book is available from the British Library

ISBN: 978-1-032-88971-9 (hbk)
ISBN: 978-1-032-88969-6 (pbk)
ISBN: 978-1-003-54058-8 (ebk)

DOI: 10.4324/9781003540588

Typeset in Times New Roman
by KnowledgeWorks Global Ltd.

**For Maggie Robbins
and in memory of Philip Bromberg,
analysts and teachers**

Table of Contents

Acknowledgments

Thanks, first and foremost, to my friends and colleagues in the University of Pennsylvania's Psychoanalytic Studies program, especially my fellow program co-directors Dr. Lawrence Blum and Professor Greg Urban, administrative coordinator Nancy Ameen, and my clinician co-teachers: Dr. Susan Adelman, Dr. David Lopez, and Dr. Mark Moore of Philadelphia and Dr. Maggie Robbins of New York. For well over a decade, it has also been my privilege to collaborate with and learn from other devoted members of our program's steering committee: Dr. Jane Abrams, Professor Warren Breckman, Professor David Eng, Dr. Patricia Gherovici, Professor Jean-Michel Rabaté, Dr. Kathleen Ross, Dr. Barbara Shapiro, Professor Stephen Steinberg, Dr. Richard Summers, and Professor Liliane Weissberg.

I've learned much by sharing thoughts concerning psychoanalysis and education with a number of extraordinary scholars and clinicians: Eyal Amiran, Gila Ashtor, Lauren Berlant, Jeffrey Berman, Philip Bromberg, Brian Connolly, Ian Curtis, Nina Cornyetz, Dennis Debiak, Marcia Dobson, Todd Dufresne, Stephen Frosh, Kelli Fuery, Nathan Gorelick, Dagmar Herzog, Carolyn Laubender, Emma Lieber, Deborah Luepnitz, Elizabeth Lunbeck, Elissa Marder, Lisa Mendelman, Brendon Nicholls, Leonardo Niro, Ann Pellegrini, Francois Rabie, Nicholas Ray, Lisa Ruddick, Vanessa Rumble, Avgi Saketopoulou, Murray Schwartz, Joan Wallach Scott, Yael Segalovitz, Jordan Stein, Neil Stillings, Adele Tutter, Antonio Viego, Marita Vyrgioti, and Tina Zwarg.

And, because our students are often our best teachers, I'd particularly like to thank Arvind Mohan, Liesl Dentlinger, Phoenix Garcia-Ramos, Yohanna Ragins, Imani Rhodriquez, and Yu Yan for their curiosity and insight.

For their astute comments on various parts of the manuscript, sincere thanks to Larry Blum, Carter J. Carter, Emma Lieber, Jean-Michel Rabaté, and Nicholas Stock. In addition to the gift of his own extraordinary books and essays, Donnel Stern's steadfast support of my work has been a blessing over the years, and I'm deeply grateful to him for including *Psychoanalysis and the University* in his "Psychoanalysis in a New Key" series. For their encouragement and guidance through the publication process, my heartfelt thanks as well to Aakriti Aggarwal, Aner Govrin, Kate Hawes, Abhishek Singh, and their other colleagues at Routledge.

Note on Citations

Full citations for all works mentioned in this book appear in the Bibliography. Author-date references to these editions are noted parenthetically within the text. Translations, unless otherwise indicated, are my own.

Introduction

Paths of Resistance and Renewal

> To speak of psychoanalysis at the university … means one has decided that
> the university is also a place of discovery, and not only of mere routine.
> —JEAN LAPLANCHE, *Problématiques V* (1987)

The relation between psychoanalysis and the university has always been one
of resistance and renewal. Shifting views (medical, intellectual, popular) of
psychoanalysis have been closely, if often indirectly, linked to the changing curricular and institutional priorities of higher education. At the same
time, conflicting perspectives on the purpose and value of higher education
have frequently, though often unconsciously, been influenced by transformations in psychoanalytic thought, training, and practice. Psychoanalysis
is both *of* and *not of* the university, depending on when and where you
look and on what you want to know—as well as on what the conditions of
knowing are in your particular part of the world, a world of shifting psychoanalytic centers and peripheries.[1] In turn, as an institution still largely
medieval in conception but functioning more and more like a transnational
corporation, the university both needs and mistrusts psychoanalysis as a
singularly "undisciplined" field of knowledge.

Indeed, it's the hazy and contingent ideal of the pursuit of knowledge
that cleaves psychoanalysis to the university while at the same time cleav-
ing them asunder. In the US, as in many other countries, the university has
long been both conservator and producer of knowledge, as well as a space
reserved for the active transmission of knowledge between teachers and
students. Yet, within the past century or so, psychoanalysis has altered the
very meaning of knowledge—that is, knowledge as what we know and how
we think we know it. After Sigmund Freud's death in 1939, W. H. Auden
said that he was "no more a person/now but a whole climate of opinion/
under whom we conduct our different lives" (1991, 275). The climate for

DOI: 10.4324/9781003540588-1

psychoanalysis is less promising now than it was in Auden's day. There is widespread disenchantment with Freud's ideas, and many psychoanalysts themselves have grown disillusioned by their own calling. For example, in her article "On Teaching Psychoanalysis in Antianalytic Times," psychoanalyst Nancy McWilliams laments that "irrespective of how much we continue to learn about human psychology and effective psychotherapy, the era in which analysis offered an exciting new way to think about the human condition is over" (2000, 375). Nevertheless, it's still very hard to imagine a world "where our 'inner lives' would not be inhabited by the 'dramas' and 'hidden meanings' that still carry [Freud's] name: the unconscious, the Oedipus complex, the ego, and the superego" (Winter 1999, 1). Whatever specific psychoanalytic knowledge particular individuals or cultural groups might possess, most of the world now lives and learns in a fundamentally Freudian epistemic era, or *episteme*.[2]

Living in a particular episteme means being governed by a certain set of rules, beyond grammar and logic, that operate outside our conscious awareness, defining the range of conceptual frameworks that determine what's possible to think in a given place and time. With the advent of the Freudian episteme, the pursuit of knowledge changed radically, for, as *subjects* of knowledge (as individual subjects who learn and know), our experience of *ourselves* has changed. Any lingering, pre-Freudian, rationalist sense of being a sovereign subject of determinate and stable knowledge will continue to give way to a sense of what psychoanalyst Adam Phillips calls "a radical and formative insufficiency, something that cannot be solved by knowledge." In other words, for the post-Freudian world, being a subject in pursuit of knowledge means searching for "good ways of bearing our incompleteness" (1996, 7), including the undertaking of a wholly new kind of education—Freud sometimes used the word "after-education [*Nacherziehung*]" (1963, 451)—called psychoanalysis.[3]

In this new kind of education, the "student" is urged, especially at first, to suspend reason and judgment. In their "teacher," such a student finds a mentor or guide whose role is not to transmit knowledge but rather to facilitate "the reliving through language of that which is known but not yet thought" (Bollas 1987, 4). Not assimilation, but free association. Not memorization but de-repression. Not interpreting the work of others, but working through one's own resistances to interpretation. Not critical thinking, but uncritical attention. Not a disinterested "profession" of knowledge, but an empathetic receptivity to "unformulated experience"—to the coming-to-mind of hitherto repressed or dissociated thoughts and feelings (Stern 2003, 36–39).

Psychoanalysis is thus a kind of pedagogy. However, its techniques and goals are antithetical to those of conventional university classrooms where groups of students (rather than normative "individuals") gather for expert instruction in the accumulated knowledge and methodological procedures of particular disciplines. These disciplines, whether traditional (e.g., biology, history, philosophy) or emergent (e.g., artificial intelligence, disability studies, environmental humanities), constitute and compartmentalize different "kinds" of knowledge for their more efficient transmission. Disciplines canalize their students' (and teachers') attention in order to concentrate knowledge, cultivate expertise, and socialize practice. "Education" is itself a separate discipline at most contemporary universities. Ironically perhaps, completing a postgraduate degree in education (if not in psychology, medicine, or social work) is a common precursor to psychoanalytic training. Yet psychoanalytic training is only very rarely offered by universities (see Chapter 5). Instead, various types of candidates enroll in independent psychoanalytic training institutes, which are affiliated not with universities but with professional organizations such as the American Psychoanalytic Association (APsA) and the International Psychoanalytic Association (IPA). Analytic candidates take university-*style* courses together, but the most important elements of their education are (as they've always been) their personal training analysis and their intensively supervised clinical work with patients.

Psychoanalysis, therefore, both *is* a kind of pedagogy and also *has* a distinct pedagogy of its own. Why, then, is such a pedagogically oriented discipline so conspicuously missing from most university campuses? Why do systems of higher education make "the teaching of psychoanalysis itself such a problematic issue" (Phillips 2004, 790)? Have things always been this way? Must they continue to be so? And what might the historically problematic relation between psychoanalysis and the university have to do with the fact that, for the past several decades, both have seemed to share a state of perpetual crisis? Fewer and fewer Americans can afford to pay either for time-intensive psychoanalytic psychotherapy or for a four-year college education. The ranks of the professoriate continue to be thinned by attrition and adjunctification, while the number of psychoanalysts dwindles as the profession ages and as the healthcare industrial complex forces patients into cheaper, short-term treatment modalities like cognitive behavioral therapy and psychotropic medication. Professionals in both fields have lost prestige and income, even as their work-loads have grown impossibly heavy. University departments of psychiatry and especially psychology have, for the most part, become overtly hostile to psychoanalysis, and almost all psychoanalytic training institutes continue to shy away from alliances with universities.[4]

The precariousness of both psychoanalysis and the university makes this an auspicious moment for overcoming mutual resistances. Indeed, one aim of this book is to suggest ways in which their respective prospects for survival could be reciprocally enhanced. For example, only a small number of psychoanalytic training institutes are part of (or even affiliated with) universities. Yet since the turn of the present century, declining numbers of both candidates for psychoanalytic training and patients seeking psychoanalytic treatment have prompted some vocal and persuasive calls from the psychoanalytic community for more institutes to forge ties with universities—to enrich training programs, to augment interdisciplinary research opportunities, and to expand and enliven interest in the field among more and younger students. Recently, psychoanalyst and philosophy professor Jonathan Lear concluded, from his long career in both realms, "that teaching psychoanalysis can play a crucial role in keeping psychoanalysis alive" (2005, 13). Just as crucially, however, the psychoanalytic profession needs to find better ways of taking advantage of student interest. Lear writes that both undergraduate and graduate philosophy students regularly ask him about becoming psychoanalysts, and that they're discouraged when he tells them that most clinical M.D. and Ph.D. programs disincentivize interest in psychoanalysis (2005, 17). But these students no longer need a clinical degree to train at a psychoanalytic institute. In New York and several other states, a growing number of institutes offer intensive Licensure Qualifying Programs for people without clinical degrees who want to become analytic candidates. That is, one can earn an advanced non-clinical degree in a field like philosophy—and even spend many years teaching philosophy at the university level—and then, if so moved, apply directly to one of the growing number of analytic institutes that offer this option. (Indeed, the crisis in academia has prompted many academics to avail themselves of such programs to switch careers.) Licensure Qualifying Programs are an important advance in the field's ongoing effort to open more routes of exchange between the psychoanalytic profession and the world of higher education.

Indeed, many contemporary analysts would like to see university-centered institutes become the rule rather than the exception. Such institutes could, for example, be created as separate schools or divisions within the university, preserving institute-style training cohorts and clinical focus while expanding the scope and reach of psychoanalytic research and teaching through engagement with other schools and divisions. In 2007, Adela Leibovich de Duarte, chair of the IPA's committee on Psychoanalysis and the University, concluded that

> psychoanalysis needs to reposition itself in the University. Regarding the complexity of our subject matter, working at the university on the interface between psychoanalysis and other disciplines facilitates exchange and provides the opportunity for cross-fertilization and for gaining better understanding of the human being .... It is necessary to renew and expand our involvement as psychoanalysts within academic life in order to transmit our theory and technique whose efficacy in alleviating human suffering has been demonstrated by clinical results and systematic research.
>
> (qtd. in Gilman 2009, 1105)

In the same year, the *Journal of the American Psychoanalytic Association* (*JAPA*) published a forum on psychoanalytic education in which Robert Wallerstein, Robert Michaels, and Robert Paul debated the potential advantages and disadvantages of university placement (see Michaels 2007; Paul 2007; Wallerstein 2007a, Wallerstein 2007b; see also, Wallerstein 2009). In a 2011 article in the *International Journal of Psychoanalysis* (the principal journal of the international psychoanalytic community), psychoanalyst and Cornell University psychiatry professor Otto Kernberg wrote about how "the pressing need for psychoanalysis to establish or re-establish a strong relationship with universities and academic centers of higher learning has become broadly acknowledged and accepted by the psychoanalytic community in recent years" (2011, 609). And six years later, in the same journal, South African psychology professors Carol Long, Gillian Eagle, and Garth Stevens noted that, worldwide, "there have been increasing calls for closer alliances between psychoanalysis and the university" in order to "revitalize the discipline" (Long et al. 2017, 518).

Unfortunately, there has been far much less discussion emanating from universities themselves—from professors, researchers, administrators, and students—about how they would benefit from such institutional alliances. Teaching, interdisciplinary innovation, and psychological well-being on campus would all be enhanced if universities were to formally embrace and materially support psychoanalytic research and training. Psychological and intellectual well-being are, of course, inextricably interwoven, and intellectual and pedagogical maladies abound, not least, because of an abiding general failure to recognize the scene of pedagogy as what T. R. Johnson calls "a complex ecology, divided by—and linked to others through—unconscious desire" (2014, 2). It's been over a century since Freud identified teaching and psychoanalysis as two of the "impossible professions," and it's been over forty years since Shoshana Felman (building on the rich history of psychoanalytic thinking about education to be sketched in Chapter 1) reminded us that "it is precisely in giving us unprecedented insight into the impossibility of teaching, that psychoanalysis opened up unprecedented teaching possibilities" (1982, 22). Yet those potentialities remain almost entirely untapped. At the very least, twenty-first-century universities need to recognize their essential role in communicating the importance of psychoanalysis for understanding intrapsychic and psychosocial phenomena beyond as well as within the classroom, just as the field of psychoanalysis needs to reassert its necessity, not only as a mode of treatment but also as the richest theoretical account of our subjectivation and intersubjectivity.

Ψ

To understand how current epistemological, pedagogical, disciplinary, and institutional conditions have emerged, it's necessary to look back at the long, rich history of psychoanalysis and education. Thus the first chapter of *Psychoanalysis and the University* traces the origins and vicissitudes of the relation between psychoanalysis and education at all levels—pre-K to postgrad—from the early years of the twentieth century to its closing decades. Subsequent chapters then chart and interpret the various forms of resistance and renewal that have characterized the most recent decades, especially after the resolution of the landmark 1985 class-action lawsuit that vastly expanded non-physicians' access to accredited psychoanalytic training in the US—a seismic shift with profound consequences for psychoanalytic training, research, practice, and theory throughout the country, including on university campuses.

Other late-twentieth-century developments include the dazzling advances in neuroscience that led to the 1990s being dubbed "The Decade of the Brain" (see, e.g., Jones and Mendell 1999, 739). One salient feature of that decade was the explosion of new, safer, and ostensibly more effective classes of psychotropic medications (chiefly SSRIs and SSNRIs), which had far-reaching social as well as clinical consequences, especially for the millions of people suffering from psychiatric illnesses and their pervasive stigmatization. In intellectual and cultural terms, the 1980s and 1990s also brought to much wider public attention and debate new academic critiques of positivism, rationalism, and empiricism. Reactionaries like Allan Bloom and E. D. Hirsch, Jr., penned bestselling jeremiads on the decline of American education, blaming Freud along with Jean-Jacques Rousseau, John Dewey, and the like for what they saw as Western civilization's long descent into relativism and nihilism, while, under the broad banners of critical theory and postmodernism, many scholars in the qualitative and quantitative sciences, as well as the humanities, ramped up their counter-reactionary challenges to the lingering force of the prior, Kantian episteme and its associated norms, values, and verities.

Major shifts in the theory and practice of psychoanalysis itself have also had important consequences for the relation between psychoanalysis and the university. Beginning in the latter half of the twentieth century, in the US and elsewhere, psychoanalysis underwent a kind of sea-change, moving further and further away from a largely monadic and intrapsychic focus to attend more closely to interpersonal, or relational, dynamics. By the 1980s, the work of many interpersonal and relational psychoanalysts was yielding tremendous insights into the extent and consequences of our minds' mutually informing conscious and unconscious relations. The subjectivities of both analyst and patient, for example, grew more commonly to be regarded as co-participants in an interactional scene of reciprocal recognition (a subject-subject relationship, rather than a subject-object relationship). Increasingly, psychoanalysis was understood and practiced as the co-constitutive interplay of the patient's transference and the analyst's (counter)transference, with an enhanced focus on shared, dialogic efforts to bring the thematic patterns, structures of meaning, and associated affects of unconscious organizing activity into conscious, reflective awareness.

This intersubjective turn has entailed, for many, a substantial shift in thinking—away from what Freud believed to be the motivational primacy of the drives and toward *affectivity*. As Robert Stolorow explains,

> unlike drives, which are claimed to originate deep within the interior of a Cartesian isolated mind, affect—that is, subjective emotional

experience—is something that from birth onward is co-constituted within ongoing relational systems. Emotional experience is inseparable from the intersubjective contexts of attunement and malattunement in which it is felt. Therefore, locating affect at its motivational center automatically entails a radical contextualization of virtually all aspects of human psychological life.

(2013, 385)

Intersubjective psychoanalysis, as theorists like Stolorow readily concede, both draws on and has implications for other disciplines and other theoretical approaches to subject-subject (self-other) relations. Its propositions, according to analyst Jessica Benjamin, "reach across disciplinary barriers and enable non-psychoanalysts to access the social and philosophical implications of intersubjective psychoanalysis," including its implications for "unmasking hidden pathologies of power and domination as well as … processes of social healing and witnessing of collective trauma" (2018, 1–2).

Following the psychoanalytic discourse of intersubjectivity through the twenty-first century, this book will demonstrate how it has not merely augmented but reshaped the ways in which professionals in many fields and disciplines discover, understand, and exchange forms of knowledge—including knowledge of the mutually constitutive affective/emotional states upon which our experiences of discovery, understanding, and communicative exchange are predicated. Feminism and parallel social movements, along with other critical-theoretical interventions, have worked in tandem with psychoanalytic researchers and theorists to overcome the traditional (and still commonly gendered) separation of the "rational" from the "emotional" in intellectual life. This, in turn, has helped to augment and justify the place of affect and affectivity in higher education, without unwarranted disruptions of epistemological continuity.

Still, the interdisciplinary study of psychoanalytic history, theory, and practice is anything but well established at most colleges and universities. The intellectual resistances and practical challenges to achieving this goal are significant but not insurmountable, and there are some strong incentives to overcoming them. While this book focuses primarily on the relation between psychoanalysis and higher education in the US, the history of this relation would be unintelligible without reference to circumstances and developments elsewhere in the world—and to the international as well as national histories of both psychoanalysis and the modern university. What's more, the digitization and globalization of knowledge-economies in our era continue to accelerate, causing the sheer amount of knowledge to grow immeasurably and often to overwhelm us with the inconceivability of its limits and potential uses. Since the 1990s, the ways in which knowledge is evaluated, stored, and disseminated have been transformed to an extent not seen since the respective ages of Johannes Gutenberg and Francis Bacon. Meanwhile, the human psyche has had to adjust rapidly—perhaps *too* rapidly—to unprecedented existential crises: chiefly, the real possibility of imminent and total environmental and societal collapse.

How the human psyche keeps pace—and makes some kind of peace—with this unprecedented explosion of knowledge and its various wondrous as well as devastating potentialities should be recognized as one of humanity's greatest concerns and therefore as one of higher education's most important challenges. The university is both the principal seat of knowledge-production and the primary custodian of future generations of knowledge-workers. Yet the university—as Bill Readings observed so presciently in 1997—is "in ruins," inasmuch as it continues, in the US and elsewhere, to be increasingly diminished and dismantled by declining enrollments, increasing operating costs, and its own massive concessions to techno-bureaucratic expediency, neoliberal economics, and sociopolitical conservatism.[5] In this light, the broad refusal to engage psychoanalysis must be seen not only as the suppression of a single field of knowledge but also, crucially, as a defensive refutation of the determinations of unconscious experience throughout all aspects of human affairs.

Of course, psychoanalysis is not a solution to the world's ills. It cannot answer all the questions over which we anguish nor claim priority or authority or even reliability in the safe conduct of individual lives or collective affairs. And, if it still has a role to play—as I hope to demonstrate—in helping to pull the university back from the brink of total ruin, it will certainly not be by restructuring the university as a kind of hypertrophied analytic institute or, worse still, a mass clinic. As Peter Taubman points out, the pairing of psychoanalysis and education can and should provoke anxieties about reductionism, "imposed therapy," and other "dangerous intimacies" (2012, 13; see also, Guerra in Jagodzinski 2002, 3–10). Indeed, such concerns about psychoanalytic education are as old as psychoanalysis itself, as Chapter 1 will demonstrate. But what psychoanalysis can (continue to) do—especially if given a role commensurate with its broad relevance to both curricular content and pedagogical practice—is to temper, mitigate, and perhaps even reverse some of the greatest threats to contemporary higher education: naïve empiricism, normative idealism, social developmentalism, technological utopianism, and neo-rationalism.

Making room for the nonrational—for what Taubman (2012) calls higher education's "disavowed knowledge" of the unconscious—may be the university's last, best hope. For it would mean acknowledging that the conscious, thinking mind flourishes not, as philosopher Amy Allen puts it, "with the coercive mastery of inner nature but rather with the ego's expansion and enrichment through the ongoing incorporation of more and more unconscious content." It would, moreover, require "a robust conception of the unconscious, one that takes seriously precisely its foreignness … its inability to be translated into rational, communicative thought without remainder" (2021, 15). As a society, we've been pushing that "remainder" further and further beyond the realm of education at all levels. Yet many of us continue to be angered and mystified when, inevitably, this remainder crops up elsewhere and in ways with which we are ill-equipped to contend, including: attention disorders, frustration, intellectual apathy, diminished creativity, rigid identitarianism, communication-skill deficits, curricular disarray, anxiety, acting out, harassment and abuse, diminished empathy, infantilism, technological determinism, student distress, avoidance of difficulty, and teacher burnout.

Ψ

While *Psychoanalysis and the University* is addressed primarily to readers in the US, the UK, and other English-speaking countries, the regimes of higher education in numerous non-anglophone countries also share many of the same challenges and opportunities—thanks not least to the long, international history of the relation between psychoanalysis and education, as the overview in Chapter 1 will show. Following that overview, Chapter 2 ("Psychoanalysis and the Curriculum") will describe and evaluate psychoanalytic content in higher education over the past several decades. Where and how is psychoanalysis being taught in our colleges and universities? What sorts of departments and programs most often tend to include psychoanalytic content in their courses, and of what does that content consist? Who are the principal psychoanalytic thinkers students are asked to read? What would an expansion of psychoanalytic curricula look like from the perspective of different areas of study, and how might such enhancements be implemented and justified in light of the crises we now face?

Chapter 3 ("Psychoanalysis among the Disciplines") will consider the ways in which universities "discipline" knowledge and whether psychoanalysis itself is—or should be—treated as a distinct discipline, with its own institutional infrastructure. Where do psychoanalytic studies already have such an infrastructure, and how are these programs faring, both at the undergraduate and graduate levels? Is psychoanalysis inherently interdisciplinary, and, if so, with how many different disciplines does it—or could it—interact? To what extent—and in what sense—is psychoanalytic research empirical? And how does it balance the empirical and the theoretical or speculative? What are the descriptive, heuristic, and epistemological roles played by psychoanalysis in different areas of research and teaching? And how might the enhancement of psychoanalytic education help mitigate or even reverse the effects of increasing standardization, accountability metrics, and other forms of *naïve* empiricism regarding the assessment of instructional quality and learning outcomes?

Scenes of instruction and learning will be the particular focus of Chapter 4 ("Psychoanalysis and Pedagogy") as it describes and evaluates the activities of teaching and learning from a psychoanalytic perspective. How might the individual experiences of teachers and students, as well as the collective experience of the classroom group, be better understood in psychodynamic terms? How might such experiences be even better facilitated by actively incorporating certain psychoanalytic concepts and techniques into existing pedagogical practices? Of primary significance to such questions are the mutually informing phenomena of transference and countertransference—the often powerful emotional currents that flow, unconsciously, between teachers and students, as well as between students themselves, in classrooms, office-hours, labs, and other educational settings. What are the advantages as well as the potential risks of the emotional attachments, erotic feelings and fantasies, and forms of mistrust, love, anger, emulation, and jealousy that tend to remain unavowed and therefore unaddressed in the pedagogical situation? The pursuit of knowledge itself has its own affective dimensions that tend not to be openly discussed as part of the learning process. But what if they were? How might psychoanalysis help teachers and students make better use of their "passion" (or "hatred" or "boredom," etc.) for a particular object of study or entire field of inquiry?

The considerable cost—in time as well as money—of both psychoanalytic treatment and higher education prompts the very reasonable question: "Are they worth it?" Will either one make life better? Would an enhanced relation between the two yield further, unanticipated advantages? Chapter 5

("Psychoanalysis, the University, and the Professions") will address these questions of value with respect to both psychological well-being and professional achievement, suggesting ways in which higher education could better prepare students for a variety of careers by augmenting the curricular and pedagogical roles of psychoanalysis on campus. It will describe various post-graduate possibilities for students of psychoanalysis and explain how advantageous a psychoanalytically informed education can be in the pursuit and development of many different sorts of professions and careers. This chapter will also addresses the often conflicting claims of metapsychological theory and caregiving practice in psychoanalytic training, while also considering how psychoanalysis could enhance the university's own pastoral role—not only by improving the quality of campus-based mental healthcare but also by developing the capacities of all students for compassionate self-understanding and ethical relations with others.

Finally, the Appendix will offer some further practical information for educators, including a database of syllabi from various courses taught by academics and clinicians in a multitude of fields, information about professional psychoanalytic organizations with demonstrated interest in psychoanalytic education, and a supplemental list of sources not already cited in the Bibliography.

Notes

1 Because of its limited length and its projected audience, this book concentrates chiefly on North America and Europe, where the histories of both psychoanalysis and higher education share many commonalities, interests, and institutional forms. For example, both the modern university and the psychoanalytic training institute are European inventions that have been closely replicated in the US Yet, like the concept of the university (Lat: *universus* whole, entire), the fundamental precepts of psychoanalytic training have, at the very least, transcultural pretensions. They might, in fact, have transcultural applicability. Each has indisputably taken root and flourished in many other parts of the world, and their potential universality isn't automatically negated by the fact that both education and psychoanalysis have been (and continue to be) instrumentalized by Western powers for various imperialist and authoritarian purposes.

2 According to Michel Foucault, an "episteme" is a contingent, historical field "in which knowledge, envisaged apart from all criteria having reference to its rational value or to its objective forms, grounds its positivity and thereby manifests a history ... of its conditions of possibility" (1994, xxii).

3 "This work of overcoming resistances is the essential function of analytic treatment; the patient has to accomplish it and the doctor makes this possible for him with the help of suggestion operating in an *educative* sense. For that reason psycho-analytic treatment has justly been described as a kind of *after-education* [*Nacherziehung*]" (Freud 1963, 451). As Alain de Mijolla observes, Freud repeatedly likens psychoanalysis to

"after-education" while also maintaining "that the psychoanalyst must not fall into the role of an educator" (2005, 359).

4 Psychodynamic training has already virtually disappeared from clinical psychology doctoral training programs at US universities (see Levendosky et al. 2023). The psychoanalytic profession's own training institutes have, through their balkanization and resistance to change, helped to compound the field's marginalization. According to Erika Schmidt, "the insularity of psychoanalytic education, along with confusion within the field about the definition of psychoanalysis and what constitutes the essential theory, have also added to the troubled position of psychoanalysis in the culture" (2018, 182). In his recent, comprehensive proposal for restructuring psychoanalytic education, Otto Kernberg, too, is highly critical of its current "stagnation" and its excessive reliance on what he calls the "trade school" model of most training institutes (2016, 44, 59). See also Willock (2007), Kirsner (2009), Stepansky (2009), and Fonagy (2015).

5 See, for example, Childress (2019), Ginsberg (2013), Hamilton and Nielsen (2021), Hunt (2018), Barnard-Naudé (2022), Rosenberg (2023), Ambrose and Nietzel (2023), and Means and Slater (2023). Often erroneously accused of being the bastion of leftist radicalism, most modern universities are actually home to faculty members and administrators of all political persuasions who share a keen desire at least to appear morally progressive. For example, as Robert Samuels points out, the US professoriate includes "many 'liberal' professors who became quite aggressive when … confronted with the reality of the exploitive labor system that supports their work" (2020, 154). Roger Kimball's notorious "tenured radicals" (1990) tend chiefly to be exhausted or disaffected liberals who avoid directly confronting issues of labor and inequality even within their own institutions.

Chapter 1

Psychoanalysis and Education
A Brief History

> None of the applications of psycho-analysis has excited so much interest and aroused so many hopes, and none, consequently, has attracted so many capable workers, as its use in the theory and practice of education.
>
> —SIGMUND FREUD, "Preface" to August Aichhorn's
> *Wayward Youth* [1925]

The question as to whether psychoanalysis should be taught in universities is almost as old as psychoanalysis itself. Throughout his life, Sigmund Freud—who took his university degree in medicine and worked initially as a university researcher and lecturer in neuropathology—considered psychoanalysis to be a thoroughly creditable scientific research program with numerous applications to other fields, including education. Yet he also maintained that psychoanalysis was a distinct field with professional standards of its own that should remain separate from medical education, and he strongly resisted the prospect of a medical-school monopoly over psychoanalysis. Consistently supportive of lay (i.e., non-physician) analysts—including his daughter Anna Freud—he favored a broad, liberal education for future analysts, writing in 1913 that "the practice of psycho-analysis calls much less for medical training than for psychological instruction and a free human outlook" (1958b, 330–31).

Freud doubled down on this position in a later pamphlet, arguing that if

> one had to found a college of psycho-analysis, much would have to be taught in it which is also taught by the medical faculty: alongside of depth-psychology, which would always remain the principal subject, there would be an introduction to biology, as much as possible of the science of sexual life, and familiarity with the symptomatology of psychiatry. On the other hand, analytic instruction would include

DOI: 10.4324/9781003540588-2

branches of knowledge which are remote from medicine and which the doctor does not come across in his practice: the history of civilization, mythology, the psychology of religion and the science of literature. Unless he is well at home in these subjects, an analyst can make nothing of a large amount of his material.

(1959c, 20: 246)

This passage appears in Freud's *Question of Lay Analysis* (1926) and was written in defense of Theodor Reik, who had been frivolously charged for practicing psychoanalysis without a medical degree (Jones 1957, 3: 292). The case's flawed jurisprudence and flimsy evidence were easy for Freud's authority to overwhelm. But he didn't make light of its implications. For in this episode, as Nancy Luxon perceptively argues,

the crisis of [psychoanalytic] authority is on full display, where the facts of regulatory power are unclear, where justice must nonetheless pronounce on them, where the problem is less one of accuracy … than of *how to regulate the new and the unforeseen.*

(2013, 50; italics added)

Arguably, both formal education and psychoanalysis are authoritative modes of regulating the "new and unforeseen." Yet the psychoanalytic clinical relationship, in which "the experience of authority that ostensibly structures it" is *itself* a matter for interpretation (Luxon 2013, 51), also poses a challenge not merely to the prescribed and codified authority of schooling in particular subjects and methodologies but also to the nature and justification of authority as such. The new and unforeseen question as to whether psychoanalysis should be taught in universities was part of the much larger and more fundamental dilemma posed by psychoanalysis to education generally. For, in light of increasingly verifiable psychoanalytic insights into the predominantly unconscious nature of human experience and the lasting, often neurotogenic, consequences of early psycho-sexual development, the challenge facing all educators became how to strike the proper balance between freedom and constraint—between what Freud called, with respect to education, "the Scylla of non-interference and the Charybdis of frustration" (1964b, 149). Moreover, would achieving such a balance for the individual also best serve the needs of the classroom group and of the larger society?

During the first half-century of psychoanalysis, these questions seemed especially urgent with regard to the most formative stages of life and thus the learning environments of the youngest children, in both home and school. As Freud's friend and colleague, Ernst Kris reflected,

> the contact between psychoanalysis and education was established when, in the progress of his work with the adult neurotic, Freud discovered that for "an understanding of his condition or to effect a cure" it was necessary to "trace the determination of his symptoms … back into his early childhood."
>
> (1948, 624)

The university remained in view from the beginning. But the chief focus, at least until World War II, was on early childhood instruction. The education of children was "an organizing goal" for the "Wednesday Psychological Society" that Freud began hosting in 1902 and later became the Vienna Psycho-Analytic Society (Cohen 2018, 231). Psychoanalytic insights into infantile sexuality and the enduring psychic influence of "archaic" experiences, along with the emergence of the field of child psychoanalysis in the 1910s, helped sustain this focus, inspiring a wide range of psychopedagogical experiments at the nursery, kindergarten, primary, and secondary levels.

For the founders of both psychoanalysis and psychopedagogy— including the Freuds, Kris, Sándor Ferenczi, Ernest Jones, Dorothy Burlingham, Marie Bonaparte, Siegfried Bernfeld, Willi Hoffer, August Aichhorn, Eva Rosenfeld, Oskar Pfister, Hans Zulliger, Otto Rank, Hanns Sachs, Alfred Adler, Carl Jung, Laura Polányi, George Green, Alice Bálint, Vera Schmidt, Melanie Klein, Frieda Fromm-Reichmann, Wilhelm Reich, Sabina Spielrein, and Nelly Wolffheim—the primary concern was the negative influence on the youngest schoolchildren of traditional, authoritarian schooling. And their principal hope was that progressive psychoanalytic pedagogies would liberate them from that schooling's inhibiting, neurotogenic effects. This also meant revisiting questions as to when formal schooling should begin, how it should proceed, and toward what ends it should be directed. Definitive answers were not forthcoming. Yet the philosophy and psychology of education would never be the same, and many of the psychopedagogic principles and practices controversially introduced by these innovators have long been assimilated in classrooms and school systems around the world.

Ψ

Anna Freud was a trained teacher who embraced the progressive, "child-centered" approach of Maria Montessori.[1] She was also one of the first practitioner-theorists of child analysis and remained deeply invested in the relation between psychoanalysis and education throughout her professional life.[2] She was apprenticed and later certified as a teacher, and she continued to teach while being analyzed by her father and beginning her own career as a psychoanalyst (Young-Bruehl 2008, 76). Even after resigning her teaching post in 1920—and while systematizing the field of child analysis—she remained actively involved in pedagogy and teacher-training, sponsoring courses, writing articles, and delivering lectures on psychoanalysis for Vienna's schoolteachers.[3]

The audience for her lectures included teachers from the city's working-class *Kinderhorte* (Danto 2023, 5, Young-Bruehl 2008, 159, 176). At the *Kinderhorte* (a kind of daycare and after-school center), teachers had to contend, Freud writes,

> with children who have already had a whole series of more or less profound experiences and who have passed through the hands of numbers of educators [each of whom] must note that these children, at any rate at first, do not in the least react to his real individuality and to his actual behavior toward them. They simply bring with them a preconceived attitude of mind, and may approach the teacher with the suspicion, defiance, or feeling of having to be on guard which they have acquired through their personal experience of other adults.
>
> (1935, 14)

Unable adequately to observe, engage, and understand the lives of these children, their teachers—and by extension all teachers, Freud implies—are left merely to "correct" the non-conforming behaviors of even the youngest of these "complex miniature personalities" (1935, 16). Thus it would help teachers immeasurably to understand, from a psychoanalytic perspective, where such behaviors come from—to understand, for instance, that students who are prone to fighting are often "fighting out ... conflicts which they were not able to finish in their own homes" and that the "longings" and "wishes" they harbor with respect to their parents are "transferred to you ... with the resultant anguish and surrender" (1935, 32–33).[4]

The chief purpose of Anna Freud's *Kinderhorte* lectures—later published as *Psycho-Analysis for Teachers and Parents* (1930)—was to introduce some basic elements of psychoanalytic theory and its perspective on both child development and student-teacher interactions. She explained that children, like adults, have powerful unconscious drives, wishes, and fantasies; that seemingly arbitrary behaviors are always motivated, whether or not the motive can be discerned; that education demands psychically costly renunciations that children often deeply resent and against which they frequently rebel; that children project onto their teachers aspects of their parental relationships; and that children's memories function very differently from those of adults. Freud concedes that she has little *practical* advice for making use of these insights in the classroom, but nevertheless cautions her readers that, in the regimentation, inhibition, and judgment typically imposed upon school-age children, psychoanalysis sees "quite definite danger" (1935, 93).

Freud was speaking not only for herself but for many of her colleagues in both Europe and America, including Ferenczi, Jones, and Pfister.[5] Pfister's *What Can Psychoanalysis Offer to the Educator?* (1917) further emphasizes the "quite definite danger" posed to students who are "languishing in the bonds of the unconscious" and directly confronts their teachers' general ignorance of the psychodynamic factors endemic to learning: the intertwined nature of intellectual and emotional development; the influence of each child's distinct personal experiences, needs, and unconscious defense mechanisms on their cognitive functioning; the unapparent meaningfulness of acts of both compliance and disobedience; and the inevitability of student-teacher transference. Pfister rails that many teachers

> know more of beetles and mushrooms than of the souls of their pupils, more of the law of the expansion of gases than of the child mind. Can he be called a trained educator who cannot distinguish between an obsessional liar and a morally feeble-minded one? Between a tormentor of animals driven by neurotic compulsion and a similar culprit who has no pitying counter will? …. The customary rewards are regular poison for hundreds of pupils who are languishing in the bonds of the unconscious, and punishment a torture as cruel as it is useless.
>
> (1922, 29)

With similar concerns, Ferenczi's first psychoanalytic publication, "Psychoanalysis and Education" (1908), warned against the era's authoritarian educational practices, calling "present-day education" a "hothouse for various neuroses." He worried that educative regimentation and its emphasis on sublimation interfered with children's ability to take "unselfconscious pleasure in the natural joys of life," chiefly by burdening their minds with further compulsions and by strengthening already powerfully ingrained sociocultural inhibitions (2002, 280–82). Like Anna Freud, Ferenczi envisioned a "future experimental pedagogy," based on psychoanalytic insights, that would serve the pleasure principle rather than civilization's repressive requirements (2002, 286).

Other early analysts, too—though largely uncertain as to what psychoanalysis could do, systematically, to improve education—were vocal in their criticisms of what Jones calls the "harmful effects of faulty education" (1910, 497). These "harmful effects" were thought to include the thwarting and distortion of children's libidinal impulses and the disavowal and punitive suppression of the richness—both physical and mental—of their erotic lives (1910, 504). Pfister notes that "psychoanalytic pedagogy lays great stress on prophylaxis" (1915, 545), and his Romanian disciple Constantin Narly, professor of the philosophy of pedagogy at the University of Czernowitz, explained that "not only the normal child, but especially the large number of nervous children, those from whom future neuropaths will be recruited, find in psychoanalytic education an early cure, and are thus protected from later complications" (1933, 190; see also, Petrin 2018).

Because of both the dynamic idiosyncrasy and the lasting consequences of every child's psychosexual development, Jones also adamantly opposed the uniformity of "additive" models of education, with their strict imposition of undifferentiated standards of knowledge. A child's education, he maintained, should be "a more individual matter than it is at present," a "drawing out, of his special potentialities" and the "free development of his latent qualities"—most crucially, through the incorporation of "sexual enlightenment" into the curriculum (1910, 506, 512). Jones, like Ferenczi and the Freuds, had to concede that, in those early days, psychoanalysis had "less to say about how to instruct a child than about how not to." Yet he was confident that "when one appreciates what dangers are to be avoided, the problem of how to instruct the child presents no serious obstacles" (1910, 512).

In a follow-up paper, Jones emphasized how the psychoanalytically informed guidance and thoughtful facilitation of the sublimation of children's "primary interests and tendencies" could better help them follow their own intellectual inclinations, instead of being bullied or cajoled into pursuing objects or occupations for which they had no real desire:

> A child, for instance, who has conquered a sadistic love of cruelty may when he grows up become a successful butcher or a distinguished surgeon, according to his capacities and opportunities. One in whom the exhibitionistic fondness for self-display was pronounced my develop into an actor, an auctioneer or an orator.
>
> (1912, 250)

Jones realized he was calling for modes of attentive observation, uncomfortable frankness, and time-intensive guidance and support (not to mention sophisticated teacher-training) that were highly incompatible with mass public education. But he believed that the early-twentieth-century world had reached a kind of ethno-psychic tipping point—a plateauing of society's tolerance for the ever-increasing degrees of repression it must to some extent endure but beyond which loomed a Nordau-like prospect of social degeneration and madness.[6]

Meanwhile, others continued to theorize and experiment with various forms of psychopedagogy—among them, Switzerland's Hans Zulliger, whose authoritative and experience-rich writings were widely praised and lastingly influential. Zulliger was a fulltime teacher and practicing analyst who also wrote numerous articles and books abounding in both practical suggestions and shrewd insights into children's psyches. Zulliger had been analyzed by Pfister but developed a distinctive style of psychotherapy for very small children. Like Klein and Anna Freud, he was an early practitioner of play therapy, about which he writes vividly in *Healing Powers in Children's Play* (1952). Gifted and tireless as both child analyst and schoolteacher, Zulliger became one of the first true experts on the application of psychoanalysis to the practice of teaching, spending most of his life as a primary school teacher in a working-class town outside Bern. He immersed himself not only in studying how children learn but also in reflecting on their personal development and behavior, including such problems as stuttering, bedwetting, and kleptomania. His pioneering work was published widely—in Swiss teaching journals, in the *French Review of Psychoanalysis*, in the *Journal for Psychoanalytic Pedagogy*, and in books including *Psychoanalytic Experiences in Public School Practice* (1921), which is full of student case studies and teaching anecdotes richly embellished with actual classroom dialogues.[7]

Still, there were few such committed psychopedagogues, and when Anna Freud told Vienna's schoolteachers that psychoanalysis saw "quite definite danger arising from education," she anticipated her father's observation, in his *New Introductory Lectures* (1933), that "hitherto education has fulfilled its task very badly and has done children great damage" (1964b, 149)— chiefly, the damage done by failing to acknowledge childhood sexuality and by teachers' heavy-handed suppression of children's aggressive as well as libidinal drives.[8] Like his daughter, Freud had already devoted much thought to the potential educational benefits of psychoanalysis, beginning with early writings on childhood sexuality, such as his write-up of the case of "Little Hans" in 1909: "Hitherto education has only set itself the task of controlling, or … suppressing, the instincts [with results] by no means gratifying." Freud also complained of the failure to examine "by what means and at what cost the suppression of the inconvenient instincts has been achieved." Freud proposes that educators aim at "making the individual capable of becoming a civilized and useful member of society with the least possible sacrifice of his own activity," and that the knowledge "gained by psycho-analysis … can claim with justice that it deserves to be regarded by educators as an invaluable guide" (1955a, 146). Freud also expressed reservations concerning the application of psychoanalysis to education:

> The work of education is something *sui generis*: it is not to be confused with psycho-analytic influence and cannot be replaced by it. Psychoanalysis can be called in by education as an auxiliary means of dealing with a child; but it is not a suitable substitute for education.
>
> (1961c, 274)

However, Freud's insistence here and elsewhere on a separation of spheres probably stems less from humility regarding his lack of expertise in the field of education than from his fiercely felt need to protect the scientific integrity and professional autonomy of psychoanalysis.

Nevertheless, Freud was keenly alert to "the overmastering interest which must be felt in psycho-analysis by the theory of education." He charged Europe's scientific community and its educators to devise and implement a workable, psychoanalytically informed teaching practice, for psychoanalysis, he insisted, "has brought to light the wishes, the thought-structures and the developmental processes of childhood," including "the inestimably important factor of sexuality in its physical and mental manifestations"

(1955b, 189). Freud urged teachers, especially, to help overcome the failures of the educational system by familiarizing themselves with "the findings of psycho-analysis" and by reconciling themselves to the realities of
early psycho-sexual development—including the fact that

> the forcible suppression of strong instincts by external means never has
> the effect in a child of these instincts being extinguished or brought
> under control; it leads to repression, which establishes a predisposition
> to later nervous illness [and] in loss of efficiency and of capacity for
> enjoyment, which has to be paid for the normality upon which the
> educator insists.
>
> (1955b, 189–90)

Moreover, Freud advised, if children's "asocial and perverse instincts"
aren't subjected to repression, they can instead be "diverted from their original aims to more valuable ones by the process known as 'sublimation.'"
Indeed, he argued, "our highest virtues have grown up, as reaction formations and sublimations, out of our worst dispositions" and concluded that
"education should scrupulously refrain from burying these precious springs
of action" (1955b, 190). Freud even gave public lectures on education at the
University of Vienna during the winter terms of 1915–1916 and 1916–1917
(Gay 1998, 368). But it remained to be seen just what a thoroughgoing
"psycho-analytically enlightened education" would look like and what sort
of individual and societal benefits it might yield.

Ψ

Fortunately, the time was ripe. By the end of World War I, a broadly felt
spirit of progressive change promoted rebellion against the authoritarian
pedagogical regimes for which submission (to the state, the class structure, the church, etc.) was education's principal goal. According to Austrian
writer and Freud family friend Stefan Zweig,

> the [Hapsburg] state exploited the school as an instrument of its
> authority. Above all, we were to be educated to respectfully regard
> what existed as perfect, the opinions of teachers as infallible, the words
> of our fathers as incontrovertible, and the provisions of the state as
> absolute and eternally valid.
>
> (1994, 54)

Whether at school or at home, Zweig recalled, "young people were not to have things too easy." Their foremost lessons were duty and docility, and "we were simply to be thankful for all that was granted to us and had no right to make requests or to demand anything" (1994, 54). But now that both the war and the Hapsburg monarchy were finished, a less docile, more demanding Austrian populace clamored for change, and a more liberal system of education became one of its top priorities. In Austria's postwar republic, as in many other parts of the modernizing world, prominent educational reformers—many of them spurred on by socialist experimentation—were ready and eager to act on the new insights of psychoanalysis.

Crucially, it seemed to them, the rigid suppression of students' libidinal and aggressive drives must be relaxed. With regard to its students, the new psychoanalytic pedagogy would, in Anna Freud's words, "rather risk the chance of their being somewhat uncontrolled in the end instead of forcing on them from the outset such a crippling of their individuality" (1935, 98). And according to Rank and Sachs, "an understanding sexual education" would have to be "the foundation for the prosecution of the positive pedagogic task." "So far as possible," they continued, "one should leave the child alone, with as complete withholding of direct injurious influences as possible, and inhibit him as little as possible in his natural development" (Rank and Sachs 1916, 329). They rejected the state-imposed emphasis on duty, docility, and submission in traditional pedagogy, which, in Zulliger's words, "ultimately represents the defense of the adult generation against the Oedipal desires of the children's generation" (2018, 74). Instead, they encouraged independence, curiosity, and self-discovery. Rote learning and a fixed curriculum were to give way to education in its root sense of "drawing out" (Lat. *ex*: "out" + *ducere*: "to lead"), and teachers were urged to take curricular cues from students' own needs, desires, and life-experiences and the content and manner of their expression.

Thus there were at least three major pedagogical interventions that even basic psychoanalytic teacher-training could facilitate. First, the psychoanalytic critique of existing, excessively regimented and punitively erotophobic methods. Second, the creation of a teaching force with an enhanced understanding of child development and the human condition generally. And third, a progressive educational mandate to help repair injuries already inflicted by unenlightened parents and educators (A. Freud 1935, 104). Teachers, after all, were authority figures with whom many children spent as much (or more) time as they did with their parents. Inevitably, students'

teacher-objects would be incorporated as part of their super-ego formation, making teachers especially well-positioned to help students find a "*via
media*" between unchecked drive-gratification and neurotogenic drive-
inhibition (A. Freud 1935, 102–03). Moreover, they could do so, at least to
some extent, independently and of their own volition until more systemic
changes were implemented. While, "for the present, no analytic pedagogy
exists … for general use," individual teachers who were interested in psychoanalysis (and who had perhaps been analyzed themselves) could, in
their own classrooms, "apply to the education of children the understanding
that psycho-analysis has brought to them" (A. Freud 1935, 103).

This is Barbara Low's main point as well, in her 1923 lecture on "Social
Aspects of Psychoanalysis" (Council 1924, 262). One of the first British
psychoanalysts and a founding member of the British Psychoanalytical
Society, Low warned, "so long as educators take into account only the conscious mind, whether their own or that of those to whom they speak, they
remain unequipped for the task" (1924, 172). Recognition of the unconscious lives of both students and teachers, she argued, should be the *sine
qua non* of education—especially of younger children, for whom fantasies
prompted by unconscious drives, wishes, and traumata play so much more
prominent a role as "explanation of the unknown and non-understood"
(1924, 184). Teachers who overlook, misapprehend, and even recoil from
the abundant manifestations of children's unconscious lives, Low argues,
tend indiscriminately to impose external compulsions "too far removed
from the standard of civilisation *which the child has reached within himself*" (1924, 181). Moreover, to "become acquainted with the unconscious
in his pupils," the teacher "must first know something of his own unconscious." Despite the practical obstacles, Low concludes, all teachers should
be psychoanalyzed as part of their preparation (1924, 201).[9]

Six years later, Low saw encouraging signs of progress and acceptance
of psychoanalysis in the educational field, including, at least to some extent,
"in the ordinary school and in the ordinary classroom," as well as in "the
teaching of educational ideas now being carried out in colleges [and] training colleges." Since 1920, she claims, "not a book written by any serious
psychologist or educationist … has been uninfluenced by the work of Freud
and his followers" (1929, 315–16). Indeed, because teaching was becoming
increasingly professionalized, many educators were eager to associate their
work with the scientific prestige of various forms of psychology, including psychoanalysis. Edith Kurzweil suggests that, because of its emphasis on parental influence in early childhood, psychoanalysis also offered a

reprieve to teachers accustomed to being blamed for their students' intellectual and behavioral deficiencies (1989, 129). Psychoanalysis held out the
promise of addressing student resistance and delinquency more effectively
and compassionately in the classroom.

During the interwar period, numerous analysts—including the Freuds,
Hermine Hug-Hellmuth, Ferenczi, Pfister, Sachs, Adler, Jung, and Low—
lectured on psychoanalysis to teachers in Austria, Germany, Switzerland,
England, and the US. In addition, an abundance of books on psychopedagogy were published, including Pfister's *Psycho-Analysis in the Service
of Education* (1917), Herbert Ellsworth Cory's *The Intellectuals and the
Wage Workers: A Study in Educational Psychoanalysis* (1919), Wilfrid
Lay's *The Child's Unconscious Mind: The Relations of Psychoanalysis
to Education* (1920), Pfister's *The Treatment of Difficult to Educate and
Abnormal Children* (1921), Hugh Crichton-Miller's *The New Psychology
and the Teacher* (1922), George Herbert Green's *Psychanalysis* [sic] *in
the Classroom* (1922), Jones's *Social Aspects of Psychoanalysis* (1924),
Fritz Wittels's *Set the Children Free!* (1927), Low's *Psycho-Analysis and
Education* (1928), Caroline Zachry's *Personality Adjustments of School
Children* (1929), and Adler's *Guiding the Child: On the Principles of
Individual Psychology* (1930) and *The Education of Children* (1930).

In 1926, German analyst Heinrich Meng and Swiss educator Ernst
Schneider co-founded the *Journal for Psychoanalytic Pedagogy*, which—
before political upheaval forced its closure in 1937—published more than 300
articles, constituting the largest single record of early efforts to combine the
fields of psychoanalysis and education and to explore the psychodynamics of
teaching and learning: Reich on "Parents as Educators"; Erikson and Bernfeld
on the pedagogy of sexuality; Aichhorn on delinquency; Zulliger on "Fear
of Confession and the Compulsion to Confess in Children"; Felix Boehm on
lying and misbehavior; Imre Hermann on obedience; Nelly Wolffheim on
children's erotic friendships; multiple special issues dealing with "Onanism,"
"Menstruation," and other post-pubertal phenomena; Felix Schottländer on
the question "Does Psychoanalysis Destroy Guilelessness?"; Felix Preisswerk
on student failure; Siegfried Kraus on orphanhood; Heinrich Hoffmann on students hating teachers; and Melitta Schmideberg on "intellectual inhibition."[10]

Ψ

In this era of educational reformism, coordinated efforts were made to
promote psychoanalytic pedagogy and even to create psychoanalytically

minded institutions for school-age children. Thanks largely to Ferenczi's influence, Budapest became a center of such activity as early as 1911, when his friend Laura Polányi opened an experimental kindergarten (Szapor 2005, 130–36). In 1927, analyst Lilly Hajdú opened the Special Education Institute and Children's Holiday Centre (Borgos 2021, 34). Indeed, during the interwar period, a large network of Hungarian professional women coalesced around psychoanalytic pedagogy. Formal and informal seminars for teachers and parents were held at the free Polyclinic of the Hungarian Psychoanalytical Society by Alice Bálint,[11] Edit Gyömröi, Lillián Rotter, Margit Dubovitz, Klára Lázár, Kata Lévy, Alice Hermann, and others, many of whom also contributed to the psychoanalytically oriented educational journals—including *Paths to the Future* and *Early Education*—established in Hungary in the 1930s. Effectively, however, the integration and development of psychoanalytic pedagogy was restricted to private schools, which, in addition to Polányi's, included Margit Hrabovszky Révész's Forest School, Emma Domokos Löllbach's New School, Márta Nemes Müller's Family School, and, immediately after World War II, Emmi Pikler's Lóczy nursery home (Borgos 2021, 24).

Back up the Danube in Vienna, educator and psychoanalyst Siegfried Bernfeld had been, before the war, the student leader of the short-lived Austro-German Anfang Movement—the century's first leftist youth movement, which sought independence from adult authority and promoted antiauthoritarian educational reform. As the war brought tens of thousands of refugees to Vienna—many of them Polish Jews—Bernfeld helped house and educate their children and was able, as head of the Zionist Central Council for Western-Austria, to open the Kinderheim Baumgarten in 1919 (Utley 1979, 207–11). Anna Freud later hailed this residential school for postwar refugee Jewish orphans as "a first experiment to apply psychoanalytic principles to education" (1968a, 7; see also Cohen 1999, 166–68). Bernfeld's experiment was short-lived, but from it sprang the Vienna Kinderseminar—a kind of think-tank that brought Anna Freud and Bernfeld together with Hoffer, Aichhorn, Burlingham, and Rosenfeld to share ideas and plans. Their achievements included the publication of Bernfeld's *Kinderheim Baumgarten* (1921) and his subsequent treatise *Sisyphus; or, The Limits of Education* (1925); Hoffer's establishment of Vienna's Psychoanalytic Training Course for Educators; and the 1926 launch of the *Zeitschrift*.

By the later 1920s, members of the Kinderseminar were ready to experiment with a school of their own. Aichhorn, in particular, shared invaluable insights derived from his leadership of Austrian welfare institutions for so-called "delinquents." His revolutionary treatment of these boys—many with severe behavioral and personality disorders—was guided in large part by his psychoanalytic understanding of the developmental damage they had experienced at the hands of others. Their aggressive, often destructive impulses, Aichhorn recognized, were in many cases expressions of developmental deficits and repressed longings for withheld parental love and recognition. In his bestselling book, *Wayward Youth* (1925), Aichhorn wrote:

> It is above all the tender feeling for the teacher that gives the pupil the incentive to do what is prescribed and not to do what is forbidden. The teacher, as a libidinally charged object for the pupil, offers traits for identification that bring about a lasting change in the structure of the ego-ideal.
>
> (1935, 235)

Many analysts as well as educators—including Anna Freud, Hoffer, Erikson, Margaret Mahler, Kurt Eissler, Peter Blos, and D. W. Winnicott— were indebted to Aichhorn's creation of a novel analytic framework for connecting with and treating adolescents (Houssier and Marty 2009; see also, Schowalter 2000).

Yet while the progressive socialist ideals that inspired Bernfeld and Aichhorn were widely shared among other members of the Kinderseminar, the first school they established was nothing like Aichhorn's large, public reformatories or Bernfeld's charitable Kinderheim Baumgarten. Instead, in 1927, with Burlingham's financial support, she and Anna Freud established the small, private, psychoanalytically informed Matchbox School for "children of different nationalities whose parents were undergoing analysis or who were perhaps in analysis themselves" (Erikson 1987a, 3). Indeed, with 15 to 25 students attending at any one time, many had near-daily sessions, although any clinical discussions were held apart from school staff meetings (Danto 2018, 137, 144). As one student (Burlingham's own daughter Katrina) later recalled, "there was a connection between analysis and the school's educational ideas but personal analysis and analysis in general were not brought into the classroom" (qtd. in Danto 2018, 143). In addition to Anna Freud and Burlingham, the faculty included Aichhorn, Blos, Marie Briehl, Kurt Eissler, Erik Homburger (the future psychoanalyst Erik H. Erikson), Joan Erikson, and Esther Menaker (Midgley 2008, 33; Danto

2018, 142). Most were either analysts or analysts-in-training, and they shared a psychoanalytic perspective on the need for a progressive, even permissive, approach to matters of sexuality and a nonpunitive attitude toward manifestations of aggression and other potential sources of guilt. They did their best to strike an ideal balance between monitored freedom and non-authoritarian discipline.

But what was their pedagogy actually like? In "Psychoanalysis and the Future of Education" (1930)—one of two early articles on his work at the Matchbox School (see Erikson 1987b and 1987c)—Homburger (Erikson) shared his recollection of a discussion motivated by watching students' occasional angry outbursts during outdoor play. Back in the classroom, Homburger asked the students to talk about their own experiences of anger and to compare them with some historical examples from their recent studies, including a story about Roald Amundsen's anger at Umberto Nobile during the recent *Italia* expedition to the North Pole:

> We discussed examples of rage, justified and unjustified, and examples of the social control of this emotion. With this acceptance of rage as a general fact, that is, as something that is not merely the fault of the individual who carries it within him, a variety of thoughts began to stir in the children's minds. They spoke of aggression that is displayed and of aggression that is felt, of guilt and the desire for punishment, with an inner comprehension of which adults are hardly capable. They even discovered "civilization and its discontents" in our little progressive school. They admitted openly that their desire for punishment was not satisfied by us. One of them said, "In the other schools it was fun to pin a paper on the teacher's coat. Here there's no fun in it any more." Another declared, "We're like balls that are all ready to explode and suddenly are put into an air tight room."

> Then we were able to discuss what one should do with this desire for punishment. The Puritans were mentioned—men who though expelled for their belief became the grimmest of religious tyrants as soon as they had the power to exercise tyranny. The older children discovered that their behavior towards the smaller ones represented a tendency to abreact their feelings regarding control by the teachers. This began to make it clear that valuing fairness so much more than mutual suppression, as we did, only one thing was possible—submission through understanding

of the situation. Finally the children came to the conclusion that the only thing possible would be to speak often and penetratingly about the force which endangered this understanding from within until it lost its power.

(1987c, 27–28)

This vignette of a student-centered pedagogy might seem adroit but unremarkable today. However, in early-twentieth-century Europe, this sort of exchange represented a complete overturning of traditional classroom practice. Even now it still feels fresh and plausible and clearly demonstrates that teachers like Homburger were not—as some feared—turning pedagogy into psychotherapy. Nor was Homburger letting the students run wild and failing to address disciplinary matters. Instead, he was helping them understand, and discover ways of correcting, their own bad behavior—and even to use this enhanced self-understanding to interpret curricular content.

But many teachers were unable or unwilling to practice Homburger's (and Aichhorn's and Freud's) "middle way." Rumors of unchecked permissiveness at certain other psychoanalytically minded experimental schools threatened to taint the entire enterprise. One of the most permissive was Moscow's Children's Home and Psychological Laboratory, run by Vera Schmidt from 1921 until 1924 as one of many experimental schools sponsored by the Bolshevik intelligentsia (see Hai et al. 2020). At Schmidt's school,

children were free to satisfy their sexual curiosity among themselves. Nudity was the rule in warm weather. Children's questions about sexual matters received clear, truthful answers. Punishments of any kind on the part of the teachers was forbidden .... Since there was no need on the children's part for secrecy or shyness ... teachers had every opportunity to observe the sexual development of the children step by step. By such means, Schmidt hoped to learn whether the various phases of infantile sexuality postulated by Freud arise spontaneously and then disappear without any educational influence.

(Cohen 1999, 170)

Leon Trotsky himself encouraged the school's efforts to combine psychoanalysis and communism to forge a new Soviet citizenry. On staff were the young neuropsychologist Alexander Luria and famed Russian psychoanalyst Sabina Spielrein. Yet the experiment was radical even by early

Soviet standards, and public outcry prompted accusations and investigations. Gossip about the school's sexual permissiveness was confirmed by one of Schmidt's own published reports, in which she affirmed the importance of allowing children to express their sexual interests openly and that "the educator must first free herself through analytical work from the prejudices [of] her own upbringing" (1924, 18).[12] But there were teachers who hadn't been psychoanalyzed who found the atmosphere unsettling, and even those who had been analyzed were of different minds about its propriety (Cohen 1999, 170).

It wasn't only in such exceptional settings that dissension grew and public trust faltered. By the 1930s, the world of psychoanalysis was growing uncomfortably fractious—due, not least, to debates about the expansion and even the very legitimacy of child analysis as such. Also, despite some promising developments, like Hoffer's new three-year training course in psychoanalytic pedagogy at the Vienna Psychoanalytic Institute, many analysts professionally involved with education were growing dubious and even disillusioned. They argued about how the specific achievements of psychopedagogy could reliably be measured and whether certain promised goals were even possible. Most controversial, perhaps, was the claim—grounded in Freud's *Three Essays*—that, because strict upbringings led to the repression of libidinal drives, early, permissive sexual enlightenment was bound to have a prophylactic effect against later neurotic illness. This problematic thesis was translated into a range of psychopedagogical theories by prominent figures including Rank, Sachs, Bernfeld, Schmidt, and Spielrein. But practical, political, and theoretical challenges made its scattershot implementation increasingly difficult to defend, especially when even less radical pedagogical experiments were so hard to sustain and justify.

Once the Matchbox School had closed in 1932, it "dropped out of most histories of both psychoanalysis and education" (Midgley 2008, 37).[13] Indeed, most of the era's experimental psychoanalytic schools and nurseries—including Adler's first Viennese child guidance center, opened in 1922, and the Dutch psychoanalytic children's home run by analyst Max Levy-Suhl and his pediatrician wife Hildegard Levy-Suhl from 1933 to 1937—have been largely forgotten. Yet the psychopedagogical efforts of their creators persisted in many ways. Anna Freud, for instance, continued her work of institution-building, teaching, lecturing, and writing in the field of child education for the rest of her life, even under the most difficult circumstances. In 1937, with the financial help of fellow child analyst Edith Jackson, she created the Jackson *Kinderkrippe* (according to Freud, "something between a crèche and a nursery school") for children under the age of two, who were selected from poor Viennese families in which both parents worked outside the home. Freud's biographer notes that a nursery for children so young was "unheard of at that time."

To a great extent, it was Freud and her colleagues who were still the principal learners: "What we need to see now," Freud wrote, "are the actual experiences of the first years of life, from the outside, as they present themselves" (qtd. in Young-Bruehl 2008, 218). The Jackson Nursery survived only for a year, due to the 1938 *Anschluss* and looming world war. But, having escaped to England with her father, Freud enlisted Dorothy Burlingham to help her revive the experiment in their Hampstead War Nursery, which opened in 1940. Building on its wartime success, Freud went on to create the Hampstead Child Therapy Course in 1947 and, in 1952, formally established the Hampstead Child Therapy Course and Clinic—the first fully-fledged center for child analysis, observational research, education, and training.[14] All the while, she continued to train subsequent generations of child analysts, lecture on psychoanalysis to members of the Nursery Schools Association of Great Britain and other groups of child educators and caregivers, publish numerous articles and books of her own, and help found the annual journal *The Psychoanalytic Study of the Child*.

Ψ

The Psychoanalytic Study of the Child was launched in 1945 (the final year of World War II), almost as if to signal a kind of rebirth or resurrection after years of global conflict and mass death. In addition to reviving the work of the defunct *Journal for Psychoanalytic Pedagogy*, it was also, for many émigré analysts, part of their work of mourning for countless other dislocations and losses they'd suffered (Thompson 2023, 17). By that year's end, the world could look back on the allied victory over Hitler's Germany, the revelation of the scope of Nazi genocide, and the atomic bombings of Hiroshima and Nagasaki. The psychoanalytic world could also look back on what had been its own most tumultuous and divisive "war" thus far: the so-called Controversial Discussions of 1942–1944. This protracted series of meetings of the British Psychoanalytical Society involved heated struggles over the future of psychoanalysis in the wake of Sigmund Freud's death in 1939. Anna Freud led the traditionalists and Melanie Klein the revisionists, and longstanding debates over treatment, training, and theory were volatilized as much by the clash of these two strong personalities as by the horrendous pressures of the world war and the vicissitudes of mourning the "father" of psychoanalysis. During this period of fear, anger, uncertainty, confusion, and—crucially—helplessness, it's hardly surprising that the endeavor of child analysis, to which both Freud and Klein were devoted, was at the heart of these "Controversial Discussions."

Anna Freud and Klein held radically different views concerning the consequences of infantile helplessness for human development and understanding. From Klein's perspective, as Britzman characterizes it, this primal distress, the distress of not-knowing, "enraged and frustrated the infant to such an extent that anxiety and aggression marked every moment of normal development." From Freud's perspective, however, infants were for the most part adept (given the support of good-enough parenting) at "learning to sublimate instinctual conflict and acknowledge the demands of external reality" (Britzman 2003, 41). Which has more influence, internal reality or external reality? How best could the parent/teacher/analyst recognize and address the child's anxiety, their relation to external objects, their drives, their persistent fantasies, their rage, their projections, their defenses, their capacity to symbolize, and their existential need *to know*? As participants clashed over such questions, the Controversial Discussions frequently recurred to the topic of education (from the learning and schooling of the youngest children to the training of adult psychoanalysts) and to "the status and boundaries of epistemology and ontology in learning and teaching" (Britzman 2003, 37).

Most of the theoretical, or metapsychological, differences between Freud and Klein derive from their respective work as pioneering child analysts. Each spent years observing, listening to, interacting with, and writing about children, whose intrapsychic and interpersonal lives differ so markedly from those of the adult patients and self-analyzing practitioners upon which the foundational principles of psychoanalysis were constructed. One of the heightened challenges they faced in their work with children was what Britzman calls "the dissonant, uneasy place of education within psychoanalytic thought" (2003, 46), and they both faced it, in part, by experimenting with psychoanalytic principles in non-domestic spaces of education. For example, like Anna Freud, Klein had come out early and strongly for school-based approaches to the facilitation of children's psycho-sexual health, concluding her first major essay, "The Development of a Child" (1921), by asking: "How can upbringing on psycho-analytic principles be carried out in practice?" Her provisional answer was: "the founding of kindergartens at the head of which there will be women analysts" (1975a, 53).

Klein envisioned a primarily reactive role for the analyst-head, as someone who could "observe a whole crowd of children so as to recognize the suitability of analytic intervention and to carry it out forthwith" (1975a, 53). But others approached psychoanalytic pedagogy more pro-actively—including, notably, Alexander S. Neill at the famous Summerhill school (founded in 1921 in Germany but moved to England in 1923) and Susan Isaacs at the shorter-lived Malting House School (1924–1929) in Cambridgeshire. Unlike Isaacs, Neill was not a psychoanalyst, but he found a rationale for his own early intuitions about the dangers of "sex repression" in the controversial work of analyst Wilhelm Reich (Neill 1993, 217)[15] and created Summerhill to be a permissive, non-coercive learning environment in which children's impulses—including their erotic impulses—were encouraged rather than suppressed. Though untrained, Neill held quasi-analytic sessions with some of the students and was generally more concerned with the promotion of children's overall happiness than with the quality of their formal education. Neill's book, *Summerhill: A Radical Approach to Child Rearing* (1960), was published with a highly encomiastic foreword by Erich Fromm, in which he praises Neill and his school for upholding "the *true* principle of education without fear" (Neill 1960, xii).

Isaacs's approach to education was anti-authoritarian as well. But, unlike Neill, she was both a trained teacher and a qualified psychoanalyst (thereby meeting Klein's recommendations for a head of school). Isaacs and her colleagues were determined to listen respectfully to the Malting House School's pre-adolescent students and give them full freedom of action and emotional expression. Isaacs and her colleagues wanted to observe the children as they were, without the customary masks of fear or respectability (what Winnicott would call "false selves") imposed by traditional school discipline; to help them manage and channel their sexual and aggressive impulses, instead of enforcing their suppression; and, rather than impose rigid rules and harsh punishments, to give them room to experiment with and adapt to the vicissitudes of interpersonal relations with both their schoolmates and their teachers (Graham 2008, 10–13). The Malting House School was short-lived. But, due to the wealth and prominence of the Cambridge/Bloomsbury families from which its students came, and to Isaacs's subsequent career as an analyst and writer, its importance as an early experiment in educational psychology endured.

During its years of operation, the Malting House School attracted many visitors, including Jean Piaget, James Strachey, and, most consequentially, Klein, with whom Isaacs formed a lasting personal and professional relationship. Both Piaget and Strachey were skeptical of the school's permissive ethos. But Klein's critique was more instrumental in Isaacs' revision of her own psychopedagogical thinking—particularly after dissent among the school's leadership led her to resign in 1927. (Financial difficulties forced the school's closure in 1929.) Isaacs had helped to create Malting House School at a time when many psychopedagogues believed that, if teachers would relinquish their traditional authoritarian and disciplinarian roles and if each child were allowed to follow his or her own inclinations without fear or guilt, then even when they expressed or conducted themselves in ways that were disruptive, aggressive, or licentious, "the ego [could] be spared the necessity of repression" (Sterba 1945, 309). But Klein helped Isaacs give more consideration, not just to the inevitability, but also to the psychic *necessity* of internal as well as external conflict. It was also clear to both of them that the functions of analyst and teacher couldn't practicably be combined in one person. In 1929, Klein and Isaacs collaborated on a symposium on the psychoanalytic education of teachers in which they drew heavily on Isaacs's experience at Malting House, while correcting many of its flawed early assumptions. Isaacs's books, *The Intellectual Growth of Young Children* (1930) and the more fully Kleinian *Social Development in Young Children* (1933), helped lead to her appointment as Head of the Department of Child Development at the University of London's Institute of Education, and both books continued to be used for decades as standard texts in teacher-training colleges.[16]

Looking back in 1938, Michael Bálint observed that thus far psychoanalytically informed education, in both theory and practice, had concentrated chiefly on "a pedagogy of the super-ego" (1965, 197). The Freuds, Ferenczi, Jones, Pfister, Klein, Zulliger, Isaacs, Rank, Erikson, and the rest had hitherto, both in their writings and in their experimental teaching and institution building, been chiefly concerned with liberating children from the intrapsychic and social consequences of authoritarianism and from the suppression of their libidinal and aggressive drives. They sought, in other words, to re-educate the super-ego—or, at the very least, to mitigate the psychic incorporation of traditional schooling's "exhortations, moralizing and especially the laying down of values" (1965, 199–200). They aimed, as Anna Freud put it, "to foster in the child the development of ego forces strong enough to hold their own against the pressure of the drives" (1989, 6). But, like Bálint, Freud came to recognize the inadequacy of this "pedagogy of the super-ego." For one thing, it was impossible and indeed undesirable to "rid the child of anxiety." For when "the severity of the super-ego was reduced, children produced the deepest of all anxieties, that is, the fear of human beings who feel unprotected against the pressure of their drives" (1989, 8).

Neither Bálint nor Anna Freud nor any of their peers were able to articulate the more sophisticated psychoanalytic pedagogy that continued to stir their imaginations. At the IPA's Four Countries Conference—held in Budapest in 1937 and including members of the Hungarian Psychoanalytic Society, the Vienna Psychoanalytic Society, the Italian Psychoanalytic Society, and the Czecho-Slovakian Psychoanalytic Study Group—there was a comprehensive "Review of Psychoanalytic Pedagogy" that turned out to be, as Sol Cohen observes, "the last great conference of child analysts and psychoanalytic pedagogues before the final curtain descended on an epoch and before the diaspora of the child analysts from the continent." At this conference, "it fell to Anna Freud to read the epitaph for the movement: 'After years of intensive work by some of the best psychoanalytical research workers, we are certain only that there still exists no practicable psychoanalytical pedagogy'" (Cohen 1999, 175). Many of the conference's attendees, of course, would soon make their way to the US, where most ended up as critics of Americans' perceived overindulgence of their children generally and of the medicalized "mental hygiene" movement that flourished there during the interwar years and beyond. Yet this tremendous influx of psychoanalytic wisdom and experience would transform American thought and culture for decades to come. As the eminent behavioral psychologist Orval Hobart Mowrer later lamented, "anyone who reached adulthood prior to 1950 knows how perversely Freudian theory and practice dominated not only in the specific field of psychotherapy, but also education, jurisprudence, religion, child rearing, and art and literature, and social philosophy" (qtd. in Burnham 2012, 158).

Ψ

Meanwhile, during the interwar years—notwithstanding the much more substantial emphasis on early childhood and adolescent education—there had been a number of significant efforts toward "establishing psychoanalysis in the university, including," Eli Zaretsky observes, "by Sándor Ferenczi at the University of Budapest, Karl Abraham at the University of Berlin, Franz Alexander at the University of Chicago, and Max Eitingon at the Hebrew University in Jerusalem" (2004, 176). Sigmund Freud earnestly supported these efforts. But he also

> sought to guard the autonomy of psychoanalysis, which, he insisted, was subject to the general protocols of science but not reducible to existing paradigms such as organic psychiatry or experimental psychology. He need not have worried. All attempts to gain a foothold in the university failed.
>
> (Zaretsky 2004, 176)

Still, substantial thought was given to the place of psychoanalysis in higher education. Freud himself remained mindful, to say the least, of the academic reception of his ideas. Recalling, in 1914, his one and only trip to the US—made in 1909 at the invitation of Stanley Hall, the president of Clark University—Freud wrote that,

> to our great surprise, we found the members of that small but highly esteemed University for the study of education and philosophy so unprejudiced that they were acquainted with all the literature of psycho-analysis and had given it a place in their lectures to students. In prudish America it was possible, in academic circles at least, to discuss freely and scientifically everything that in ordinary life is regarded as objectionable.
>
> (1957b, 31)

Of course, few "academic circles" were anything like Clark's under President Hall. Indeed, Freud's new ideas advanced much more slowly in universities in the US than in his native Austria and other European and South American countries.

Nevertheless, Freud kept the faith, writing in his 1919 essay "On the Teaching of Psychoanalysis in Universities" that the application of the psychoanalytic method

> is by no means confined to the field of psychological disorders, but extends also to the solution of problems in art, philosophy, and religion …. The general psycho-analytic course should be thrown open to the students

of these branches of learning as well. The fertilizing effects of psycho-analytic thought on these other disciplines would certainly contribute greatly towards forging a closer link, in the sense of a universitas literarum, between medical science and the branches of learning which lie within the sphere of philosophy and the arts.

(1955f, 173)

Freud also persisted in his disdain for academic psychology, telling Ferenczi in 1918 that it "storms on without noticing that psychoanalysis has cut off its head" (Freud and Ferenczi 2000, 2: 306).

Freud gave fuller scope to this antipathy in a 1933 letter to Judah Magnes, president of Jerusalem's Hebrew University. Magnes had sought Freud's advice regarding candidates for the appointment of a "Chair of Psychology" and asked what Freud thought about the relation of psychoanalysis to such an appointment. Magnes *own* view was "that it would be premature to introduce psychoanalysis before a Chair of Psychology has been established" (qtd. in Bargal 1998, 56)—in other words, only upon the secure foundation of psychology's scientific legitimacy could a psychoanalytic superstructure be contemplated. Infuriated, Freud replied:

Psychoanalysis is also psychology in the sense that it is a science of the *unconscious* psychic processes, whereas what is taught as academic psychology is confined to dealing with *conscious* phenomena .... All the applications of psychology to medicine and the arts derive from deep-reaching psychoanalysis, whereas academic psychology has proved itself to be sterile.

(1961b, 418)

Sterile or not, academic psychology was only minimally receptive to psychoanalysis. As Hall puts it in his autobiography,

psychoanalysis and the study of the unconscious have been simply ignored or condemned on superficial grounds by most American psychologists of the normal. This neglect is in part explained because of a prudish reluctance to face the momentous problems of sex life. [They] balk, too, at the unconscious .... Most psychologists hover about focal consciousness or awareness like insects about an arc light.

(1923, 11)

Moreover, according to historian Nathan Hale, Jr., academic psychologists were "put off by the apparent psychoanalytic disdain for their discipline and for their laborious attempts to be scientific" (1971, 286).

Such resistance, however, wasn't absolute. In 1931, for example, Dorothy Park examined the most widely used US college psychology textbooks published between 1910 and 1930. Her intent was to determine exactly how much attention—whether positive or negative—they devoted to Freudian psychoanalysis, combing through every page of 50 such textbooks for direct references as well as for evidence of "marked indirect influence" (1931, 73). Park found that 38% made *no* direct reference to "Freudianism" and that "the average percent of Freudian influence" amounted to 4.07% (1931, 78). Nevertheless, she interpreted her findings to indicate "that Freudianism has a recognized place in academic psychology today and is becoming more and more firmly established" (1931, 84). Park found it especially meaningful that in every case but one in which an author had published a second edition, most had shown "a quite pronounced proportional increase," even among those with "unfavorable" attitudes toward psychoanalysis (1931, 80).

Subsequent studies, however, indicate that Park's optimism about psychoanalysis "becoming more and more firmly established" in academic psychology was at best misguided. A 1999 study published in *American Psychologist* reported that fewer than one percent of doctoral dissertations in psychology completed between 1967 and 1994 contained any keywords pertaining to psychoanalysis (Robins et al. 1999, 120). In 2001, Robert Bornstein observed that "in most introductory, personality, developmental, and abnormal psychology texts, psychoanalysis is described in negative terms" and that "in other domains of psychology (e.g., cognitive, biological, industrial-organizational), psychoanalysis is rarely mentioned at all" (2001, 6).

In 2006, Sandra W. Park and Elizabeth L. Auchincloss reported their far more comprehensive findings that: a 1940 "survey of the most frequently used texts in academic psychology [found that if] psychoanalysis is presented at all, it is presented incorrectly and, in an inadequate fashion, naively criticized on impertinent grounds" (2006, 1365); a 1943 study of 350 textbooks of general psychology, abnormal psychology, and psychiatry published between 1901 and 1940 featured, among other things, a catalog of what its authors called the "vocabulary of rejection" consistently deployed against psychoanalytic ideas (2006, 1365–66); a 1976 review of introductory psychology textbooks published between 1908 and 1975 found their discussions of psychoanalysis to be characterized by "a marked and steadily increasing polarization of attitudes" (2006, 1366); a 1991 assessment of ten psychology textbooks published between 1985 and 1988 concluded that "all introductory textbooks treat [Freud] superficially and simplistically" and give no account of "how Freud's thought was constantly evolving" (2006, 1366–67); that, looking back in 1992 at the range of psychology textbooks published in the first half of the century (including many from Dorothy Park's early study), another researcher found them persistently "assimilating psychoanalytic concepts into mainstream psychology without mentioning their origins" (2006, 1367); and that a 1997 study of fifteen textbooks published between 1988 and 1992 found they all tended reductively to equate psychoanalysis with Freud (2006, 1367).

Even more recently, three researchers evaluated the eight top-selling, full-length, introductory psychology textbooks in 2005. They defined psychoanalytic content as "(a) material on Freud or other prominent psychoanalytic theorists … (b) material on core psychoanalytic terms and concepts … (c) material on psychoanalysis in theory or practice; and (d) material on psychodynamic psychotherapies." In the eight textbooks—each one containing several thousand paragraphs—they found a total of 873 such paragraphs (i.e., approximately 0.05% of the cumulative number of paragraphs in all eight books). They coded such content for accuracy paragraph-by-paragraph and found that "approximately 8% of the psychoanalytically oriented paragraphs … contained some kind of inaccurate or misleading information" (Habarth et al. 2011, 17).

So persistent and pervasive have these omissions, reductions, and distortions been, throughout the twentieth century and into the twenty-first, that the preface to Stephen Mitchell and Margaret Black's superb introduction to the field, *Freud and Beyond: A History of Modern Psychoanalytic Thought* (1995/2016), is devoted to debunking several "major myths about psychoanalysis"—myths cultivated by psychology textbooks, further disseminated by mass media, and possessing "wide currency in both the popular and scholarly spheres" (2016, xvi).

Ψ

Both within and beyond the field of psychology, the twentieth-century US reception of psychoanalysis has been chiefly characterized by a toning-down of its more radical aspects—a trend heavily influenced by the rise of ego-psychology and by the medicalization of the psychoanalytic profession. Initially, however, the US had been quicker than most European countries to assimilate the basic principles of psychoanalysis—not only by way of "mass magazines and popular books" (Hale 1995, 74), but also through the academic fields of sociology, anthropology, philosophy, psychology, and education. As in popular culture, the academic use of psychoanalytic terms and concepts was often subject to dilution and distortion and frequently resisted. Yet they were nevertheless widely recognized and applied, especially in the realm of progressive education (see Herman 1995).

In Europe, liberal "child-centered" pedagogies gathered force only after World War I had broken up the old monarchies and traditions, whetting appetites for innovation and democratization. But in the US, long before the war had even begun, Charles W. Eliot at Harvard, John Dewey at the University of Chicago (and later Columbia), and other progressive educators made it possible for the nascent field of educational psychology to emerge with the new century, and during its first decade Dewey's psychoanalytically oriented peers were doing their best to bring Freud's "new psychology" into workable accord with seemingly antagonistic approaches like behaviorism.

By the 1920s, "powerhouse" educational psychology programs like Ohio State University's were proving in their teacher-training courses that, rather than being wholly antithetical, "psychoanalysis and behaviorism were complimentary and consolidated" (Petrina 2004, 525). Public lectures and national periodicals helped to rationalize "applied psychoanalysis" for classroom purposes among the rank-and-file.[17] In 1926, for instance, Isador H. Coriat—one of the first American psychoanalysts and founder of the Boston Psychoanalytic Society—explained the pedagogical value of transference in an article for the national journal, *Progressive Education*:

> In school the teacher becomes a substitute for the father or mother of the child and in the emotional tie which exists between teacher and pupil, the earlier parent-child relationship is re-lived and re-animated. Teachers must understand their own unconscious, for if they fail to do so, they will never realize why they are acting in certain manner towards the pupil or the effects of their daily contacts. The moulding must not be according to the teacher's prejudices or resistances but along the lines of the best possibilities inherent in the pupil's mind, both conscious and unconscious.
>
> (1926, 21)

However, in the US, entire schools that were based even in part on psycho-analytic principles—the most notable of which was Margaret Naumburg's New School (which opened in New York in 1915 and later changed its name to the Walden School)—remained very few in number. For the most part, psychoanalytic pedagogy for mass public education remained a fantasy. Moreover, the progressive education movement, generally, was focused on mass public instruction below the college level. Thus psychoanalysis made little headway in higher education, either as a foundation for pedagogy or as a field of knowledge, even in disciplines like psychology and philosophy where it might have found a proper home.

Freud himself had always been wary of what he called the "narrow-mindedness of academic philosophy" (1964b, 31), and as early as 1905 he felt the need to defend psychoanalysis against various forms of philosophi-cal positivism:

> I am aware that anyone who is under the spell of a good academic philosophical education, or who takes his opinions at long range from some so-called system of philosophy, will be opposed to the assumption of an "unconscious psychical"… and will prefer to prove its impossibility on the basis of a definition of the psychical. But definitions are a matter of convention and can be altered. I have often found that people who dispute the unconscious as being something absurd and impossible have not formed their impressions from the sources from which I at least was brought to the necessity of recognizing it.
>
> (1960a, 161–62)

Of course, Freud's debts to the philosophical tradition, from Plato to Schopenhauer, are as clear as they are profound (and frequently referenced in his writings)—as are his debts to history, literature, art, and many of the qualitative social sciences. But just as early twentieth-century acad-emicians (with a few important exceptions) tended to hold psychoanalysis at arm's length, so too did Freud seek to maintain the independence of psychoanalysis from the intellectual and bureaucratic Balkanization of aca-demic disciplines.

Thus, the first major step in forging an alliance between psychoanalysis and the university was the creation of the Psychoanalytic Institute in 1929 as part of Frankfurt's Institute for Social Research. One of the Frankfurt School's founding members, Leo Löwenthal, observes in his autobiography that "the mere fact that a psychoanalytical institute was allowed to use rooms on a university campus was then almost a sensation" (1987, 51). Among its core members, Erich Fromm was himself a psychoanalyst, and other members, including Löwenthal, Theodor Adorno, Max Horkheimer, and Herbert Marcuse, considered psychoanalysis essential to their critical investigations of philosophy and sociopolitical theory. Following leftist psychoanalysts like Adler, Fenichel, and Reich, they sought to combine various orthodox and unorthodox versions of psychoanalysis and Marxism. Horkheimer told Freud in 1932 he was convinced "that our task cannot be carried out fruitfully without the use of psychoanalytic knowledge, but I also believe I can hope that such participation in social-scientific research will not be without value for the development of psychoanalysis itself" (Ruggieri 2012, 293–94). Freud in turn, despite his ambivalence, congratulated the Institute's members for their pioneering introduction of psychoanalysis into the university setting (Horkheimer 2007, 366).

Successive generations of Frankfurt School members transformed higher education around the world, beginning with their early attempts to bring together, in the service of human emancipation, the Marxian critique of political economy and the psychoanalytic theory of the mind. Subsequent shifts and permutations of critical theory and immanent critique linked as well as transformed many branches of philosophy and the qualitative and quantitative social sciences—from cultural anthropology to economics, history, linguistics, literary criticism, media studies, political science, psychology, and sociology. Frankfurt School members' approaches to psychoanalysis varied considerably, including efforts to domesticate the radical alterity of the unconscious and, as in the later work of Jürgen Habermas, to reject psychoanalysis in favor of the empiricist framework of cognitive psychology. Yet even Habermas's rationalistic models of development and sociality are predicated on an understanding of the self "as founded upon the mastery or suppression of the drives" (Allen 2021, 12). In many academic disciplines, debates over the relation between the empirical and the theoretical, the rational and the irrational, and the utopian and reformist have continued to be— both explicitly and implicitly—debates over the place of psychoanalysis in higher education.[18]

Conversely, some psychoanalytic theorists of education have questioned the psycho-social value of higher education as such. For example, at the First International Conference on Student Mental Health, held in Princeton in 1956, Erikson presented a paper on "Late Adolescence" in which he claimed that

> among the special institutions designed for this stage, college education is probably the greatest organized artificial postponement of adulthood, emotionally speaking, that could be imagined …. It fosters particular forms of extended childishness even as it cultivates certain forms of one-sided precocity.
>
> (1987d, 633)

Erikson himself never attended college, and, while he doesn't suggest that young Americans shouldn't either, he is less sanguine than most of his colleagues about the consequences for identity formation of the "choice" of college-attendance at such a critical developmental stage.

Yet Americans were flocking to college like never before, and the number and size of public institutions expanded dramatically to accommodate the unprecedented demand. Postwar enrollment was surging by the end of the 1940s. In the 1950s, college enrollment rose by 49%; in the 1960s by 120%; and in the 1970s by another 45%. By 1980, almost half of all 18-to-24-year-olds were matriculants, and the number of older and returning students was also increasing, both at the undergraduate level and at the postgraduate and professional levels (Snyder 1993, 66–70). During the same period, the institutionalization and medicalization of psychoanalysis became a *fait accompli*. In 1925 and 1927, respectively, APsA and the New York Psychoanalytic Society began requiring a medical degree for membership. In 1938, APsA started requiring a psychiatric residency as well. And in 1954, APsA, the American Psychiatric Association (APA), and the American Medical Association (AMA) issued a joint declaration against lay (non-physician) practitioners, insisting that "the application of psychological methods to the treatment of illness was a medical function and should take place under medical supervision" (Hale 1995, 215). According to Peter Taubman, "as psychoanalysis's absorption into the medical profession by way of psychiatry deepened, the power of its original insights … decreased" (2012, 79).

Still, thanks in large part to the Rockefeller-funded "Mental Hygiene" movement, with its normative emphasis on adaptation and optimism, the educational influence of a watered-down, ego-psychological psychoanalysis expanded at all levels (Taubman 2012, 79–80). The founder and first president of APsA, neurologist James Putnam—who Freud once called the psychoanalytic movement's "most influential representative in America" (1955g, 269)—sought to "temper the darker aspects of psychoanalysis and its radical skepticism with an idealism and a belief in the power of education … to transform human beings" (Taubman 2012, 38). By 1925, Freud was already raising a red flag regarding Putnam's influence, thanks chiefly to the latter's desire to make psychoanalysis "the servant of moral aims" (1959c, 52). By the 1930s, the philosophy of "Moral Hygiene" had become thoroughly allied with the newly professionalized medical establishment—which would continue to control the practice of psychoanalysis in the US for decades—and used its association with medicine's scientific prestige to disseminate its influence over other fields, including social work and education.

Taubman points out that the well-intentioned efforts of the Mental Hygiene movement not only yielded real health benefits but also ushered more liberal attitudes into American schools. "The complication in terms of psychoanalysis," however, was that the movement's version "stripped it of its more radical insights and questions, and, in sustaining its alliance with medicine, edged it closer to becoming a male profession …. Psychoanalysis, which had been one of the few professions with a high number of women, became after World War II [in the US] completely male dominated" (2012, 83).

In the postwar US, psychoanalysis was "translated," as Taubman puts it,

> into the social conservatism of ego psychology and psychiatry, reduced by academic psychology to a series of experimentally tested concepts and hypotheses, and turned by clinical psychology into a cure-all, an expedient therapy, and a way to maximize human potential.
>
> (2012, 86)

Nevertheless, the postwar rise of clinical psychology embedded the study of psychoanalysis—albeit a limited version of psychoanalysis focused on "development" and "adjustment"—in academic departments of psychology. Efforts to combine psychoanalysis and behaviorism and the scientific aura of experimentalism in this hybridized psychology had the effect of reinforcing various psychoanalytic terms in the textbooks assigned in psychology and education courses, even though these terms were deracinated from the psychoanalytic theory that gave rise to them, and Freud's name went largely unmentioned.

The postwar alliance between clinical psychology, psychiatry, and psychoanalysis garnered a great deal of prestige within and beyond the university. Popular acceptance of psychoanalysis reached an all-time high in the US, including its glamorization in popular culture (see, e.g., Taubman 2012, 95–96)—even though mental illness itself remained heavily stigmatized. Vastly increased government funding for behavioral studies motivated at least nominally psychoanalytic research in various academic fields, including anthropology and sociology as well as psychology. Even elementary- and secondary-school teachers and guidance counselors started speaking a threadbare and misinformed patois of psychoanalytic buzzwords.

American psychoanalytic practice itself was largely commandeered by ego psychologists like Heinz Hartmann. Hartmann was the last person to complete his training analysis with Freud, but his understanding of the mind couldn't have been more unlike his analyst's. Hartmann turned the ego into what Taubman calls "a muscular organ for social adaptation" (2012, 103), collapsing the distinction between Freud's "reality principle" and the normative demands of America's Cold War social order. In effect, American ego psychology operationalized psychoanalysis for conservative ideological purposes, and its critics—which included the dominant wing of the American Communist Party (CP)—were accused not only of being "unscientific" but also politically dangerous. Suspicion (and confusion) cut both ways: the CP accused psychoanalysis of deflecting attention away from class struggle and effectively blaming individuals for social inequities, while the FBI and the House Un-American Activities Committee (HUAC) associated psychoanalysis with socialist Jewish refugees, subversive intellectuals, and sexual deviants. The FBI surveilled known Marxist analysts, while recruiting other analysts to inform on their own patients (see Danto 2012; see also Herzog 2017). As Dagmar Herzog sums it up for the Cold War US, psychoanalysis "could have both normative-conservative and socially critical implications," and the institutional response, for example from APsA and the IPA, was a plea/directive to analysts in many parts of the world to retreat from the extrapsychic as much as possible (2017, 2–3).

However, during the 1960s and 70s especially, the more politically conscious ranks of the profession (not to mention the irrepressible unruliness of psychic life itself) helped dispel the analytic authoritarianism of the 1950s, inspired and abetted in many ways by the rise of the New Left and the radical campus movements in North America, South America, and Europe. The international revitalization of psychoanalysis was to a great extent a youth movement, both on university campuses and among the new ranks of analytic candidates. Yet even as the revolutionary content of psychoanalysis itself was spilling into the streets, it was still being heavily excluded from the classroom. As late as 1969, ego psychologist Bruno Bettelheim's article on "Psychoanalysis and Education"—one of very few articles on the subject published in the postwar US—could begin by lamenting that "we are still without any psychoanalytic theory of learning" (1969, 73). Bettelheim blamed this on earlier experiments in psychoanalytic pedagogy (e.g., Bernfeld's) that sought, in his view irresponsibly, "to uncover and free the unconscious, the id" without proper attention to what Bettelheim, in a startling neologism, calls the "ego correct" (i.e., an intelligible ego that had "a meaningful message to others" [1969, 75]). Moreover, for conservatives like Bettelheim, education meant taking children beyond the pleasure principle—not in Freud's sense, but by disciplining them with a proper amount of "fear" and "respect for the external superego," so that they could "move from id expression to ego achievement" and from the self-chastening of irrational superego to conscience modified by "reason" (1969, 78–80).

Unsurprisingly, Bettelheim supported the US war in Vietnam (then at its height) and expressed dismay that "the young generation feel that those over thirty have nothing of importance to say to them." They've begun life "in a dream world," he insisted, and were now, having been so badly miseducated, simply mystified by the world, with insufficient ego strength to do anything but blame society and "drop out or seek oblivion in drugs" (1969, 80–81). Such were the fruits, in his view, of what earlier critics had called the "over-permissiveness" of the pedagogical experiments conducted by Bernfeld, Aichhorn, Anna Freud, Neill, Isaacs, and others.

Bettelheim seemed wholly unaware that his alternative recommendation for a proper psychoanalytic pedagogy amounted to little more than infantilizing conservative propaganda:

> If we want our children to feel that life in our society is worthwhile, we must see that it comes across to them, when they are young, that things are essentially all right, though sometimes difficult and in need of improvement. And it must come across to them through symbols like the President or the police, symbols they can easily grasp in visual form.

> (1969, 83)

Having been imprisoned in both Dachau and Buchenwald toward the end of the war, Bettelheim's social conservatism, which grew increasingly aggressive in the 1960s, may have been, in part, a reaction formation directed against what he perceived to be a dangerous faith in human betterment on the part of the American left and in the opinions of some of his European socialist colleagues, including Alfred Adler (Fisher 2008, 82–84).

Another Austrian refugee from Hitler who settled in the US, ego psychologist Ernst Kris, published an article immediately after the war, outlining a very different, transferential approach, inspired by Harry Stack Sullivan's interpersonalism. In Kris's view, "every step of learning in early childhood, as are many steps of learning in later life, is co-determined by object relations and involve conscious and unconscious identification" (1948, 634). But this precocious appeal to focus on the transferential dynamics of the teacher-student relationship was out of step with the postwar ego-psychological mainstream, of which Bettelheim was such a visible and popular figurehead, and Kris's more object relational/interpersonal perspective on teacher-student dynamics had scant influence at the time.

In the 1950s, psychology professor Arthur T. Jersild, also influenced by Sullivan, published several books, including *When Teachers Face Themselves* (1955), in which he stressed the importance of psychoanalytic self-reflection for teacher-training. Yet in 1957 his colleague at Columbia's Teachers College, education professor Goodwin Watson, was still lamenting "that the discipline of psychoanalysis, which for over a half century has revealed so much about the dynamics of a child's life, should have so little direct impact on education." Few educators, Watson observed, had more than a cursory impression of fundamental psychoanalytic concepts: "Freud's influence has filtered into teacher education by indirection. Resistance has been reduced by dilution" (1957, 241). Despairing of the present, Watson nevertheless hoped that, "eventually," the current, one-sided view of teaching would be supplanted by recognition of what he saw as six lines of necessary development toward a psychoanalytic psychology of education: encountering resistance, using transference, understanding group psychology, attending to unconscious communication of affect, recognizing internal conflict, and making psychotherapy an integral part of teacher-training (1957, 242–45).

But throughout the 1940s and 50s, notwithstanding the insights of Kris, Jersild, Watson, and others, the nexus of ego psychology, medicine, and Cold War politics helped perpetuate Bettelheim's brand of institutionalized psychoanalytic conservatism in US academic psychology. If, in the late

1950s, Philip Rieff could marvel at Freud's "intellectual influence" across the US and claim that, more than "any other modern thinker," he "presides" over "the college classroom" (1959, xi), it was nonetheless a domesticated version of Freud, co-opted by medical authorities and made to conform to the escalating empirical requirements of the social sciences.

Thus it was left to professors in other disciplines—chiefly in the humanities—to make room in higher education for the untamed and unsettling insights of psychoanalysis: Norman O. Brown (at Wesleyan and Rochester), Dorothy Dinnerstein (at Rutgers-Camden), Erich Fromm (at Michigan State and NYU), Norman N. Holland (Buffalo), H. Stuart Hughes (at Stanford and Harvard), Herbert Marcuse (at Brandeis and UC-San Diego), Philip Rieff (at the Universities of Pennsylvania and Chicago), and Lionel Trilling (at Columbia).

Norman Holland's work as a psychoanalytic literary critic in books like *The Dynamics of Literary Response* (1968) made him a key figure in the development of reader-response criticism. In 1970, he founded the Center for the Psychological Study of the Arts at SUNY Buffalo. This interdisciplinary center didn't grant degrees of its own but, as Murray Schwartz puts it, "supplemented undergraduate and graduate education in many fields" (2018, 137). Like Holland, Schwartz was one of the center's many psychoanalytically oriented faculty affiliates, and he describes the curriculum as having included

> theoretical and applied psychoanalysis, bridges between medical and humanistic education, opportunities for clinical experience, and, perhaps most importantly, a pervasive spirit of collegial, critical inquiry and commitment to interdisciplinary dialogue related to psychoanalytic education.
>
> (2018, 138)

The pedagogical method of the center's core seminars was patterned after clinical models and

> designed to encourage and consider every response, even the most "irrelevant" and "outrageous," as a statement from which something could be learned …. We remained aware that unconscious processes are always at work, setting fluctuating limits to the possibilities for thought and knowledge.
>
> (2018, 139)

As psychoanalysis continued to retreat in most segments of US culture, the Buffalo Center endured—and still exists today, as the Center for the Study of Psychoanalysis and Culture (Schwartz 2018, 146).

Ψ

Even now, very few academic programs and centers for psychoanalytic studies exist, either in the US or elsewhere. (Those that do will be discussed in Chapter 2.) But, beginning in the 1960s, psychoanalysis became more and more a part of university discourse in less formalized, institution-directed ways. Indeed, both on and off campus, it was the social justice movements of the 1960s—feminism in particular—that were instrumental in keeping psychoanalytic thought alive and under lively contestation in higher education. And while movement-based critiques of psychoanalysis contributed to the decline and eventual demise of the field's social prestige and medical influence, they nevertheless helped to forge an interdisciplinary psychoanalytic discourse that restored the radical, critical, and speculative dimensions of psychoanalysis suppressed and displaced in previous decades. Of course, the field of psychoanalysis itself, along with its closest interlocutors (from Frankfurt School members like Marcuse and Fromm to other great thinkers such as Norman O. Brown, Ernest Becker, Frantz Fanon, Paul Ricoeur, and Juliet Mitchell), had been doing extraordinary, transformative work all along, especially in the areas of object relations and interpersonalism. And it was Mitchell's book, *Psychoanalysis and Feminism* (1974), that—at the height of the feminist movement's opposition to the patriarchalism of both Freud's writings and the male-dominated psychoanalytic profession— argued that psychoanalysis was an essential foundation of the *critique* of patriarchy and its oppression of women.

Mitchell wrote *Psychoanalysis and Feminism* amidst the sociocultural upheavals and controversies of the 1960s and the 1970s and, in doing so, courted controversy herself—risking, as one early reviewer put it,

> accusations of apostasy from her fellow feminists. Her book not only challenges orthodox feminism, however, it defies the conventions of social thought in the English-speaking countries (with which feminist thought is thoroughly entangled)—cultural relativism, historicism, an empiricism hostile to theory in almost any form.
>
> (Lasch 1974, 17)

Indeed, Mitchell was among the first major scholars to help broaden awareness among Anglophone readers of Jacques Lacan—one of many French psychoanalysts and psychoanalytically engaged thinkers (including Louis Althusser, Gilles Deleuze, Jacques Derrida, Michel Foucault, Luce Irigaray, and Julia Kristeva) whose diverse works transformed the intellectual and cultural landscape of late-twentieth-century America and Britain. Chapter 4 of this book will have more to say about how Continental theory and movement politics affected the place of psychoanalysis in this period's academic contests over disciplinary methodologies. But, here, it will be helpful to compare the history of psychoanalytic education in the US and the UK to what was transpiring in France—including, crucially, the consequences of the civil protests and strikes of May 1968, in which university students (and some of their professors) played a major role.

According to Elisabeth Roudinesco, between 1945 and 1968, psychoanalysis was "present" in French universities "in the manner opened up by Lagache" (1994, 552). Daniel Lagache had in fact pioneered the introduction of psychoanalysis into the French university system as a lecturer in psychology at the University of Strasbourg in 1937. Articulate and charming, with a humanistic sensibility and a sterling scientific reputation, Lagache (a full member of the Paris Psychoanalytic Society) assuaged academicians' anxieties while also helping to disseminate psychoanalytic ideas more broadly in publications for general readership.[19] In 1947, he left Strasbourg to head the psychology department at the Sorbonne, where he championed what turned out to be, in practice, the untenable notion of a unified discipline of psychology that included psychoanalysis—which continued to be taught, as Roudinesco writes, "under the rubric of psychology and after a tradition that owed more to Janet than to Freud" (1994, 552). Thus the path opened up for psychoanalysis within the French university system only ever led to the greater reach and legitimation of clinical psychology, in which psychoanalysis continued to occupy a marginal position (1994, 554)—until, that is, the extraordinary period of civil unrest and student protest throughout France commonly known as May 68.

Ironically, the marginal position of psychoanalysis within the university found its counterpart in the much more vainglorious (and largely self-imposed) institutional marginalization of France's most influential psychoanalyst, Lacan, who for three decades, beginning in 1952, delivered a series of "Seminars" in which he developed his theories and promulgated his teachings extramurally—until 1964, that is, when their venue shifted from the Sainte-Anne Hospital (where Lacan was a staff psychiatrist) to the École Normale Supérieure (ENS), and in 1969 to the Sorbonne. But if the 1960s were the decade of Lacan's tentative affiliation with the French university system, they were also the decade of his complicated disaffiliation from and disaffection with both the French Psychoanalytic Society and the International Psychoanalytical Association—punctuated in 1964 by the founding of his own professional organization, the Freudian School of Paris. If Lacan's highly unorthodox practice alienated him from his analytic colleagues, his even more highly interdisciplinary (and theatrical) teachings drew almost all of France's leading intellectuals to his Seminars, and their hurried transcription and publication, along with his previously published *Writings*, made his provocative and challenging work available to others, like Juliet Mitchell, elsewhere in the world.

Like Mitchell and other major theorists and philosophers of the era, many of France's young *soixant-huitards* ('68-ers) developed and sustained a complex relation to Lacan's teachings. Lacan's own initial support for the uprising soon became an indictment of the revolutionaries' impingements on certain aspects of his distinctive, crypto-Marxian "return to Freud" and his ongoing battle with institutionalized psychoanalysis as such. In fact, Lacan's earlier criticisms of France's psychoanalytic training institutes helped inspire the soixant-huitards' own rebellion against hierarchical institutions, including the French university system. But, after his initial excitement ebbed, Lacan came to feel that his psychoanalytic views on power, knowledge, and desire had been woefully misconstrued and erroneously linked to the "libidinal revolutionism" of figures like Reich and Marcuse. Lacan famously ridiculed the students' ostensive goal of liberating the subject's desire for knowledge as a kind of hysterical symptom of their own unconscious desire for a master (1991, 239), and he foresaw that their demands for university reform would play very nicely into the hands of President de Gaulle's swiftly drafted and implemented plan for the neoliberal expansion of the proto-corporate university.

Because by the mid-1960s Lacan had been excluded from the professional psychoanalytic community, he sought recognition and authority from the wider intellectual world and, with ambivalence, from academe. His own Freudian School welcomed non-analysts as well as trained analysts, thereby attracting members from fields including philosophy, linguistics, anthropology, and literary studies. Later, in the wake of May 68 and amidst other hurried reforms, de Gaulle's minister of education created the University of Paris at Vincennes—an "experimental" university meant to test some of the soixant-huitards' demands for educational reform, including greater curricular flexibility and student participation in administrative affairs. Vincennes' academic divisions included a Department of Psychoanalysis—the first such university department in France and thus the first official French recognition of psychoanalysis as an autonomous academic discipline.

Initially chaired by Serge Leclaire, its faculty included François Baudry, Jean Clauvril, Luce Irigaray, Michel de Certeau, Claude Dumezil, Jacques-Alain Miller, Michele Montrèlay, Jacques Nassif, Claude Rabant, and René Tostain—all of whom were members of Lacan's Freudian School (Dosse 1997, 148). Lacan himself was relieved of his teaching position at the ENS in 1969, and he thereafter sought to wield even greater control over the department at Vincennes. He dismissed Irigaray and several other faculty members, persuaded Leclaire to resign, and installed his son-in-law Jacques-Alain Miller as a kind of proxy ruler (Robcis 2013, 190).

The creation at Vincennes (Paris VIII) in 1968 of a department of psychoanalysis "established for the first time on a French university campus a psychoanalytic curriculum free from any indebtedness to medicine or psychology" (1994, 557). And in 1980, at what was then Paris V, Jean Laplanche[20]—who had taught psychoanalysis at the ENS and the Sorbonne before moving, in 1969, to the Clinical Human Sciences department at Diderot (Paris VII)—established France's first, non-clinical doctoral degree program in psychoanalysis. This too, Roudinesco writes, was "something completely new in France, and perhaps in the world: the existence of a faculty composed of psychoanalysts speaking as such—not under the cover of another discipline, whether psychology, literature, or philosophy—about psychoanalysis in an authorized manner within the university" (1994, 556).

About Laplanche's various achievements in university-based psychoanalytic education from the 1960s to the 1980s, Dominique Scarfone wrote in 1997 that,

> today, this might all seem quite banal; psychoanalytic studies at the university level are in fact now quite widespread, not just in France, but in the Anglo-Saxon world as well. Nevertheless, such programs … can easily lead to misunderstandings.

(1997, 46)

But Scarfone's suggestion that, between 1980 and 1997, psychoanalytic studies had become "quite widespread" in French, American, and British universities is an exaggeration. For despite the continuing influx of Continental, or postmodern, philosophy during those two decades—an influx that included psychoanalytic theory and related discourses—institutional recognition, in the form of program-building, faculty hiring, and awarding of degrees, remained quite rare in all three countries. In the US and the UK, a handful of colleges and universities managed to establish and, in some cases, sustain formal psychoanalytic studies programs. But most of these were non-degree/non-certificate programs with little institutional support or infrastructure and small student cohorts. (The dozen or so currently existing programs will be discussed further in Chapters 2 and 3.)

In a 2004 article, Laplanche outlines several common areas of misunderstanding and controversy: 1) The epistemological status of psychoanalysis: Is it a legitimate scientific discipline or branch of knowledge, and would it be open to critique and refutation like other such formations? 2) What would be the proper relation between academic psychoanalysis and academic psychology? 3) Will university-based "theoretical" or "applied" psychoanalytic research be compromised and devalued by its separation from clinical practice? 4) Can psychoanalysis be taught by and to those who are not themselves—or have never been—in analysis? 5) Would advanced university degrees in psychoanalysis be mistaken for qualification to practice psychoanalysis and potentially compromise the authority of analytic institutes?

In outlining these questions, Laplanche is dismissive of the qualms he understands to be behind them. Thus he concludes the article by insisting that university-based research would facilitate rigorous debate precisely through the recognition of psychoanalysis as a distinct epistemological field and that, paradoxically, this would serve as "a guarantee of the extraterritoriality of analytical practice in relation to *any* institution" (2004, 12).[21] This "extraterritoriality" is

a corollary of the fundamental rule in psychoanalysis: the suspension of goal-representations. Without it, analysis quickly falls back on the adaptive aims of these institutions, even when these aims are directed at the training of analysts. Laplanche is therefore not only far from wanting to train analysts at the university, but also fiercely opposed to the so-called "didactic" psychoanalysis maintained even to this day, in various psychoanalytic institutes throughout the world, for those training to become analysts.

(Scarfone 1997, 48–49)

Laplanche's wariness of all professionalizing institutions stems in part from his early commitment to socialist politics. In 1948, he helped to found the radical libertarian socialist group, "Socialism or Barbarism," and he channeled his commitment to its principles into his participation in the events of May 68. But, as he explained in 1999, "analysis took the place of the political things. They are difficult to keep together" (2000, 32).[22] Nevertheless, he remained wary of the normative and coercive nature of institutions, including psychoanalytic institutions, and resisted the notion that the goal of psychoanalytic treatment was "a renewed capacity to inhabit institutions, to assume the symbolic mandates determining our identity in the eyes of community and tradition" (Santner 1999, 3).

In elaborating his fundamental contribution to psychoanalytic theory, the concept of the "enigmatic message," Laplanche posits that the infant-parent relation is always

an encounter between an individual whose psycho-somatic structures are situated predominantly at the level of need, and signifiers emanating from an adult. Those signifiers pertain to the satisfaction of the child's needs, but they also convey the purely interrogative potential of other messages—and those other messages are sexual. These enigmatic messages set the child the difficult, or even impossible, task of mastery and symbolization and the attempt to perform it inevitably leaves behind unconscious residues.

(1989, 130)

Indeed, these "residues" *inaugurate* the unconscious, giving birth to the self's otherness to itself. As Eric Santner explains,

the traumatic encounter with the dense, enigmatic presence of the other's desire as constitutive of the inner strangeness we call the unconscious. Because adult ministrations to an essentially helpless child are always permeated by this enigmatic quality, seduction is, in a very broad sense, *constitutive* of the adult-infant relation.

(1999, 8)

But infants aren't the only recipients of enigmatic messages that, somehow, have to be metabolized. As Santner points out elsewhere, some aspects of the family situation are recapitulated at the level of the social, for every "social formation is itself permeated by inconsistency and incompleteness, is itself punctuated by a lack by which we are, in some peculiar way, addressed, 'ex-cited,' and for which we are in some fashion responsible" (2005, 86–87). That is, our adult selves, too, are inundated with enigmatic messages—unintelligible communications of a sovereign other's desire, including messages from authoritative institutions endowed with the crypto-parental power to recognize and regulate many aspects of our lives and identities.

Thus, Laplanche's deceptively simple autobiographical statement that, at a certain point in his life, "analysis took the place of the political things" clouds what he knew (from his own turn "away" from "political things") to be the potential political force of psychoanalysis itself—its "extraterritorial" potential as a means of resistance to hidden or distorted institutional mandates. The major part he took in the post-68 infusion into the French university system of psychoanalysts and psychoanalytic research was itself an extension of sociopolitical resistance to "existential dependency on institutions which are themselves in some fashion sustained by sovereign acts of foundation and augmentation" (Santner 1999, 2). Yet institutions—like families—can't simply be done away with, and along with Lagache, Lacan, Leclaire, Baudry, Clauvril, Irigaray, Certeau, Dumezil, Miller, Montrèlay, Nassif, Rabant, Tostain, and others, Laplanche helped steer one of the most significant pushes any country has thus far seen to establish a viable and enduring relation between psychoanalysis and the university.

Ψ

There had, of course, been important precedents to the post-68 French academic infusion elsewhere in the world—including in nearby Belgium where, at the French-speaking Catholic University of Louvain, the study of psychology and medicine had been heavily influenced by psychoanalysis since the end of World War II.[23] As noted in this book's introduction, the dynamic of resistance and renewal between psychoanalysis and the university is as old as psychoanalysis itself, and since the interwar period this dynamic has been playing out in many different and asynchronous ways throughout the world—in Austria, Germany, France, England,

Hungary, Argentina, Brazil, and the US, of course, but also in Belgium, the Netherlands, Lebanon, Turkey, Japan, Greece, Canada, Syria, Serbia, China, South Africa, Morocco, and elsewhere. While there isn't room in these pages to offer a comprehensive, culturally comparative history, it's important to acknowledge at least some of the widely dispersed efforts to find and maintain mutually beneficial intellectual and professional relations between the psychoanalytic field and the world's various centers of higher education—its universe of universities.

One of the first of these efforts was made during the final months of World War I, in Budapest, where Ferenczi had organized the Fifth International Psychoanalytic Congress. Several officials of the short-lived Hungarian People's Republic attended the Congress because of their interest in the psychoanalytic treatment of war neuroses and in the prospects for the psychoanalytically oriented reform of higher education. In 1918, medical students at the University of Budapest formally petitioned for psychoanalysis to be recognized as a university subject, and Ferenczi, along with Lajos Lévy, enlisted Freud's support, which he provided in an article for the Hungarian medical journal, *Medicine* (Mészáros 2012, 83). The conservative university council initially resisted these changes. But the Bolshevist putsch that established the Hungarian Soviet Republic helped pave the way for their temporary success—including Ferenczi's appointment at the University of Budapest as the first full professor and chair of the world's first university department of psychoanalysis.[24] Thus, writes Ágnes Szokolszky, "at a time when psychoanalysis was at the periphery of international academic life and nowhere in the world was it present in universities, the short-lived Hungarian Soviet Republic presented an unprecedented opportunity for psychoanalysis to establish itself as an academic discipline" (2016, 26; see also, Mészáros 2014, 43–46). Unfortunately, the internationalist avant-garde political spirit of the 1920s and the 1930s was reversed by the rise of conservative nationalism in Hungary and elsewhere. Influential analyst Michael Bálint succeeded Ferenczi as head of Budapest's Psychoanalytic Polyclinic, but soon thereafter many Hungarian analysts were either exiled (like Bálint) or killed by the Nazis, and the postwar Soviet regime quashed any further efforts at the revitalization of what had been one of Europe's most important psychoanalytic centers. It wasn't until 1989 that the Hungarian Psychoanalytical Association was restored to IPA membership, making it simultaneously one of the oldest and one of the youngest in the world.

One Hungarian refugee, Franz Alexander, spent the 1920s at Berlin's eclectic Psychoanalytic Institute. But what he really sought was some hospitable place in which to create for psychoanalysis the kind of institution that would fulfill many of the roles of both the university and the analytic training institute. In 1930, while attending a conference in Washington, D.C., he was invited to consider a visiting appointment in psychiatry at the University of Chicago. During negotiations there, he gave a lecture and was pleasantly surprised by the audience's response, reflecting later that "such a dispassionate discussion of an address on this contested field—psychoanalysis—would have been unthinkable at any European university" (1960, 98). In subsequent negotiations it was agreed that his title at Chicago would be Visiting Professor of Psychoanalysis, rather than Psychiatry—making it, like Ferenczi's, one of the world's first such appointments.

As soon as he started teaching, however, he realized that the psychiatry department wanted nothing to do with psychoanalysis; it was in the university's Social Sciences Division that Alexander found his students and colleagues. "This was the group," he wrote, "which originally supported my attempts to introduce psychoanalytic thought into the university. Their comprehension of psychoanalysis was far advanced in comparison with that of the medical faculty, where I scarcely succeeded in making a dent" (1960, 103). Soon, though, Alexander realized that he was stuck between the indifference of the university's psychiatrists and the instrumental positivism of most of its social scientists, who sought to incorporate psychoanalysis as a science of social adjustment (Gitre 2010, 241). Alexander left the university after only one year, going on to establish Chicago's Institute for Psychoanalysis as a home for divergent views that could function as a training institute while also supporting research and serving as a center for intellectual exchange and debate—which made it an attractive destination for many other émigré analysts.

In Germany itself, Berlin—like Vienna, Budapest, London, Prague, and Zurich—had been a vital early center of psychoanalytic thought and practice. During the Weimar Republic, Jews were allowed to hold high office in universities, and there were hopes for the creation of a professorial chair of psychoanalysis at the University of Berlin. Max Eitingon's father wanted to endow a chair in psychoanalysis at the University of Leipzig but withdrew the provision from his will in 1931 in response to mounting antisemitism (Schoonheten 2016, 105). Then, in 1933, the new National Socialist government brazenly began "Aryanizing" psychoanalysis, so that it would no longer be a "Jewish" science. By 1936, almost one hundred analysts had left Germany, and many more would either follow or perish. The purged institutes were reconstituted as the new German Institute for Psychological Research and Psychotherapy, under the leadership of Nazi psychiatrist Matthias Göring (see Cocks 1985; Sokolowsky 2022). The genocidal anti-semitism and anti-intellectualism of the Third Reich compelled most psychoanalysts and large numbers of their colleagues and allies (e.g., at the Frankfurt Institute) to flee the country: Max Eitingon went to Jerusalem; Ernst Simmel, Otto Fenichel, Frances Déri, and Theodor Adorno to Los Angeles; Karen Horney, Clara Happel, and Therese Benedek to Chicago; Siegfried Bernfeld to San Francisco; Hans Lampl and Jeanne Lampl-de Groot to Amsterdam; Hanns Sachs to Boston; and Edith Jacobson, Sándor Rádo, Wilhelm Reich, René Spitz, Erich Fromm, Theodor Reik, George Gero, Herbert Marcuse, Leo Löwenthal, Henry Lowenfeld, and Max Horkheimer to New York.

Wherever they went, new psychoanalytic societies and institutes sprang up, and many of the émigrés took up university teaching posts—by and large in departments of psychiatry and psychology. Some sought, and even found, institutional recognition as professors of psychoanalysis as a distinct discipline. Eitingon, for example, arrived in Jerusalem in 1933 hoping to establish a professorial chair of psychoanalysis at Hebrew University. But the university's rector opposed the idea—even after receiving a chastising letter from Freud himself (1960b, 418–19).[25] Fromm, who emigrated to North America in 1934, held numerous academic appointments, including Adjunct Professor of Psychoanalysis at New York University and, starting in 1951, Professor of Psychoanalysis at Mexico City's National Autonomous University of Mexico.

Of course, more than a few German analysts left Germany before Hitler's rise. In 1925, for example, Melanie Klein had moved to England, where both Sigmund and Anna Freud would end up as refugees in 1938. Fredric Wertham moved to the US in 1922, practicing psychoanalytic psychiatry first in Baltimore and then in New York, where in 1946 he joined with Ralph Ellison and Richard Wright (both of whom were immersed in psychoanalytic thought) to establish the psychoanalytic Lafargue Mental Health Clinic in Harlem. Like Fromm, Wertham rejected the conservatism of psychoanalysis in the US, where he also recognized the connections between American white supremacism, Euro-American colonialism, and

European fascism. Wertham published psychoanalytic critiques of segregation and anti-Black and anti-Puerto-Rican racism, lent his support to *Brown v. Board of Education*, advocated for affordable mental healthcare (what Freud had championed as "psychotherapy for the people" [1955d, 168]), and wrote several books about capitalism and the psychology of violence (Gaztambide 2019, 92–93). Toward the end of his career, Wertham became a professor of psychiatry at New York University. But his more important link to the world of higher education began with his activist and intellectual collaborations with Wright and Ellison—part of a network of what Daniel José Gaztambide calls "liaisons between intellectuals of color and White psychoanalysts [that] form a missing link in psychoanalysis' cultural history" (2019, 95). This network reached from Harlem to the Caribbean to North Africa and culminated most influentially in the writings of Martinican psychoanalyst Frantz Fanon—an oeuvre that has remained foundational to the psychoanalytic dimensions of academic research and teaching in the fields of postcolonialism, diaspora and subaltern studies, African American and Afro-Caribbean studies, critical race theory, and antiracist revisionism in psychoanalytic studies.

The psychoanalytic diaspora of the 1930s and 40s was itself largely a racial phenomenon, created by antisemitism and other forms of racial and ethnic hatred. From all over Europe, analysts and their colleagues and allies who were Jewish, and those targeted for being undesirable in other ways (queers, Romani, unionists, Blacks, the disabled, certain intellectuals, etc.), sought refuge in other parts of the world, thereby seeding new ground for psychoanalytic ideas and institutions and also for new forays into the realm of higher education. In the mid-century US, university-affiliated analysts were typically appointed as professors of psychiatry or psychology. But some, including Robert Waelder and Paul Ornstein, secured positions that formally recognized psychoanalysis as a distinct field. Like the Freuds, Waelder fled Vienna in 1938—in his case, to emigrate to the US where, in 1963, he was appointed Professor of Psychoanalysis in the psychiatry department of Philadelphia's Jefferson Medical College. Ornstein was a Hungarian refugee whose mother and three brothers were murdered at Auschwitz while he was studying medicine. He fled to Cincinnati, where he met fellow-Hungarian Michael Bálint, who had escaped Budapest shortly after his parents committed suicide to avoid capture by the Nazis. While at Cincinnati, Ornstein also met the distinguished analyst Heinz Kohut— another Austrian survivor of the Holocaust who settled in Chicago—with whom he did his psychoanalytic training before going on to become Professor of Psychiatry and Psychoanalysis at Cincinnati's Medical School.

Like North America, Latin America was a primary destination for uprooted analysts. Indeed, decades of mass European emigration to Argentina—along with that country's relative economic prosperity during the global financial crisis of the 1930s and its cultural progressivism after the 1955 overthrow of Peronism—helped psychoanalysis to thrive both within and beyond its universities. As early as 1925, psychoanalyst Julio Pires Porto-Carrero predicted that it would become "standard practice to apply psychoanalysis … to pedagogy" (qtd. in Mijolla 2005, 1295). By the end of the 1920s, psychoanalysis had entered the curriculum at the University of Buenos Aires and thereafter maintained a strong presence in university curricula. There was even a short-lived journal, *Psyche at the University* (1958–59), established to "promote and disseminate the study and knowledge of psychology with deep and dynamic criteria for students in all Faculties at the university" (Huertas-Maestro et al. 2022, 1012). Perón's dictatorship temporarily suppressed the progressivism of the country's universities, but in its wake intellectual life resurged, and by the 1960s psychoanalysis had recovered its well-established place at both the undergraduate and graduate levels in the field of psychology.

A deliberate separation of roles seems to have precluded substantial tensions such as those experienced elsewhere between university-based programs and independent training institutes. For example, when Argentinian analyst José Bleger became the first Chair of Psychoanalysis at the University of Buenos Aires in 1962, he took care to distinguish between the academic study of psychoanalysis at the university from clinical training as the province of the institutes:

> It is impossible to teach at university the same things and in the same way as at the analytic institutes. What is to be taught exists in relation to both the nature of the subject and the particular objectives to be pursued.
> (1962, 56)

Nonetheless, the psychoanalytic orientation of academic psychology—sustained by the alliance of progressive psychoanalysts, reformist psychiatrists, and overwhelmingly leftist student interest—also helped direct the clinical orientation of mental healthcare throughout the country (Dagfal 2018, 259–62).

Moreover, the 1966 coup radicalized many of the country's universities just as the works of Lacan and Althusser were being disseminated in Argentina, harmonizing Marxian and Freudian revolutionism with consequences for both university curricula and clinical practice. As Mariano Ben Plotkin observes, "whereas knowledge of Lacanian psychoanalysis in the United States has been limited largely to the academic world ... in Latin America, and in particular in Argentina, it has become ... a widely used therapeutic technique" (2001, 212). For a time, the 1976 coup quelled the political force of the Argentine psychoanalytic movement, but not its intellectual and clinical vitality. The restoration of democracy in 1980s and 90s saw a further massive influx of psychology students at the universities of Buenos Aires, Rosario, Córdoba, Tucumán, and La Plata, where almost every clinical chair had a Lacanian orientation and where Lacan was taught at the undergraduate as well as graduate/professional level (Dagfal 2018, 266–67). In 2018, Alejandro Dagfal wrote that "a new professional identity emerged: that of the psychologist-psychoanalyst with Lacanian orientation that, although deprived of its former political connotations, is still in force today" (2018, 264). In Argentina, the university teaching of psychoanalysis continues to dominate the study of psychology, and the practice of psychoanalysis continues to thrive, even as it dwindles in the US. Indeed, Dagfal concludes that "the steady growth of psychoanalysis in Argentina, its extension from the upper classes into the middle classes, its feminization, and its persistence as a theoretical framework and as a prototype for most psychotherapies (well after its decline in most of the Western hemisphere) are all the result of a historical process beginning by the establishment of a 'psychoanalytic hegemony' in university psychology programs" (2018, 256).

Lacan's influence on Argentinian psychopedagogy was reinforced and supplemented by the work of other major figures in the Lacanian movement, including the child analysts Françoise Dolto and Maud Mannoni, the latter of whom established the Experimental School in Bonneuil-sur-Marne for psychotic and autistic children in 1969 (see Mannoni 1999).[26] In turn, the Lacanian Argentinian psychoanalytic and psychopedagogic fields also had a tremendous impact on other Latin American countries, including Chile, Mexico, Peru, Uruguay, and Brazil. Beginning in the 1910s, Freud corresponded with a number of Latin American doctors and intellectuals, including the Peruvian psychiatrist Honorio Delgado and the Brazilian physician Durval Marcondes. Marcondes had been practicing as a lay analyst since the early 1920s and was one of the founding members of the short-lived Brazilian Psychoanalytic Society. After serving as a physician for the Education Department of the state of São Paulo, he became the first director of the school system's newly created Section of Mental Hygiene and, by 1936, was a psychiatrist working for the Education Department. One of the first Brazilian analysts to be recognized by the IPA, Marcondes also taught courses on psychoanalysis at São Paolo's prestigious Free School of Sociology and Politics (Plotkin 2022).

In Brazil, there was at first significant tension between members of the psychiatric community, who sought to use psychoanalytic psychotherapies as "civilizing" instruments for taming perceived "wild" or "primitive" human tendencies in portions of the population, and the cultural and intellectual avant-garde, which "welcomed psychoanalysis not only as a controversial doctrine appropriate to *épater les bourgeois* but also as the body of ideas that dealt with the wild and savage tendencies in human nature" (2001, 36). The former wanted to domesticate these tendencies; the latter wanted to understand and thereby celebrate them. Psychoanalytic ideas continued to circulate in the academic (chiefly psychiatric) and intellectual milieux of São Paolo and Rio de Janeiro, and by the 1950s both cities had IPA-recognized psychoanalytic institutes. According to Jane Russo, psychoanalysis also continued to be enlisted in the pedagogical and cultural projects of Brazil's elites, who saw it as a "modernizing and 'civilizing' tool" (2007, 68). Psychiatry departments had begun to lose their hold on psychoanalysis in 1939, when it was incorporated by Marcondes into the sociology curriculum at São Paulo's Free School of Sociology and Politics. By the early 1950s, sociology and psychology departments at many Latin American universities were teaching psychoanalytic content (Oliveira 2012, 125), although the "invasion" of Lacanian theory, beginning in the late 1960s, had the effect of undermining the authority of the university degree as a criterion for candidacy at the proliferating Lacanian institutes (Russo 2007, 74; see also, Elia 2016).

Early in the twentieth century, psychoanalysis had also been taken up enthusiastically in Russia, and long before the European flight from both Russian and German depredations in the 1930s and 40s psychoanalysis played a significant role in Russian intellectual life. Freud's writings were quickly translated and assimilated to an extent that caused Freud himself to write, in 1912, of a Russian "epidemic of psychoanalysis" (1912, 495). The first Russian psychoanalysts included Moshe Wullf, Max Eitingon, Sabina

Spielrein, Freud's close friend Lou Andreas-Salomé, and others who had been trained in Europe and, in many cases, returned home as practitioners and members of the pre- and post-Soviet intelligentsia. After the Bolshevik revolution, Moscow's psychoanalysts were, according to Alexander Etkind, "supported and employed in the country's highest political circles, most intensively by Leon Trotsky" (1997, 5). Formally, the state-approved Russian Psychoanalytic Society, created in 1922, wasn't dissolved until 1933. But after Lenin's death and Trotsky's exile and murder, psychoanalysis in Russia was effectively smashed along with many other revolutionary projects—at least until Stalin's death paved the way for glasnost and, ultimately, the fitful psychoanalytic revival of the post-Soviet era.

Before the 1930s, however, psychoanalysis played a significant role in Bolshevik experimental schooling, including Schmidt's Children's Home. Although Freud's writings were "rarely used in university courses on psychiatry" (Etkind 1997, 6), psychoanalysis was both an inspiration and a challenge to the development of a distinctly Soviet "pedology"—a term coined (coincidentally, by Clark's President Hall) to designate what would always be a marginal and dubious scientific field for the study of child behavior and development. Pavel Blonsky, a chief theorist of Soviet pedology, defined it as "the study of the entire set of symptoms of the various eras, phases, and stages of childhood, their temporary consequences, and their dependence on a range of conditions" (qtd. in Etkind 1997, 261). But Soviet pedology also diverged sharply from child psychoanalysis and psychopedagogy in being overtly ideology-driven and goal-oriented. Speeches at the First Pedological Conference in 1927 by Soviet education minister Anatoly Lunacharsky and politburo member Nikolai Bukharin made clear that, in Bukharin's words, "we need to direct our strength not into abstract chatter, but into an effort to produce a certain number of living workers in the shortest possible time frame; qualified, specially schooled machines that we can start up right away and set in motion" (qtd. in Etkind 1997, 265). The antithetical priorities of exploring character, on one hand, and regimenting it, on the other, drove early Soviet psychoanalysis and Soviet pedology further and further apart.

Nevertheless, even so radical and anti-authoritarian an analyst as Spielrein seems to have remained associated with the Soviet pedology movement. After her return to Moscow in 1923, where she spent a year working at the Children's Home, she moved back to her native Rostov-on-Don and seems to have spent part of the rest of her short life as a pedological educator. She continued publicly to defend psychoanalysis, but there is very little documentary evidence of her final years (before her 1942 murder by the SS) and none at all to indicate what sort of accommodation she made between pedology and psychoanalysis in her teaching. The oblivion that swallowed Spielrein is representative of the pervasive, violent suppression of psychoanalysis in authoritarian Soviet Russia over the next three decades, until glasnost and the reopening of scientific debate made it possible to use words like "unconscious" again. By the 1970s, Moscow-based academics including philosopher V. M. Leibin, sociologist V. N. Dobrenkov, and philologist Nataliya S. Avtonomova were able more freely to challenge the Soviet distortion and suppression of psychoanalysis by introducing works by Fromm, Lacan, Sullivan, and Marcuse, and, in 1979, a major psychoanalytic conference was held in Tbilisi, where guest-speakers from Europe and North America helped reopen Russia's psychoanalytic dialogue with the rest of the world.

The mid-century Soviet embargo on psychoanalysis extended to other countries as well. Poland, for example, had a thriving psychoanalytic community during the interwar period—a community that included "literary scholars and pedagogues who not only looked to the psychoanalytical theories of Freud, but also of Adler and Jung, for sources of inspiration in developing new concepts for educating children and youth" (Dybel 2020, 51). A treatise by the pioneering analyst Leopold Wołowicz (1914) included the first Polish attempt to conceptualize the relation between psychoanalysis and university pedagogy. But when, after World War II, Poland came under Soviet control, the "bourgeois science" of psychoanalysis "was removed from the curriculum at the universities and its private practice was forbidden" (Dybel 2020, 51). As in the USSR, the era of glasnost brought Poland's psychoanalytic community slowly back to life, including the restoration of psychoanalytic courses to university curricula.

As in other Soviet bloc countries, psychoanalysis was prohibited in Romania (where Constantin had made such an auspicious beginning), and it wasn't until the end of the dictatorial Ceaușescu regime in 1989 that the teaching and practice of psychoanalysis again became possible with the establishment of the Romanian Society for Psychoanalysis. However, despite some initial receptivity, Romania's universities failed to embrace it, and psychoanalysis was eliminated from the curriculum in psychology, to the ongoing dismay of many academics. Writing in 2013, for example, Gabriel Balaci, a lecturer in psychology at the Vasile Goldiş Western

University, urged the reintroduction of psychoanalysis into the curriculum as

> extremely important, not just for future psychologists, but for all the other professions, in which the main activities involve direct contact with other persons, found in different existential moments, or that face different problems which disrupt their psychic comfort and equilibrium.
>
> (2013, 114)

Balaci's sense of urgency was triggered in part by student interest and demand. For instance, he reports being solicited by his students to create a psychoanalytic study group as a supplement to their psychology courses and that student interest only grew as the study group itself grew larger and larger (2013, 115).

In many other countries, too, there had been fitful signs that psychoanalysis might find a meaningful place in higher education. For example, Girindrasekhar Bose made courses in psychoanalysis mandatory for all students in the University of Calcutta's psychology department, which he chaired from 1929 to 1949. In 1922, Bose had founded Calcutta's Indian Psychoanalytic Society (which became a training institute in 1930). Of the Society's fifteen original members, nine were college lecturers in psychology and philosophy (Nandy 1995, 96). Bose and his fellow educators and analysts "created a lively intellectual space for psychoanalytic inquiry in Calcutta" (Akhtar 2005, 11), and such spaces were created in other parts of India as well. By 1945, for example, there was a second institute in Bombay (now Mumbai), as well as a "psychoanalytically oriented school and college counseling center" (Akhtar 2005, 17).[27]

In post-revolutionary Mexico, philosopher Samuel Ramos sought to "diagnose" the Mexican national character in a series of psychoanalytically informed publications, including *Profile of Man and Culture in Mexico* (1934), which became for a time required reading in most Mexican secondary schools (Gallo 2010, 58). Having begun his career at the National Preparatory School and the National Teachers School, he went on to earn his doctorate in philosophy and rose to head of the Faculty of Philosophy and Literature at the National Autonomous University of Mexico, where his Adlerian reform-mindedness and biologistic theories of "inferiority" and the "masculine protest" (which Freud had vigorously refuted) informed his teachings on the Mexican "national character" and on the prophylactic and even redemptive powers of education (Gallo 2010, 69–70).

Psychoanalysis also made inroads into higher education in pre-revolutionary Iran, where Freud's works were being translated into Persian as early as 1936 (Barzin 2010, 163). Following World War II, Iranian sociopolitical life was divided between religious belief and a secular, Marxist ideology. By 1950, a department of psychology had been established at Tehran University, and its head, British-trained psychoanalyst Mahmoud Sanaie, set up a library for psychoanalytic literature. In 1951, Sanaie's colleague in the sociology department, Marxist sociologist Amirhossein Arianpour, published the first book on psychoanalysis written in Persian. The 1979 revolution had only a briefly marginalizing effect on psychoanalytic psychiatric training and practice, and, according to Nader Barzin, psychoanalytic theory continues to find its way into universities—including Tehran's Shahid Beheshti University—chiefly through their literature departments (2010, 166).

Throughout Islamic West Asia and North Africa, the reception of psychoanalysis remained uneven and contentious in most university settings, as well as more comprehensively, in countries and regions that, until the later twentieth century, were chiefly occupied colonies. Frequently, an exaggeratedly Eurocentric psychoanalytic/psychiatric discourse was imported to these regions as an ideological instrument of colonialism, racial exclusion, and psychic expropriation—and only gradually (if at all) transformed into a decolonial discourse and practice (see, e.g., Gana 2023, Khanna 2003, Sheehi and Sheehi 2022). Yet the study and practice of a less perverted, even counter-colonial psychoanalysis in the Arab world began at least as early the interwar period. According to Omnia El Shakry, "an article in *Al-Hilal,* a popular cultural journal, noted in 1938 that a new generation of Egyptian students were imbibing Freud and Freudian ideas on the unconscious and the sexual drive" (2018a). Shakry also notes that psychoanalysis served many Egyptian scholars as "a metonym for broader Arabic debates surrounding the status of the unconscious in psychic life" (2017, 1). Sufism, with its own ancient concept and discourse of the unconscious, has been a particular focus of research in the post-World War II era, and there's a substantial scholarly tradition of interdisciplinary, comparative work on psychoanalysis and *'ilm al-nafs*, the modern form of Islamic psychology. Yūsuf Murād's scholarship, for example, focuses in part on what Stefania Pandolfo calls "looking for 'another scene' of the Freudian unconscious in the vocabulary of Sufism" (2018, 128–29).[28] By the mid-twentieth century, psychology was an academic subject at most of the major universities in Egypt (Shakry 2017, 126n.9), and in the early 1950s Mustafa Radwan Ziywar established the psychology department at Cairo University. Muhammad Fathi Bey, a Cairo University professor of criminal psychology, published *The Problem of Psychoanalysis in Egypt* in 1946. In 1958, the Egyptian Lacanian analyst Moustapha Safouan published an Arabic translation of Freud's *Interpretation of Dreams*, and Sami Mahmud Ali's Arabic translation of Freud's *Three Essays on the Theory of Sexuality* appeared in 1963.[29]

In the 1950s, it was Fanon who introduced the possibility of a decolonial, activist culture of psychodynamic inquiry and practice—first in Algeria and subsequently in Tunisia. In addition to his clinical work, he formed psychoanalytic study groups in Blida and taught psychoanalytically informed psychiatry at Tunis's School of Medicine. At the University of Tunis, he also taught a course on "Society and Psychiatry" for students in sociology and psychology (see Fanon 2018). Crucially, Fanon was among the first to articulate the difficulties inherent in both universalist and particularist theories of the psyche with special regard to colonialism, ethnocentrism, race, and nationalism. For example, in *Black Skin, White Masks* (1952) he asks, what holds people together against ideological and sociopolitical exclusionisms? That is, what is the basis, not of universality, but of a "solidarity" that would transcend the self-alienation of rigidified identities? In the book's valedictory chapter, Fanon writes that "it is through the effort to recapture the self and to scrutinize the self, it is through the lasting tension of their freedom that men will be able to create the ideal conditions of existence for a human world" (1967, 231). To the extent that psychoanalysis (understood by Fanon as always, itself, under scrutiny) is a means by which the self can be "recaptured" and "scrutinized," it would, among other things, have to transcend the historical particularities of all the various nationalisms in which it has been embedded and from which it has been excluded, while, simultaneously, being able to serve, in the immediacy of the clinical setting, as a holding environment for particular, historically contingent selves forever being undone in their relation to internal and external others.

Ψ

Could this also be a contemporary blueprint for the relation of psychoanalysis to the university? That is, could there be a kind of solidarity stemming from the nonbelonging of psychoanalysis among the particular, often fragmented disciplines that constitute the university, and could psychoanalysis serve as a kind of holding environment for the alienating and exclusionary properties of specific fields of knowledge? If May 68 had at last enabled psychoanalysis "to take root in the universities as a teachable subject," it didn't end up addressing the perennial question posed by students (and their parents) about all subjects, including psychoanalysis, perceived as esoteric: "What is it good for?" How did psychoanalytic studies augment the curriculum? And what, after all, could one "do" with a non-clinical degree in psychoanalysis? In other words, the university's recognition of psychoanalysis as a legitimate discipline helped stoke the flames of controversy regarding the utilitarian value of a liberal education and the very legitimacy of the university. Is psychoanalytic education education with a purpose? And, if so, what purposes does it serve? Practical skills or lofty ideals? Compliance or criticism? Observation or reflection? Conversion or liberation? New beginnings or indeterminate ends? Augmented incomes or uncertain outcomes? Doctrine or dissent? Reason or revolution? Eros or Thanatos?

The following chapters pursue these and other questions in more recent decades leading up the present moment and beyond. Are there still sound intellectual and social benefits to be derived from sustaining and enhancing the place of psychoanalysis in college and university science and humanities curricula? What would those curricula look like, and how would they be administrated? To what extent would the escalating campus mental-health crisis be mitigated by expanding the roles of psychoanalysis and psychodynamic psychotherapies in student mental health centers, and in what ways might caring for students' psychological well-being and tending to their intellectual and social maturation be beneficially linked? Do we still have the kinds of universities that we want—universities that fully serve both individual and collective needs? Are the ruins of the university salvageable? Or, is it time to begin again?

Notes

1 In the early twentieth century, physician and educator Maria Montessori developed an innovative "scientific pedagogy" in which teachers concentrated on observing students left at liberty to act according to their inclinations, in classroom environments fitted out to meet their emerging interests and needs. Montessori's belief that facilitating children's spontaneous activity in such environments was the key to fostering their natural development quickly became an educational movement, leading to the creation

of tens of thousands of Montessori schools all over the world. Approximately fifteen thousand are active today (see De Stefano 2022).

2 In a 1917 letter to Montessori, Sigmund Freud told her that "my daughter, who is an analytical pedagogue, considers herself one of your disciples" (1960b, 320). (Montessori herself had little interest in psychoanalysis.)

3 The Hungarian Psychoanalytical Association had already done something similar in Budapest, and "there was a large audience who regularly attended the meetings: mothers, teachers, doctors, and university students among them" (Erös 2023, 21).

4 Isador H. Coriat, one of the first American psychoanalysts and a founder of the Boston Psychoanalytic Society, shared the same insights in a 1926 article for the journal *Progressive Education*: "In school, the teacher becomes a substitute for the father or mother of the child and in the emotional tie which exists between teacher and pupil, the earlier parent-child relationship is re-lived and re-animated. Teachers must understand their own unconscious, for if they fail to do so, they will never realize why they are acting in certain manner towards the pupil or the effects of their daily contacts. The moulding must not be according to the teacher's prejudices or resistances but along the lines of the best possibilities inherent in the pupil's mind, both conscious and unconscious" (1926, 21).

5 Pfister, a Swiss minister, lay analyst, and psychopedagogue, coined the term "Pädanalyse" in his 1913 book, *The Psychoanalytic Method*.

6 Two World Wars later, analyst and educator Lawrence Kubie amplified Jones's warning to humankind in his 1953 commencement address at Goddard College. Thus far, Kubie proclaimed, humanity has, "in spite of a growing knowledge of the world around [us] … repeated like an automaton" the unconscious errors of the past—and repeated them "in forms which become increasingly destructive and catastrophic as [we become] more educated. Whether [our] erudition has been in history, art, literature, the sciences, religion, or the total paraphernalia of modern culture, this has been the limiting factor in our Culture of Doom" (1954, 350). Our "ancient slavery," he warns, "to those repetitive psychological processes over which at present [we have] no control" can only be overcome through fundamentally new techniques of education, at all levels, that would direct self-awareness toward the workings of the unconscious" (1954, 351).

7 Selections from the book have been translated into English; see Zulliger (1940) and Zulliger (1941).

8 Freud's late-life conviction in the existence of what he called the "death drive" raised his misgivings regarding education and innate aggressivity to a sarcastic pitch: "That the education [*Erziehung*] of young people at the present day conceals from them the part which sexuality will play in their lives is not the only reproach which we are obliged to make against it. Its other sin is that it does not prepare them for the aggressiveness of which they are destined to become the objects. In sending the young out into life with such a false psychological orientation, education is behaving as though one were to equip people starting on a Polar expedition with summer clothing and maps of the Italian Lakes" (1961a, 134n.).

9 At the following year's International Congress of Education, Carl Jung delivered three lectures on "Analytic Psychology and Education," in which he insists that it is "absolutely essential for any teacher who wishes to apply the principles of analytic psychology to have a first-hand knowledge of the psychopathology of childhood and its attendant dangers" (1981, 74).

10 Other contributors included Sigmund and Anna Freud, Ferenczi, Pfister, Spielrein, Klein, Alice Bálint, Bonaparte, and Fromm-Reichmann.

11 Alice Bálint was an especially prominent and prolific contributor, teaching public courses on psychoanalytic pedagogy and analytic child psychology and speaking and publishing regularly on related topics (Erös 2023, 21). In his foreword to the 1931 Hungarian edition of Bálint's book, *The Psychology of the Nursery: A Psychoanalytic Study*, Ferenczi credited Bálint as one of those responsible for the fact that "psychoanalysis has hurled heavy stones into the long-stagnant waters of children's education" (1931, 5).

12 For more on the Children's Home, including its relation to other experimental pedagogies of the Bolshevik era as well as to the Soviet elite, see Cohen (1999, 169–71), Hai et al. (2020, 113–47), and Etkind (1997, 202–14).

13 On the Matchbox School, see also Danto and Steiner-Strauss (2019), Erikson and Erikson (1980), Heller (1992), and Midgley (2013, 32–53).

14 Upon her death in 1982, it was renamed the Anna Freud Centre.

15 Neill didn't begin reading Reich's books until the 1930s. They first met in 1935, and Neill was Reich intermittent patient from 1937 to 1939 (Croall 1983, 250–64).

16 For more on Susan Isaacs and the Malting House School, see Gardner (1969, 54–75), Graham (2009), and Bar-Haim (2017).

17 The term "applied psychoanalysis" may refer to the application of psychoanalytic theory and methodology to sociocultural aims, challenges, or problems in contexts other than the analytic consulting room. For example, psychoanalytic theory might be "applied" to the interpretation of literature (as in Freud's reading of Wilhelm Jensen's *Gradiva* [1959b]) or to the writing of a biography (as in Freud's psychobiography of Leonardo da Vinci [1957a]). In the classroom, certain psychoanalytic techniques—such as free association, mirroring, and reverie—might be applied pedagogically to enhance spontaneous thinking or to encourage reflection. The term is sometimes used and/or perceived as pejorative, connoting something superficial, mechanistic, or diluted. Psychoanalytically informed education is very commonly referred to—whether pejoratively or not—as a form of "applied psychoanalysis."

18 For more on the Frankfurt School's integration of psychoanalysis, see Jay (1996, 86–112).

19 For example, Lagache's primer, *La psychanalyse, first published in 1955 in the popular series "Que sais-je?"*, not only sold widely at the time but remains in print 70 years and 22 editions later.

20 Laplanche began his personal analysis and psychoanalytic training with Lacan in 1947. But by the 1960s, he had broken his intellectual and institutional ties with his mentor.

21 Ironically, until quite recently, Laplanche was known to anglophone readers almost exclusively as the co-author, with Jean-Bertrand Pontalis, of *The Language of Psycho-Analysis*, originally published in 1967 and in a highly successful English translation in 1973. Over half a century later, it remains one of the most frequently cited works of French psychoanalytic writing. Yet it wasn't until the early twenty-first century that Laplanche's many other major contributions to psychoanalysis started to gain recognition in the US, and the first US conference on Laplanche's work didn't take place until 2021. "Laplanche in the States: The Sexual and the Cultural" (October 2–3, 2021) was sponsored by New York University, Columbia University, the Association for Psychoanalytic Medicine, and La Fondation Jean Laplanche de l'Institut de France.

22 As if in illustration of this difficulty, the recent 700-page *Cambridge Handbook of Democratic Education* (2023) contains not a single reference to psychoanalysis or the political history of psychoanalytically informed education.

23 By the 1950s, Louvain had shed its strictly Thomist orientation and, philosophically at least, turned toward phenomenology and welcomed the Freudian perspective on

the nature of human subjectivity. One of its most esteemed faculty members, Antoine Vergote, had studied with phenomenologist Maurice Merleau-Ponty and completed his psychanalytic training with Lacan. Vergote was one of the founders of the Belgian School of Psychoanalysis, and at Louvain he and other faculty members brought their interest in psychoanalysis not only to the field of psychology but to those of philosophy and theology as well—establishing psychoanalysis as part of a tradition of intellectual catholicity, as it were, that was still being celebrated at the turn of the twenty-first century. In 2000, Louvain hosted a conference on "La psychanalyse à l'université [Psychoanalysis at the University]," with dozens of speakers from the fields of anthropology, cognitive science, law linguistics, literature, medicine, philosophy, and theology (Florence 2002).

24   Even the Hungarian Marxist philosopher and critic Georg Lukács supported Ferenczi's appointment; for, despite his intellectual disdain for psychoanalysis, he recognized its importance as part of the counter-authoritarian wave of revolutionary reforms (Damousi and Plotkin 2012, 186).

25   Almost 50 years later, in 1977, Joseph Sandler was appointed as the first Sigmund Freud Chair in Psychoanalysis. Sandler was born in South Africa and earned his medical degree there, but, due to his anti-apartheid stance, he was forced to flee to London in the 1940s, where he became part of Anna Freud's circle. Anna Freud herself gave the "Inaugural Lecture" for the newly established chair, reminding her audience that "psychoanalytic work fares best in the freedom which it has arrogated to itself from the beginning, and some of which it wishes to retain even within a university curriculum" (1981, 145). Sandler taught intermittently as a Visiting Professor of Psychoanalysis at Leyden University in the late 1960s before the Hebrew University appointment. In 1984 he left Jerusalem to become the Freud Memorial Chair at University College London (see Chapter 2). As Harriet Basseches has recently pointed out, "named chairs of psychoanalysis give recognition not only to a particular distinguished psychoanalyst but equally to the field itself." In 2003, Basseches and her colleagues counted the then currently serving chairs of psychoanalysis in the US and UK and found a total of eight (Basseches 2003, 9).

26   John Seligman's now rarely seen film about Mannoni's school, *Vivre à Bonneuil* (1975), was at the time a *succès de scandale*, thanks to its depiction of emotionally disturbed children freely going about their business in the open, mixed setting of Mannoni's self-styled "institution éclatée" (1973). Mannoni had been trained by Winnicott and was affiliated both with Lacan and with the anti-psychiatry movement of Laing and others. Thus she made sure that her "exploded institution" dispensed with conventional asylum practices of sequestration and segregation-by-illness and treated psychosis not so much as a pathology but more as a reaction to severely conflictual circumstances (see Vanier and Malone 2017).

27   More recently, the University of Delhi has become a center for psychoanalytic thought and training, though currently only Delhi's Ambedkar University offers an M.Phil. program in psychoanalytic psychotherapy, while certificate courses are offered at West Bengal State University's Centre of Psychodynamic Studies (Salam et al. 2022, 306). More broadly, according to Arka Chattopadhyay of Gandhinagar's Indian Institute of Technology, "there is more psychoanalysis in the university than in the clinic!" (Rousselle 2022).

28   Murād also authored a popular book, *Shifāʾ al-Nafs* (*Healing the Psyche)* (1943), which introduced general readers to various psychoanalytic concepts and techniques.

29   For an extended reading of this translation, see Shakry (2018b).

Chapter 2

Psychoanalysis and the Curriculum

Teacher, teacher, teach me love;
I can't learn it fast enough.

—EDDIE PHILLIPS AND KENNY PICKETT,
"Teacher, Teacher" (1980)

The specter of psychoanalysis continues to haunt higher education. These days, it's true, psychoanalysis as an academic topic has never seemed less visible in the curriculum or more thoroughly disavowed by departments of psychology in particular. Yet Freud and a very few other psychoanalytic thinkers (chiefly Lacan, Klein, and Winnicott) continue to appear on individual course syllabi in a wide range of disciplines. Certain works—for example, Freud's *Three Essays* and *Civilization and Its Discontents*, Lacan's *Four Fundamental Concepts of Psycho-Analysis*, Klein's pair of essays on manic-depressive states, and Winnicott's *Playing and Reality*—tend to crop up frequently on otherwise disparate course syllabi in anthropology, cinema, cognitive science, criminology, economics, English, health, history, history of medicine, law, neuroscience, nursing, philosophy, political science, religion, and sociology. However, courses devoted to psychoanalysis itself are very rare. Psychoanalysis is a body of knowledge with no proper academic home—the rootless cosmopolitan of the modern university, able as such to cross disciplinary boundaries with ease, often extending their horizons and creating new connections among them while maintaining its own heterodox identity through its *extramural* institutions and practitioners.

Thus its ghostlike relation to academia. Psychoanalysis *pervades* the university but has no locatable place *within* it. It serves many interdisciplinary purposes, yet few claims are made for its proper disciplinarity. It depends on institutional hospitality, yet the profession fiercely guards the independence of its autonomous, monodisciplinary training institutes. It craves

DOI: 10.4324/9781003540588-3

intellectual recognition, even though it has forever displaced the conscious intellect as the preeminent subject of knowledge (Lacan's famous "subject supposed to know" [1968, 46]). And while academia's resistance to psychoanalysis continues to wax and wane, the edifice of higher education (like the rest of civilization and its discontents) continues, ineluctably, to be grounded in the language of the unconscious—the special "gift" that Freud pandoraed into the world over a century ago and that contemporary education theorist T. R. Johnson calls "the other side of pedagogy" (2014).

Of course, Freud wasn't the first to recognize the unconscious. As he himself liked to say, the poets always "got there" before him. Saint Augustine, for example, wrote of the existence of "some things in man which even his own spirit within him does not know" (1961, 210–11). But Freud radically altered the terms of self-knowledge to include these "unknowable" aspects of the self, and he and his peers developed theories and techniques meant to help us get to know them (at least indirectly). And yet, as Lawrence Kubie complained in 1954, the need to understand "unconscious as well as conscious levels of psychological processes .... is wholly overlooked throughout the entire scheme of 'modern' education, from the kindergarten to the highest levels of academic training" (Kubie 1954, 349). Moreover, even as Kubie was voicing this grievance, post-Freudian psychoanalysis was casting ever more doubt on "the very idea of the self as an object of knowledge" (Phillips 1996, 7). All that psychoanalysis could contribute to our education, in other words, was to help us better manage our lives as subjects of uncertainty.

In other words, psychoanalysis wasn't a way *out* of that uncertainty. Still, for better or worse, it continues to be the best way we have of recognizing, accepting, investigating, and even instrumentalizing that uncertainty, no matter what dimensions of human incompleteness—that is, no matter what kinds of knowledge—we choose to pursue. This is why (despite the impression of esoterism given by its currently diminished, spectral presence on our college and university campuses) the need for psychoanalytic education that Kubie expressed so many decades ago has never been greater than it is today. A steady stream of scholarly books and articles, along with more "public facing" pieces in periodicals like *The New Yorker*, *The Chronicle of Higher Education*, and the *Wall Street Journal*, attest to, or at least broach the question of this need (see, e.g., Emre 2023; Gutkin 2023; Mintz 2023; Bloom 2023a; and Zeavin 2023). Writing for the *Journal* in 2023, Toronto psychology professor Paul Bloom begins by acknowledging student dissatisfaction with their psychology courses: "Most of all, the undergraduates wonder: Why isn't anyone talking about Freud?" (2023a, C3).

Such dissatisfaction pervades twenty-first-century academic psychology. Yet, with regard to most other disciplines in the humanities and social sciences, a better question would be: Why isn't anyone talking about *anyone other than* Freud (and, perhaps, Lacan, Klein, and Winnicott)? In courses with any sort of psychoanalytic content, writings by Freud and Lacan appear by far the most frequently, and generally to the exclusion of other and more recent psychoanalytic writers—and often in the absence of any clarifying curricular context whatsoever. As Ulster University professor Noreen Giffney reports, she initially encountered Freud as a first-year undergraduate in the following way:

> Freud's (1933) lecture, *Femininity*, was assigned as part of a literary theory module. There was little context provided and Freud's assertions appeared bizarre. I was appalled by what I perceived to be its gauche misogyny, with the result that I did not read any further pieces by Freud for the duration of my degree.
>
> (2023, 5)

Giffney eventually made her way back to Freud in graduate school, where she read other writers—including Luce Irigaray, Juliet Mitchell, and Jacqueline Rose—who "provided context to Freud's ideas in the process of articulating their own." This prompted her "to read Freud's 1915 essay, *The Unconscious*, and [appreciate] its nuance and complexity" (2023, 5). In turn, this led to further study and training, so that now, in addition to teaching psychoanalytic and psychosocial theory at Ulster, Giffney is also a practicing psychotherapist.

While it's relatively uncommon for such a latecomer to Freud to become a psychoanalytic clinician, it's all too common for undergraduates to be presented with decontextualized snippets of Freud or Lacan—isolated artifacts of psychoanalysis routinely presented as if it were a closed, outdated, misogynistic field, more than adequately represented by archaeological fragments of these two great thinkers, rather than as a dynamic field that continues to grow and change by building on, and also radically *rethinking*, Freud and Lacan's contributions. A more adequate curriculum would emphasize the field's continuous self-criticism and renewal. Syllabi would include works not only by Freud, Lacan, Klein, and Winnicott, but also by the likes of Anna Freud, Ferenczi, Erikson, Jung, Mahler, Hartmann, Horney, Kohut, Fairbairn, Kernberg, Laplanche, Hanna Segal, Harry Guntrip, Masud Kahn, Hans Loewald, Juliet Mitchell, Julia Kristeva, Stephen Mitchell, Jeanne Spurlock, Philip Bromberg, Donnel Stern, Néstor Braunstein, Nancy Chodorow, Christopher Bollas, Farhad Dalal, Jessica Benjamin, Shinhee Han, Mark Solms, and many other major psychoanalysts and analytic thinkers, representing the full range of analytic schools of thought and practice. Psychoanalysis would be presented not as settled wisdom with more historical significance than contemporary relevance, but rather as a dynamic field of ongoing exchange and the continuous revision of ideas. Many stereotypes and misconceptions with regard to clinical practice also need to be overcome. The caricature of the superannuated, taciturn, "classical" analyst who authoritatively "interprets" the patient's opaque and chaotic discourse needs to give way to an appreciation of the field's numerous and increasingly interpersonal clinical styles.

The obvious place for such curricular enhancement is in courses and programs of study whose primary, rather than ancillary (or nonexistent), purpose is to teach the history, theory, and practice of psychoanalysis. Yet, student interest in psychoanalysis notwithstanding, a combination of socioeconomic and intellectual factors continues to suppress and impede a more comprehensive psychoanalytic curriculum. For example, in the realm of mental healthcare education and delivery, psychodynamic treatments have been forced to give way to less expensive cognitive and behavioral approaches—approaches legitimated by the resurgence of methodological empiricism in clinical instruction and research as well as by demonstrably overzealous faith in psychopharmacology (see, e.g., Stone et al. 2022). In the realms of teacher-training and education policy, the drive toward quantification and standardization—ideologically motivated by neoliberalism and austerity-based economic theory—has fueled disparagement of the focus on subjectivity (see, e.g., Yates 2022). And the institutional and legislative politics of higher education continue to starve and dismantle humanistic disciplines—especially those in which the specter of psychoanalysis is still most substantive—in favor of the quantitative and qualitative sciences.

In light of such conditions, it's no wonder that, among the more than 4,000 colleges and universities in the US and the UK, *little more than a dozen* of them currently maintain formal undergraduate- or graduate-level psychoanalytic studies programs. (To be clear, these are nonclinical academic programs based in colleges and universities and shouldn't be confused with psychoanalytic training institutes, which are almost always entirely separate, post-graduate entities existing [almost] exclusively to prepare and certify psychoanalytic clinicians and researchers.) Those of us who teach in these programs have seen a few of our students go on to pursue psychoanalytic training, and this is heartening because, as the statistics show, the psychoanalytic profession continues to age and therefore needs more bright young minds to rejuvenate and perpetuate it. But the vast majority of our students don't become psychoanalysts. Instead, they carry forward into all walks of life an enhanced understanding of the human condition and a stronger capacity for empathizing with themselves and with those who are different from themselves. Intellectually, they help disseminate knowledge of what continues to be the most comprehensive and nuanced account of human subjectivity—an account always being freshly energized and augmented on many fronts. In our era of extreme cultural and political polarization and exacerbated resistance to new and uncomfortable forms of knowledge, revivifying and expanding the place of psychoanalysis in college and university curricula would surely have broadly salutary effects beyond, as well as throughout, campus settings.

The Center for the Psychological Study of the Arts at SUNY Buffalo, discussed in Chapter 1, is a precursor of the handful of currently existing nonclinical programs. Those in the US and the UK designed solely for undergraduate students include:

- Colorado College's minor in "Psychoanalysis: Theories of the Unconscious"
- Emerson College's minor in "Psychoanalysis as Cultural Criticism"
- the University of Essex's "Department of Psychosocial and Psychoanalytic Studies" (launched in 2015)
- Hampshire College's "Psychoanalytic Studies Program" (launched in 2014)
- NYU/Gallatin's minor in "Psychoanalysis and the Humanities" (launched in 2018)
- the University of Pennsylvania's "Psychoanalytic Studies Minor" (launched in 2015)

Programs for graduate-level study include:

- Birkbeck University of London's Master's program in "Psychoanalytic Studies"

- Columbia University's graduate "Psychoanalytic Studies Certificate Program"
- Emory University's "Psychoanalytic Studies Program" (launched in 1996)
- Middlesex University's M.A., M.Phil., and Ph.D. programs at its Centre for Psychoanalysis (launched in 1990)
- the New School for Social Research's philosophy Master's "Concentration in Psychoanalytic Studies"
- SUNY/Buffalo's graduate "Concentration in Psychoanalysis" at its "Center for the Study of Psychoanalysis and Culture"
- Trinity College Dublin's M.Phil. in "Psychoanalytic Studies"
- University College London's "Psychoanalysis Unit" of the Department of Clinical, Educational and Health Psychology
- the University of Ulster's "Psychoanalysis and Culture" doctoral program[1]

Each of these programs has its own distinctive history and institutional configuration. At Colorado College, for example, two faculty members—Marcia D-S. Dobson and her husband John Riker—were the prime movers behind the creation of its psychoanalytic studies Minor in 2003. With connections to both APsA and the Chicago Psychoanalytic Institute, Dobson and Riker were able to create and sustain a very visible and successful program at a small liberal arts college (see Dobson 2023). At Emerson College, the "Psychoanalysis as Cultural Criticism Minor" began as a cooperative venture between Emerson College and the Boston Psychoanalytic Society and Institute (BPSI). Students enrolled in any course that fulfills the Minor are offered special membership status and access to the events and library resources of BPSI, and BPSI-affiliated psychoanalysts with special interest in the arts are often invited to teach courses that count toward the Minor (see Schwartz 2018). At Hampshire College, the "Psychoanalytic Studies Program" is one of the "Areas of Study" in which undergraduates can elect to concentrate as they follow Hampshire's non-traditional model of faculty-mentored independent study (see Pyle 2015). NYU's Gallatin School launched its Minor in "Psychoanalysis and the Humanities" in 2018, in response to undergraduate interest in non-medically oriented psychoanalytic studies. It therefore operates separately from NYU's extremely large clinical training program in Psychotherapy and Psychoanalysis.[2]

While most college and university Minor programs are created to satisfy the needs and desires of students that aren't being met by existing departments and programs, the University of Pennsylvania's Psychoanalytic Studies program was a *faculty*-driven initiative that took shape, as its co-founders recall, through a series of get-to-know-you lunches among like-minded clinicians and scholars (Blum et al. 2016, 18). It turned out that, unbeknownst to one another, a number of UPenn faculty members, across the university, had been intermittently teaching courses on psychoanalysis from a variety of disciplinary perspectives. Early discussions led to several curricular collaborations between academics and clinicians, which in turn led to the proposal of an official undergraduate minor. In 2014, anthropology professor Greg Urban and psychoanalyst Lawrence Blum met with the undergraduate deans and with the outgoing and incoming chairs of the psychology department, who, while finding nothing of interest in the endeavor, were gracious enough to understand it was not a threat. After two years of fantasy, conversation, recruitment of interested faculty, and writing by committee, a proposal was submitted to the deans and subsequently to the full faculty, who voted to approve (Blum et al. 2016, 19). Officially launched in 2015, this undergraduate Minor benefits from UPenn's longstanding relationship with the Psychoanalytic Center of Philadelphia (PCOP), one of the area's independent analytic training institutes. Clinicians from PCOP often join members of UPenn's standing faculty to team-teach courses in the Minor, and there are plans to add a graduate certificate program at a later date.

While the programs at Colorado, Emerson, Hampshire, NYU/Gallatin, and UPenn are all centered on undergraduate education, the programs at Emory, Columbia, the New School, and SUNY/Buffalo are graduate-level programs of one kind or another. Also, unlike NYU/Gallatin's undergraduate program, Emory's graduate-level psychoanalytic studies program, which was launched in 1997, maintains closer ties with its university's own analytic training institute (the Emory University Psychoanalytic Institute), while working to create an undergraduate psychoanalytic studies program at a later date.[3] Like NYU and Emory, Columbia is one of the very few US universities to have its own embedded analytic training institute. Indeed, established in 1945 in the Department of Psychiatry of the Columbia University College of Physicians and Surgeons, Columbia's Psychoanalytic Clinic for Training and Research was the first such institute affiliated with the ASA to be established in a university and medical school. Much more recently, Columbia's graduate-certificate program in "Psychoanalytic Studies" was founded in partnership between the re-named Center for Psychoanalytic Training and Research and Columbia's Graduate School of Arts and Sciences, which means that graduate students in Columbia's non-clinical "Psychoanalytic Studies" program, like their counterparts at Emory, have (or can have) more contact with their university's training institute and its faculty than the undergraduates at NYU/Gallatin.

Unlike NYU, Emory, and Columbia, neither SUNY/Buffalo (discussed in Chapter 1) nor the New School for Social Research has an embedded analytic institute. But the New School's graduate-level "Concentration in Psychoanalytic Studies" benefits from its strong ties to the institution's psychoanalytically oriented philosophy department and, since 2008, its psychology department's Sándor Ferenczi Center, as well as to the independent psychoanalytic association, Das Unbehagen, which organizes regular events across New York City.

The half-dozen or so UK programs tend to be larger and to offer a variety of full degree programs. For example, the University of Essex began admitting students to its new BA program in Psychoanalytic Studies in 2015. According to faculty member Leonardo Niro,

> this was our first flagship undergraduate programme in psychoanalytic studies, after formerly offering optional modules in the area to students in other departments. The name of the degree was updated to BA, Psychosocial and Psychoanalytic Studies after the Centre for Psychoanalytic Studies became the Department of Psychosocial and Psychoanalytic Studies, in the summer of 2017.

The department now has roughly forty to seventy students enrolled in the programme at any one time.[4] Birkbeck University of London offers a number of undergraduate and graduate degrees (BA, MA, and MPhil/PhD) in Psychosocial Studies. Since 2010, their Psychosocial Studies program maintained formal links—including faculty and student exchanges—with the Department of Social Psychology and the Psychology Institute at the University of São Paulo, Brazil. In 2015, their Institute of Psychoanalysis established a Summer School in partnership with the Birkbeck Institute of Social Research. Beginning in 1990, Middlesex University was one of the first in the UK to offer graduate degrees (MSc, MPhil, and PhD) in psychoanalytic studies, and the university's Centre for Psychoanalysis is a hub for individual and collaborative research, visiting scholars, national and international workshops and conferences, and global outreach. At University College London, the Psychoanalysis Unit has been part of the Department of Clinical, Educational and Health Psychology since 1984, when its founder, Joseph Sandler, became the university's Freud Memorial Chair of Psychoanalysis. The University of Ulster offers a PhD in "Psychoanalysis and Culture," with an emphasis on Kleinian thought and psychosocial research. And Trinity College Dublin offers an MPhil in Psychoanalytic Studies.

Of course, faculty members need not be affiliated with a formal psycho-analytic studies program to teach psychoanalytic content in the courses they offer in their respective departments and programs. Non-clinician academics may also possess a range of substantial qualifications: most are published scholars of psychoanalytic history, theory, and criticism; some have formal degrees from graduate psychoanalytic studies programs[5]; some have done non-clinical training at various psychoanalytic institutes; some have degrees in psychology or psychiatry from analytically oriented programs; and many have been in long-term psychoanalysis or psychoanalytic psychotherapy themselves. Yet it's quite rare for an individual faculty member to have the qualifications, the will, *and* the institutional support necessary to sustain singlehandedly a robust psychoanalytic curriculum. It's also extremely difficult to gather specific information about such courses or to assess accurately the nature and amount of psychoanalytic content in university-wide curricula. Unfortunately, we don't have anything like a clear and comprehensive picture of what, exactly, students are learning about psychoanalysis in these courses. To what concepts are they being introduced? Which analytic writers are they being asked to read? To what extent do are the history and theory of clinical *practice* (in addition to metapsychological *theory*) taught in such courses?

Non-paywalled/firewalled online sources yield scant data. For example, the non-profit Web site *Open Syllabus* (www.opensyllabus.org), which, as of March 2024, has aggregated information from approximately twenty million college course syllabi, doesn't even include "psychoanalysis" among the 62 "fields" it tracks. It can tell you the total number of syllabi on which a particular work has been assigned and the number of those syllabi in any of its 62 predetermined fields. It tells us, for example, that Freud's *Civilization and Its Discontents* appears on 3096 syllabi, 828 of which are from courses in "English," 529 in "History," 324 in "Philosophy," and a further 1010 in fields *other* than "Psychology" (which gets 179 hits, or just 5.8% of the total). However, there's no indication of these courses' titles or of what other content they include. From time to time, other syllabi are made publicly available by individual instructors or institutions. But this practice remains scattershot, and the work of assembling and evaluating even the intermittently accessible syllabi would be prohibitively time-consuming and still of limited documentary value. Nevertheless, the following snapshots of syllabi volunteered by standing faculty members at a variety of colleges and universities gives a sense of various kinds of contemporary courses and their specific psychoanalytic content.

For instance, a recent course in Harvard's History of Science Department on "Freud and His Legacies: Readings in the History of Psychoanalysis" featured required readings from the entire history of psychoanalysis—including works by Sigmund Freud, Ferenczi, Rivière, Fenichel, Klein, Winnicott, Fairbairn, Guntrip, Kohut, Kernberg, Juliet Mitchell, Phillips, Salman Akhtar, and Kimberlyn Leary, as well as by non-clinician theorists and critics such as Foucault, Janet Malcolm, Christopher Lasch, and José Brunner. Other courses focus on individual psychoanalysts, including:

- Duke University's advanced (and drolly titled) seminar on Lacan— "Lacan? Still?"—immerses students in Lacan's writings/teachings, which are supplemented with readings by Lacanian analysts and theorists including Bruce Fink, Jacques-Alain Miller, Catherine Malabou, Alenka Zupančic, and Tim Dean
- Emory University's "User's Guide to Freud," taught in the Department of Women's, Gender, and Sexuality Studies
- Kenyon College's French Department course, "Introduction to Lacanian Theory," in which students read selections from Lacan's *Écrits* and Seminars I, II, III, and XI, along with commentaries by Jacques-Alain Miller, Malcolm Bowie, Bruce Fink, Dany Nobus, and Patricia Gherovici
- the University of Pennsylvania's course on "Freud: The Invention of Psychoanalysis," which is cross-listed by several departments and programs including German, History, Comparative Literature, and Gender, Sexuality, and Women's Studies

Many courses are cross- or inter-disciplinary. For example,

- the Department of Law, Jurisprudence, and Social Thought at Amherst College offers a course on "Psychoanalysis and Law" that also focuses heavily on the work of Freud and Lacan, supplemented by works of psychoanalytic theory and jurisprudence by Judith Butler, Elisabeth Roudinesco, Edward Said, and Slavoj Žižek

- Barnard College's introductory course on "Literature and Psychoanalysis," which includes readings by Freud, Lacan, Bruno Bettelheim, Julia Kristeva, Luce Irigaray, Peter Brooks, Josh Cohen, Shoshana Felman, Adam Phillips, Claudia Tate, and Patricia Gherovici
- Boston College's Philosophy Department offers a course on "Freud and Philosophy" in which students spend the first half of the semester studying Freud intensively, from *Studies on Hysteria* to *The Ego and the Id*, *Beyond the Pleasure Principle*, and *Civilization and Its Discontents*. In the second half, they study post-Freudian developments in psychoanalytic theory and practice, including some of the more creative and philosophically fruitful readings of Freud by Marcuse, Lacan, and René Girard
- the University of Leeds's "Africas of the Mind," offered in the School of English as an advanced course on postcolonial studies, psychoanalysis, and the history of psychiatry and ethnopsychiatry, includes readings by Freud, Sachs, Klein, Fanon, and Lacan
- the University of Pennsylvania's course, "Psychoanalytic and Anthropological Perspectives on Childhood," offered by the Anthropology Department, features numerous cross-disciplinary readings on infant, child, and adolescent development, child-parent relationships, separation and individuation, identity formation, cross-cultural perspectives on Oedipal structures, kinship, incest, gender difference, fluidity, and identity by analysts including Winnicott, Mahler, Selma Fraiberg, Virginia Goldner, Karen Gilmore, Daniel Stern, Anne Parsons, and Fred Pine
- also at Penn, the course "Race and Psychoanalysis," offered by the Asian American Studies Program, includes works by Freud, Klein, Lacan, and Fanon, and devotes substantial space to recent and contemporary analysts, including Bromberg, Shinhee Han, Patricia Gherovici, Christopher Christian, Avgi Saketopoulou, and Michelle Stephens[6]

Ψ

Among the very small number of courses devoted to psychoanalysis offered by psychology departments is the Massachusetts College of Liberal Arts course, "Special Topics: Psychoanalysis," the required readings for which include a breathtakingly wide range of psychoanalytic works by

Freud, Ferenczi, Klein, Jung, Hartmann, Sullivan, Bion, Fanon, Fairbairn, Kohut, Robert Stolorow, Stephen Mitchell, Nancy McWilliams, David Wallin, Julia Kristeva, Peter Fonagy, Muriel Dimen, Ken Corbett, Thomas Ogden, Avgi Saketopoulou, Lynne Layton, and Guilaine Kinouani. There are plenty of psychology professors who would sympathize with the ambition reflected here to cover as much psychoanalytic material as possible, given how few psychoanalytically oriented course are offered by most departments of psychology. In 2007, a nationwide survey of 146 "highly ranked" colleges and universities conducted by APsA found that, out of a total of 1,175 course listings with *any* psychoanalytic content, a mere 13.6% were offered by departments of psychology (Redmond and Shulman 2008, 398). This is all the more significant in light of the fact that, among US undergraduates, psychology has long been one of the most popular majors, currently accounting for more than 6% of all bachelor's degrees conferred (Stamm et al. 2023, 23).[7] That's well over 100,000 new psychology degree-holders every year, most of whom don't know even the fundamentals of psychoanalytic theory and technique.

After the release of the APsA survey cited above, *The Harvard Crimson* reported, archly, that "psychology departments at Harvard and other top universities may be repressing Sigmund Freud." To support this hypothesis, the article quotes Harvard psychologist and prolific author Steven Pinker, who teaches an undergraduate "core" course on "The Human Mind." This course is taken by hundreds of students each semester and includes just two lectures on psychoanalysis. Pinker acknowledges that "psychoanalysis is not part of the mainstream psychology curriculum at Harvard or most other major universities" and adds (ignoring decades of empirical research): "the reason is that psychoanalysis falls outside mainstream science—its claims are not empirically tested, it doesn't mesh with the rest of biology" (Viswanathan 2007).

Reporting on the same APsA survey's reception in the UK, Matthew Reisz found that "here, as in America … the discipline of psychology is probably the least hospitable of any … to psychoanalytic ideas." Reisz's article quotes Peter Fonagy, a prominent professor of psychoanalysis at University College London, who says that academic psychology's hostility toward psychoanalysis is frequently reciprocated by psychoanalysts, who feel "misrepresented by an empirically oriented psychology. Psychological research is considered irrelevant, and work attempting to systematise psychoanalytic ideas is considered inherently alien to the discipline" (2008, 38).

Before moving to the University of Toronto, another prominent and prolific psychologist, Paul Bloom, spent many years at Yale teaching "Introduction to Psychology," which by his own estimate was "one of the most popular courses at Yale"—so popular, indeed, that Bloom created an online version that "has had an enrollment, so far, of about a million students." Bloom recently published an expanded version of his course lectures called *Psych: The Story of the Human Mind* (2023b). This is a 450-page book in which there's a single, fourteen-page chapter devoted to "Freud and the Unconscious." Beyond tricking unassuming readers into thinking that Freud's oeuvre stands for the entirety of the psychoanalytic field, Bloom's treatment of Freudian metapsychology is cursory and supercilious, and smugly concludes that "Freudian theory is either vague or unsupported by the evidence. This is why we no longer study Freud in most psychology departments" (2023b, 67).

If Pinker and Bloom are authoritative representatives of academic psychology at schools like Harvard and Yale, one can only imagine what "stories of the human mind" are being told to psychology majors elsewhere. The naïve empiricism they praise and practice, their caricaturing of Freud and his ideas, their refusal to acknowledge the advances of post-Freudian psychoanalysis, their omission of the empirical findings of the neurosciences, and their willed ignorance of the field of neuropsychoanalysis all highlight the moribund nature of academic psychology and the inadequacy of its curriculum—*especially* for any kind of psychoanalytic training (see Allison 2017). Yet most accredited psychoanalytic training institutes in the US and many in other countries still require non-physician applicants to have completed either a Ph.D. or a Psy.D. in clinical psychology!

Having been attacked on empiricist grounds ever since Freud abandoned his biologistic model of the mind, psychoanalysis continues even now—in both clinical and academic contexts—to be widely criticized by academic psychologists as "unscientific," despite their knowing so little about it. Moreover, the term "scientific," in academic psychology's current disciplinary formation, tends to mean little more than "statistically based," which leads psychological researchers and clinicians to promulgate an image of the mind as a complex but thoroughly logical neuromechanism whose workings are wholly amenable to quantitative measurement and experimental verification. Most psychologists simply make no room for—that is, they disavow methodologies for recording and evaluating—the contingencies of interpersonal treatment relationships and the overwhelming amounts of data they yield.

Obviously, this scientistic reductivism remains a key obstacle to the expansion of psychoanalytic education and research, and it can only be overcome through recognition of the mutually informing relation between the empirical and the theoretical (see Scott 2005). Such recognition is at the heart of the emergent field of neuropsychoanalysis, which integrates psychoanalytic theory and neuroscience in ways that were technologically impossible until quite recently and that already have tremendous implications for teaching and research—including bridging the gap between STEM fields and the humanities (perhaps even, at some point, psychology itself). For the time being, though, courses with substantial psychoanalytic content are still far more likely to be taught in humanistic disciplines, such as anthropology, English and comparative literature, film and media studies, gender and sexuality studies, history, and philosophy (see Riker et al. 2018).

Yet even humanities instructors, broadly speaking, have fewer and fewer opportunities to add psychoanalytically oriented courses to the curriculum and less and less freedom to add psychoanalytic content to the courses they're required to teach. Moreover, the relative institutional isolation of psychoanalytically oriented teachers and scholars makes it difficult for them to find and forge alliances with likeminded colleagues. Together, rather than as lone voices, they might wield some influence in curricular decision-making at the departmental or administrative level. But discovering such colleagues in other academic fields is made especially difficult by the financial as well as intellectual balkanization of departments and other divisions within the university—interdisciplinary programs and initiatives notwithstanding. At the same time, the elimination and amalgamation of more and more traditional areas of study (e.g., the closing of entire departments such as philosophy and classics, and the folding together of multiple foreign languages into single administrative units) radically narrows the scope of liberal education as such and further accelerates students' early specialization (and restricted curricular options), making even occasional elective courses all the harder to justify. And, of course, the standardization, limitation, and homogenization of curricula have the effect of anathematizing psychoanalysis, with its slippery disciplinary status. Even scholars of psychoanalysis and psychoanalysts themselves contest its ontological status, referring to it variously as a "discipline," a "field," a "science," an "art," a "hermeneutic," a "faith," a "philosophy," or, as Lacan puts it in his own peculiar way, a "science of desire" (1992, 321).

In Lacan's estimation, psychoanalysis inherently opposes the scientific-ity of psychological empiricism and that of all other "sciences" that hide or exclude the *undisciplined*—that is, the excessive unconscious desire that, in his view, informs all intellectual work, all pursuits of knowledge. According to Lacan, this excessive unconscious desire transgresses the aesthetic and ethical reasons, rationales, and arguments with which they try to "discipline" the curriculum and, in so doing, make knowledge into what is merely a "defense against truth" (qtd. in Fink, 2017, 33). Lacanian educational theorists, including Fernando Murillo, concur that "ignoring the psychoanalytic constitution of subjectivity in its core dimensions of desire, libidinal ties, suffering, and anxiety cannot go without consequences in the formative enterprise of curriculum work" (2018, 19).

But what does such a "formative enterprise of curriculum work" look like, in practice? Crucially for Murillo, "formative" doesn't mean "developmental." Rather, the curricular ethos he espouses is a kind of de-instrumentalized humanism, the purpose of which "is not to make us feel better, or 'produce' or ameliorate anything," despite the social assurances that tend to justify curricula at all levels (2018, 58). This Lacanian ethos seeks "to undermine the supposedly redemptive goals of education"—goals which, as British high school (sixth form) teacher Nick Stock points out, often involve encouraging students to identify, as subjects, "through their *subjects*: 'I am an English student'; 'Well *I* am a Biology student'" (2023, 10). In a reading-group that Stock runs for some of his students, one of his goals is to get them to think about themselves *as* subjects—to think about what they want and why they might desire it:

> When pressed about their own desires … they often draw on signifiers like "good grades," "getting into uni," "getting a good job," and so on. Though these answers are easily explained by the neoliberal agenda that haunts contemporary education … the Lacanian dimension allows us to explore the structure of schooling beyond the neoliberal managerialization of learning.
>
> (2023, 10)

Where do the fantasies that sustain these desires come from, and why do they tend to generate so much anxiety? Or does the anxiety come from somewhere else? Might its source be, in fact, another('s) desire? And, in the context of the high school or college classroom, would reading and discussing, say, Lacan's *Seminar X: Anxiety* be a curricular challenge that many students (or their teachers) would be up to? Moreover, even if they were, wouldn't that be just one more opportunity for identification "through their subject"—in this case, Lacanian psychoanalysis?

Ψ

In systems of higher education, most discussions and decisions about curriculum take place in three realms: 1) in the dedicated fields of education and curriculum studies, which are usually hived away in schools of education; 2) among upper-level administrators and their staffs; and 3) among the faculties of individual departments and programs. Some individual instructors (typically, tenured professors at wealthy and highly-ranked schools) have a great deal of freedom to choose what courses they'll teach and what content they'll include in their syllabi. Others (especially contingent or adjunct instructors) have little or no freedom in this regard. In the US, the sweeping adjunctification of the professoriate means that approximately 70% of college and university instructors are now hired on a contingent (semesterly or annual) basis to teach specific courses, usually with pre-scribed content.[8] Among the remaining ranks of the professoriate, degrees of curricular freedom range widely, depending on numerous factors (e.g., the public or private status of the institution, its Carnegie Classification, the relative size and prestige of individual departments, perceived student needs and demands, and ideological pressure from university governance and/or state and federal legislatures).[9]

Thus, more and more, the unanticipated challenges and unforeseen possibilities of both teaching and learning are being badly met by conventional curricula. Academically speaking, a student generally follows one or more prescribed courses of study, or curricula (Lat. *currere*: "to run"), in order to attain in a timely way a certain level of expertise or credentialization. These curricula usually consist of a number of individual courses (Lat. *cursus*: "running"), each with its own predetermined content and sequence of activities directed at certain specified goals (or "learning outcomes"). The plan for an individual course usually begins with some sort of syllabus (Lat. *syllabus*: "list"), which might be highly detailed and systematic; or it might be more minimal, with room to maneuver or "course-correct" by adding or modifying the content and activities, or by allowing for the emergence of new content and activities. Some content and activities may be inadvertently or unconsciously obscured or omitted, while other content and activities may be purposefully left out.

In other words, the fluid and dynamic potentialities of curriculum as a "running" or a "journey"—or as a musical "run" that exceeds its score, or the "running" roots of a rhizomatic plant expanding into larger circuits of connection—are pedagogically "sublimated," as education theorist Jason Wallin writes, "by a reactive image." "Potential modes of becoming, Wallin continues, "are reduced in complexity and difference" to curriculum's "most common and calcified representational structure," like the closed circuit of a racetrack, or a prescribed course of medical treatment (2010, 2–3). Indeed, the discourse of "cure" (despite the false etymological link) is pervasive in education and curriculum theory, as if the student body—the corporeal subject routinely supposed *not* to know—were afflicted with a disease-like ignorance that has only one proper remedy, administered by the teacher to the student in the form of prescribed content and remedial skills (see Salvio 1999).

In college-level curriculum theory, this inoculatory model has been challenged in various since the postwar era, when theorists including Louise Tyler began turning their thoughts away from prescribed content and skills toward what might more meaningfully emerge in the "course" of teaching itself: "In the selection of instructional materials, the concepts of the unconscious, of man's instinctual nature, and of the analyst's role will be of service. These concepts may not provide solutions, but they may change our understanding of the educative process—if only to deepen our understanding of its complexity" (1958, 456). In 1970, in his closing remarks at a conference dedicated to the topic of teaching, Lacan posed a fundamental question for the analytically oriented teacher: "How does one comport oneself with regard to knowledge when one puts oneself in the position of a teacher?" (1971, 208). The gist of his answer is that knowledge can't be given in the form of a pill—that it's always so far in excess of what the teacher might want or be asked to convey that its "transmission" is impossible. "Knowledge," Lacan says elsewhere, "is always in excess of what teaching can imagine" (2001a, 298)—further begging the questions: In what does teaching consist, and what is the role or purpose of that teaching's curriculum?

In his own annual seminars, Lacan's "curriculum" consisted to a great extent of his dazzling, protracted commentaries on Freud's oeuvre. Yet accounts and transcriptions by his students show him careening and gamboling his way through a vast array of other materials and topics from virtually all of the disciplines traditionally ensconced within the university, from anthropology to biology, linguistics, mathematics, music, and philosophy.[10] There could be no question of methodically "preparing" for such a class, in the conventional manner of working through a set of assigned readings before each class meeting. Lacan would often launch his annual seminar with a deceptively concise declaration of that year's topic, e.g., "I'm going to be speaking with you about anxiety" (2004, 11); "I announced that the title of my seminar this year was *The Ethics of Psychoanalysis* (1992, 1); and "This year the question of the psychoses begins" (1997, 3). Yet, once having embarked on a clearly designated path, Lacan's polymathic extemporizations tended to proceed as if to highlight the eccentric machinations of his own "thinking" unconscious, precisely in order "to let you in on something that is under way" (Lacan 2008, 4). Lacan always had a complex and deliberate "teaching" (as distinct from "knowledge") to impart. But this meant that he brought more than he could contain, and his curriculum had to "run," to a great extent, as a kind of trackless race of self-exposure.

In her book on pedagogical ethics, Sharon Todd gives a Lacanian sense of the riskiness of education from the student's point of view:

> insofar as curriculum involves introducing them to new encounters, it also asks them to change their views, perceptions, assumptions, and modes of thinking. This suggests that in asking students to produce meaningful relations to texts, ideas, or representations, we … may be provoking an ontological crisis of sorts. What appears to be at risk, therefore, is the self itself, or, more precisely … the ego, developed through its continual negotiation with external reality.
>
> (2003, 18)

At the 1970 conference, Lacan's colleague Jean Oury had characterized the teacher's situation in similarly analytic terms:

> Exposing oneself as a teacher produces analytical effects on the teacher himself—that would be where there would be a clue: in the fact that being a teacher, somewhere, and having to explain something to a difficult audience can have an effect of diffraction that can reveal the very mechanics of the enunciation.
>
> (qtd. in Chiesa 2008, 80)

Thus, for student and teacher, the risk always "runs" concurrently, and the readiness with which both student and teacher manage their inadvertent self-exposures—rather than any prescribed content—establishes the possibility of a psychoanalytic curriculum.

Ψ

In a widely cited 1982 article, Shoshana Felman enlists her knowledge of Lacan's work in order to expand upon Freud's early insight into the difference between learning "something *about* psycho-analysis" and learning "something *from* it" (Freud 1955f, 173). Felman rejects both "the positivistic and ... negativistic misinterpretations of the psychoanalytic critique of pedagogy," with their shared focus on curricular content as opposed to the pedagogical situation (1982, 24). Felman characterizes psychoanalysis as itself "a pedagogical experience: as a process which gives access to new knowledge hitherto denied to consciousness, [affording] what might be called a lesson in cognition (and in miscognition), an epistemological instruction." This lesson proceeds "not through linear progression, but through breakthroughs, leaps, discontinuities, repressions, and deferred action" (1982, 27). Like psychoanalysis, teaching contends "not so much with *lack* of knowledge as with *resistances* to knowledge" (1982, 30). Learning is commonly equated with the transmission of knowledge from teacher to student, and the "failure" to learn (as determined by metrics such as grades, course evaluations, and outcome assessments) is commonly attributed to some fault in the teacher and/or the student. Only rarely, Felman observes, are the nature and source of such "faults" given adequate attention as being inherent to the pedagogical situation itself—to the "impossibility" that both Socrates and Freud saw as the inescapable condition of pedagogy.

In Freud and Lacan, Felman finds the exhortation to turn that very impossibility into an instrument of teaching, which, in Felman's terms,

> is not the transmission of ready-made knowledge, it is rather the creation of a new condition of knowledge ... an original learning-disposition. "What I teach you,'" says Lacan, "does nothing other than express the condition thanks to which what Freud says is possible." The lesson, then, does not "teach" Freud: it teaches the "condition" which makes it possible to learn Freud.

(1982, 31)

Fundamental to this condition is the disavowal of the traditional exchange-economy of education and the willingness to recognize where received knowledge (Lacan calls it "textual knowledge") is resisted. Attending to such resistances makes knowledge something other than fixed content. As Taubman puts it:

> For the curriculum to be treated as a fixed body, a carapace, totalized and transparent to itself, rather than a living, contingent, and re-symbolizable response to our desires, fears, and dreams is to excise the teacher's and student's subjectivity. The end result ... in the packaged curricular outcomes based on standards, and in programs of cultural literacy, is a vision of two machines transmitting, receiving, and returning information.
>
> (2012, 172)

Rather than a mechanical transmission, knowledge becomes "a structural dynamic" that "comes out of the mutual apprenticeship between two partially unconscious [instances of speech] which both say more than they know" (Felman 1982, 33). This pedagogy "abolishes," in Lacan's terms, "the postulate of the subject presumed to know" (1968, 46).

Yet as Felman reminds us, "abolishing a postulate ... doesn't mean abolishing an illusion" (1982, 34). Freud's concept of transference applies

> not just to any pedagogic situation but to the problematics of knowledge as such .... Teaching is not a purely cognitive, informative experience, it is also an emotional, erotic experience .... Insofar as knowledge is itself a structure of address, cognition is always both motivated and obscured by love; theory, both guided and misguided by an implicit transferential structure.
>
> (1982, 35)

Along with its localized curricular implications, thinking of knowledge as a dynamic structure of address also raises fundamental questions about the way universities organize and disseminate knowledge. Developing a robust psychoanalytic curriculum would mean more than simply carving out a separate institutional space for Lacan's "science of desire." It would mean giving all the disciplines "the opportunity," as he puts it, "to renew themselves" (2001b, 313). It could help ensure that necessary attention would also be directed at the irrational and unconscious dimensions of the more "disciplined" fields of knowledge, without claiming a uniquely privileged position to do so. The following chapter, therefore, is about the psychoanalytic curriculum's relation to disciplinarity as such, as well as about psychoanalysis as a disciplinary possibility for the university to come.[11]

Notes

1 A formerly existing Interdisciplinary Minor in Psychoanalytic Studies at Boston College, launched in 2003, had at its peak twenty-one faculty affiliates from seven departments and roughly a dozen Minors at any given time. As a result of faculty attrition and a lack of administrative support, this program was terminated in 2020 (Vanessa Rumble, email message to author, January 5, 2024).
2 Nina Cornyetz, email message to author, November 16, 2023.
3 Elissa Marder, email message to author, November 14, 2022.
4 Leonardo Niro, email message to the author, January 10, 2024.
5 Some European and South American universities, in countries where psychoanalytically informed teaching is much more popular and widespread—including Argentina's University of El Salvador, Belgium's Catholic University of Louvain, France's University of Toulouse-Jean Jaurès, and Spain's University of València—offer courses and even graduate degrees in psychopedagogy.
6 Other recent and contemporary psychoanalytic course offerings found in online catalogues include: "Psychoanalysis and the Visual" (NYU/Gallatin School of Individualized Study); "Freud and the Literary Imagination" (University of Washington); "Dreams of Interpretation: Literature and/as Psychoanalysis" (Emory University); "The Fantastic and the Uncanny in Literature: Ghosts, Spirits, and Machines" (Penn); "Introduction to Psychoanalysis: History, Theory, Practice" (Penn); "Law and the Unconscious Mind" (Emory); "Lives of the Death Drive" (Penn); "Philosophy and Psychoanalysis: Freud and the Interpretation of Culture" (Penn); "Psychoanalysis and Anthropology" (Penn); "The Visibility of Desire: Art, Psychoanalysis, and Culture" (Emerson College); "Retelling a Life: Psychoanalysis and Autobiography" (Penn); "Sex, Society, and Other Relations that Do Not Exist" (University of Illinois, Chicago); "Social Work Practice and Trauma" (Penn); "Core Concepts of Post-Freudian Thought" (Columbia); "Psyche, Symbol, Dream: The World of C. G. Jung" (Colorado College); "Nietzsche, Freud, and Lou Andreas-Salomé" (Hampshire); "Psychoanalytic Case Studies: Childhood and Adolescence" (Hampshire); "Drives Theory: Freud, Laplanche, Lyotard" (Emory); "Psychoanalytic Perspectives on Humor" (Emerson College).
7 Other perennially popular majors include business, nursing, biology, and engineering.
8 As of 2023, more than two out of three faculty members in US colleges and universities held contingent (non-tenured, non-tenure-track) appointments (AAUP, 2023). See also, Birmingham (2017).
9 Public institutions (such as the University of California at Los Angeles and the New College of Florida) are government-funded and thus subject to legislative oversight. Private institutions (such as the University of Pennsylvania and Vassar College) are funded by endowments and other private sources. The Carnegie Classification of Institutions of Higher Education, managed by the American Council on Education,

classifies all accredited, degree-granting colleges and universities in the US, chiefly to identify groups of roughly comparable institutions.

10 On Lacan's relation to speech, pedagogy, transcription, and writing, see Roudinesco (1994, 569–70).

11 Readers might recognize "the university to come" as a prospect about which Jacques Derrida writes with what some call utopian vagary. It's true that Derrida offers no prescriptive norms for a new kind of institution. In fact, his "university without conditions ... is not situated necessarily or exclusively within the walls of what is today called the university. It is not necessarily, exclusively, exemplarily represented in the figure of the professor. It takes place, it seeks its place wherever this unconditionality can take shape" (2002b, 236). Yet, in his many writings on the university and higher education, Derrida may be said to "profess" an institutional politics of "interruption"— interruption of the political and economic forces that continue increasingly to set the material and ideological conditions for intellectual and pedagogical work in the universities of the present. See, for example, *Who's Afraid of Philosophy?: Right to Philosophy 1* (2002a), *Eyes of the University: Right to Philosophy 2* (2004), and "The University without Condition" (2002b).

Chapter 3

Psychoanalysis Among the Disciplines

> Freud extends remarkably the empire of signs and their significant decipher-
> ment, encompassing all of human behavior and symbolic action. Thus any
> "psychoanalytic explanation" in another discipline always runs the risk of
> appearing to claim the last word, the final hermeneutic power.
>
> —PETER BROOKS, "The Idea of a Psychoanalytic
> Literary Criticism" (1987)

Psychoanalysis is a conversation between two people that proceeds according to certain rules of asymmetry. As John Forrester observes, "psychoanalytic theory offers a general view of any such encounter, and it also
offers quite specific and detailed accounts of the unexpected things that
happen in such encounters." Forrester also reminds us that psychoanalysis
"is not the only theory of such conversations available [and] in that fact lies
both its suspicion of adjacent, competing accounts and the possibilities for
[the] infusion of psychoanalytic thought by models and perceptions from
elsewhere" (1991, 243). In the university, matters of theoretical and methodological competition and adjacency are largely determined by disciplinary formations, which are of course historically contingent. The academic
discipline of sociology, for example, arose from the earlier, Enlightenment
discourse of political philosophy, as the emergent nation-state became
modernity's principal integer of imaginative affiliation, collective behavior,
and social coherence and surveillance. And the academic discipline of com-
puter science emerged as a consequence of the creation of powerful computing machines in the 1940s, so as better to study automated calculation,
large-scale algorithmic processing, and mass data structuring and storage.

As early as the age of Chaucer, the English word "discipline" referred
to different branches of knowledge (medicine, law, theology, etc.) and designated something independent of mere doctrine, "its authority [deriving

DOI: 10.4324/9781003540588-4

not] from the writings of an individual or school, but rather from generally accepted methods and truths." The persistent use of the term in this sense has continued to mask "the historical specificity of the organization and production of knowledge." Indeed, the "branches of knowledge themselves, as well as what 'a branch of knowledge' even means, have changed radically" over time (Shumway and Messer-Davidow 1991, 202). With the rise of the modern university system, individual disciplines came to be defined by the different epistemological and methodological conventions that made them serviceable to the larger knowledge-economy—including extramural institutions like scientific societies and state-sponsored industries—and proliferated through increased specialization and diversified professionalization:

> The intellectual ecosystem has with time been carved up into "separate" institutional and professional niches through continuing processes of boundary-work designed to achieve an apparent differentiation of goals, methods, capabilities and substantive expertise.
>
> (Gieryn 1983, 783)

This differentiation is "apparent" because disciplinary boundaries are, of course, always more or less permeable. Such permeability can facilitate communication, collaboration, and growth (what we call "interdisciplinarity"). But it can also lead to defensive entrenchment and territorial disputation, especially when institutional resources are at stake.

Broadly speaking, what are now the scientific (or "STEM") disciplines tend to have the least permeable boundaries and also to dominate the contemporary disciplinary hierarchy. As humanistic disciplines like literature and history have watched both their status and their course enrollments diminish, they've sometimes refashioned themselves by borrowing scientific prestige. For example, beginning in the late twentieth century, augmented applications of computing technologies (e.g., data mining, digital mapping, hypertext, topic modeling) in disciplines such as literature, music, art history, rhetoric, philosophy, and linguistics have helped them, under the banner of "Digital Humanities," to garner such prestige and gain access to hitherto unavailable funding and infrastructure, as well as to extend their appeal to predominantly STEM-oriented students.

Similarly, recent advances in the neurosciences have given psychoanalysis a potential new foothold in the university, as the emergent field of neuropsychoanalysis becomes increasingly well established and also more widely recognizable on both sides of the STEM/non-STEM boundary. This rapprochement between psychoanalysis and neuroscience (Freud began his career as a neurologist) is still proceeding fitfully toward an uncertain future—a future in which the two distinct fields might eventually merge into one. Or, as two separate and dynamic fields, they might give mature life to a third. Either way, there will be significant consequences for other disciplines as well, depending on what sorts of "boundary-work"—including processes akin to the elements of psychoanalytic dream-work: displacement, condensation, and revision/reformation—transpire between this new neuroscientific/psychoanalytic field and such traditional and interdisciplinary fields as psychiatry, cognitive science, and affective neuroscience. One major consequence already manifest is the fact that a neuropsychoanalyst— Mark Solms, perhaps the leading voice in the field—was commissioned by the British Psychoanalytical Society to edit the just-released 24-volume *Revised Standard Edition of the Complete Psychological Works of Sigmund Freud* (2024).

The growth of neuropsychoanalysis and the publication of the *Revised Standard Edition* make this an auspicious moment for revisiting the question of the disciplinarity of psychoanalysis. Because of its early, largely racist, exclusion from the European university system, its creation of numerous independent analytic training institutes, and its cooptation by medicine, psychoanalysis was never established as a standard academic discipline with its own dedicated faculty, permanent infrastructure, and stable curriculum. Because it so often seems to be a discipline like no other, psychoanalysis is frequently characterized in anything-but-disciplinary terms. In her monumental *History of Psychoanalysis in France* (1982–86), analyst and historian Élisabeth Roudinesco describes psychoanalysis as: an "autonomous doctrine"; a "teachable subject"; an "institutional movement"; "extrinsic to other fields"; "extraterritorial"; a "practice of the unconscious"; and "guild oriented" (1994). Psychoanalytic researcher Justin Clemens calls it an "antiphilosophy" (2013). Analyst Arnold Richards mourns it as a formerly "subversive worldview" (2016, 126). And Forrester, who was a professor of the history and philosophy of science, can amuse and frustrate readers by calling psychoanalysis a "technique of speech," a "discourse," a form of "gossip" or "telepathy," a "science," a "cultural artefact," a "social practice," and a "discursive practice," all within a mere two pages of his *Seductions of Psychoanalysis*—a book that nonetheless earnestly seeks to demonstrate how, for over a century, psychoanalysis has managed to retain its *extramural* institutional and discursive identity (1991, 243–44).[1]

Within the university, that identity has grown almost entirely obscure, especially among undergraduates. As a consequence of its disciplinary illocality, students who approach me and my colleagues in our designated "Psychoanalytic Studies" booth at the annual Courses and Majors Fair almost invariably begin by asking some form of the question: "So, what *is* psychoanalysis?" The tattoo of this perfectly innocent question can become disheartening. But it's precisely the right question for them to keep asking—as have countless analysts themselves. Isador Coriat (1919), Ernest Jones (1928), and Barnaby Barratt (2013) have all published books with the title: *What Is Psychoanalysis?* And contention over theories, methods, and terms is the lifeblood of the field. But this is—or at least should be—true of any discipline, which continues to beg the question of psychoanalysis's seemingly unconquerable resistance to, and perennial exclusion from, broad disciplinary recognition within the university.

Ψ

In a special issue of *Critical Inquiry* on "The Trial(s) of Psychoanalysis," literary critic Peter Brooks articulates certain anxieties about the "imperialistic" tendencies of psychoanalysis in relation to other disciplines—thereby reflecting one of several very different perspectives on the disciplinary nature of psychoanalysis itself (1987, 336). In her article for the same issue, Françoise Meltzer elaborates upon the notion of psychoanalysis as a form of disciplinary cooptation:

> Psychoanalysis has infiltrated such diverse areas as literature (to which it owes its myths), linguistics, philosophy, anthropology, history, feminism, psychology, archeology, neurology, to name some. And it is in the notion of "some," perhaps, that lies the crux of the problem. For there is in psychoanalysis an overt conviction that it exists as the ultimate totality, of which everything else is a part. Not content to see itself as one in a number of enterprises, the psychoanalytic project has at its foundation a vision of itself as the meaning which will always lie in wait; the truth which lies covered by "the rest."
>
> (1987, 216)

Today, almost forty years later, such intense concerns about the potentially "imperialistic," or totalizing power of psychoanalysis to "infiltrate" all disciplines and suss out their resistances and defenses—invading their "unconscious," as it were, and "disturb[ing] from within the entire domain of the sciences of man" (Foucault 1994, 376)—seem wildly overblown. To some younger scholars they might even sound hysterical. Indeed, many members of today's professoriate weren't even born when psychoanalysis was at the center of the "theory wars" of the 1970s and 80s. Since then, the status not only of psychoanalysis but also of critical theory *tout court* has been steadily diminished by resurgent empiricism, "post-critique" sentimentalism, and the pursuit of scientific prestige by so-called Digital Humanities—leaving psychoanalysis, as an "ultimate totality," about as efficacious as Hamlet's ghost.

Certain schools of psychoanalytic theory—particularly the more recent relational and intersubjective schools—have been making a modest comeback in the humanities and qualitative social sciences (see, e.g., Ruddick 2022, 257; Berlant 2022, 195n.2). Certain elements of the psychoanalytic profession, too, have renewed their commitment to the humanities. For example, the psychoanalytic division (Division 39) of the American Psychological Association recently created a Humanities and Psychoanalysis Committee (HPC) to advance "the creation, communication, and cross-fertilization of knowledge in the humanities and psychoanalysis to the mutual benefit of both domains." But what exactly are those "domains"? In his description of HPC's mandate, Spyros Orfanos wryly gestures at his own professional organization's contentiousness about what their "domain" really is:

> The humanities were defined as scholarship encompassing philosophy, literature and languages, the arts, history, and also biography and theology. We figured we would outmaneuver the psychoanalytic police by avoiding definitions of psychoanalysis.
>
> (2013, 46)

Indeed, among the boundaries that the "psychoanalytic police" are anxious to guard and defend are precisely those that separate psychoanalysis from humanities disciplines.

Both within and beyond the university, the question of the disciplinary status of psychoanalysis remains unresolved. Historian Fred Weinstein claims that psychoanalysis "is too fragmented to be constituted as a unitary discipline" (1990, 26), whereas analyst Nancy McWilliams refers to psychoanalysis as both an "art" and a "discipline" (2000, 371–72). The editors of *The Routledge Handbook of Psychoanalysis in the Social Sciences and Humanities* refer to the overall growth of psychoanalysis as a "field," but they question its contemporary relevance "to the academy" as both a "science of subjectivity" and a "remarkably generative discipline" (Elliott and Prager 2016, 2–8). The editors of *Psychoanalytic Trends in Theory and Practice* characterize psychoanalysis as "a very diverse field with multiple schools of thought … and no unified theory" (Etezady et al. 2018, 476–78). Literary scholar Lisa Ruddick calls for her own discipline to engage more fully with "the range of psychoanalytic theory" and refers to the "subfield of literature and psychoanalysis" (2022, 257–58), while also referencing "disciplines such as psychoanalysis" (2022, 270n.2). Historian Júlia Gyimesi observes that psychoanalysis has struggled to define itself as truly scientific, due to former collaborations with spiritualism that were "typical in psychoanalysis" and in "other fields of early psychology" (2010, 468). And persistent associations with religiosity lead contemporary analyst Paul Marcus to argue that psychoanalysis is still a "spiritual discipline" or form of ascesis (2021).

In their volume on *Disciplinarity at the Fin de Siècle* (2002), editors Amanda Anderson and Joseph Valente draw a sharp distinction—one also made by numerous analysts—between two psychoanalytic aims: interpretation ("applied psychoanalysis") and cure ("therapeutic psychoanalysis"):

> The location of a pathogenic interplay of conflicting modes of desire (sexual vs. social, erotic vs. egotonic, eros vs. thanatos) proved crucial to the development of psychoanalysis as a hermeneutical discipline, but it threatened to compromise … the possibility of the truly critical self-consciousness essential to the perfection of psychoanalysis as a therapeutic discipline.
>
> (2002, 4)

Of course, as Anderson and Valente remind us, there are many counter-disciplinary formations under the aegis of which researchers pursue "an eclectic combination of fields, methods, and theories" (2002, 1). Freud himself, in his 1919 essay "On the Teaching of Psycho-Analysis in Universities," emphasizes what we'd now call the "interdisciplinarity" of psychoanalysis and makes a crucial distinction between learning "something *about* psycho-analysis" and learning "something *from* it" (1955f, 173). Like biological species, disciplines emerge, evolve, and go extinct as the result of various endogenous and exogenous factors, including the influence of other disciplines. One could say, after Winnicott, that "there is no discipline"—or at least, with Anderson and Valente, that disciplines "are always constituted in relation to, and in a kind of dialogue with, other disciplines" (2002, 5).

Moreover, the epistemological significance of disciplinarity can't be separated from its material circumstances. University budget allocations, fundraising, and infrastructure tend to be heavily determined by traditional disciplines. Emergent or reconfigured disciplines often meet considerable resistance on other-than-intellectual grounds. Resistance to recognizing psychoanalysis as an academic discipline is further compounded by its own longstanding institutional configurations apart from and independent of the university. Indeed, psychoanalytic institutes and societies are often far *more* resistant to the academization of psychoanalysis than academics themselves. As Robert Wallerstein puts it, "psychoanalysis may be unique among scholarly disciplines … in having been born, and having grown, as a developing educational and training enterprise, in a private part-time setting, outside the university" (2009, 1107).

Some might argue this is precisely what disqualifies psychoanalysis from being a discipline, balking at Wallerstein's use of the adjective "scholarly" because it seems to privilege research over practice. I myself have team-taught courses with several brilliant analysts who've made a point of being deferential with regard to what I do as a "scholar" of psychoanalysis as distinct from what they do as "practitioners" of psychoanalysis (as if I were a neuroscientist and they were "mere" neurosurgeons). Of course, such deference is performative—in some cases defensive, in others likely ironic. Yet it's a consistent enough phenomenon from which to infer an earnest professional prioritization of practice *over* research and theory. At the same time, as a non-clinician scholar of psychoanalysis, I'm haunted by the rhetorical question Sherry Turkle poses: "Can there be psychoanalytic researchers who do not practice as analyst and who are not part of the professional organization of analysts?" (1978, 172). The answer, of course, is yes. But lacking the experience of clinical practice and supervision must be acknowledged as a certain deficit or a kind of blindness that can't always be overcome by other hard-won forms of insight. This is one of the reasons why—in our psychoanalytic studies program at Penn—we prefer to offer courses that are team-taught by an academic and a clinician. Whether we're teaching an intricate case-study, a rigorous paper on technique, or a dense meta-psychological essay, we want to be sure we're doing our best to keep track of the unpredictable, visceral, interpersonal dynamics of analytic relationships as such.

Yet various logistical, financial, and even ideological constraints make opportunities for this sort of pedagogical collaboration highly uncommon, and psychoanalysis remains for the most part *undisciplined*. That is, psychoanalysis remains largely extrinsic to constellations of both traditional and emergent academic disciplines, which continue largely to resist even its hermeneutic encroachments. The dozen-or-so formal psychoanalytic studies programs in contemporary British and American universities (see Chapter 2 and the Appendix) are the exceptions that prove the rule: the relation of psychoanalysis to the epistemological precincts of the university continues to be one of "extraterritoriality" (Roudinesco 1994, 556). Whether as a rootless cosmopolitan traversing the campus at will or as a wandering exile perpetually in search of departmental hospitality, psychoanalysis, with few exceptions, remains without a permanent university home of its own. Even within the ever-diminishing number of psychoanalysis-friendly departments of psychology and psychiatry, psychoanalysis is rarely treated as anything more than a sub-field.

In his vast oeuvre on the history of knowledge, Foucault characterizes psychoanalysis in various ways—for example, as "the possibility of a dialogue with unreason … an experience of unreason that psychology, in the modern world, was meant to disguise" (2006, 339), and as a "critical function," an "inexhaustible treasure-hoard of experiences and concepts, and above all a perpetual principle of dissatisfaction, of calling into question, of criticism and contestation of what may seem, in other respects, to be established" (1994, 373–74). Yet while Foucault recognizes psychoanalysis as a manifestation of disciplinary society, he, too, regards it not as a discipline in the academic sense but, rather, as an assemblage of heterogeneous elements, such as types of expertise, systems of classification, a discourse of truth, the production of sexuality, nosologies of identity, the universalization of the subject, modalities of training, a family of treatments, governing bodies, figures of authority, and shifting goals, stratagems, and targets of opportunity as an instrument of biopower.

Lacan also asserts the exceptionality of what he calls "this science of desire," concluding his seminar on *The Ethics of Psychoanalysis* by saying that psychoanalysis doesn't "belong to the field of the human sciences"—a field in which a debased and instrumentalized "passion for knowledge" has come to occupy the place of desire:

> Throughout this historical period the desire of man, which has been felt, anesthetized, put to sleep by moralists, domesticated by educators, betrayed by the academies, has quite simply taken refuge or been repressed in that most subtle and blindest of passions, as the story of Oedipus shows, the passion for knowledge.
>
> (1992, 321–24)

In the language of academic disciplines—here, philosophy—Lacan may be said to distinguish between two ethics: an ethics of desire and an ethics of goods. For him, the former is the province of psychoanalysis and the latter is the province of education, precisely because "desire" is that which cannot be disciplined (shaped, directed, confined, explained).

Nonetheless, both Freud and Lacan are fundamentally concerned with the subject's relation to other desiring subjects, or with what Eric Santner calls "an ethics pertaining to my *answerability to my neighbor-with-an-unconscious.*" In Santner's terms,

> what makes the Other *other* is not his or her spatial exteriority with respect to my being but the fact that he or she is *strange*, is a *stranger*, and not only to me but also to him- or herself, is the bearer of an internal alterity, an enigmatic density of desire calling for response beyond any rule-governed reciprocity.
>
> (2001, 9)

Freud's late thesis (e.g., in *Beyond the Pleasure Principle* [1920] and *Civilization and Its Discontents* [1930]) is that the attempt to discipline the drives generates an unending cycle of conflict and compromise; that a loss of freedom is both the cost and consolation of community; and that the "rule-governed reciprocity" of conventional ethics gives us security at the price of guilt (1961a, 140–44). In his view, the project of psychoanalysis is both to lament and to resist this ethos of discontent—to find a less "disciplined" way to heed the call of the "enigmatic density of desire" that arrives both from within and from all around us. Thus, the project of the university—ideally, at least—is to serve as a kind of social laboratory for the "education" of the "enigmatic density" of what Freud, Lacan, Klein, Bion, and many other psychoanalytic thinkers have postulated as a discrete *desire to know*.

Ψ

He was born in Greece, the land of Oedipus. A bright and eager neurochemistry major, Ari (as I'll call him) was handsome, athletic, good-natured, and presumptively straight. Relatively early in the semester, during our class discussion of Freud's *Three Essays on the Theory of Sexuality*, Ari listened intently as my co-instructor, psychoanalyst Susan Adelman, described Freud's early notions of phallic striving and psychosexual development, in which the penis is the object of both boyish anxiety and girlish envy. In Freud's preliminary view, Susan explained, a girl's "penis envy" is transformed by a compensatory mechanism of displacement into desire for a baby—in other words, the baby is the girl's consolation prize for not having a penis. Ari raised his hand and asked: "But who wouldn't rather have a baby than a penis?"

In addition to being a good joke, Ari's half-serious question is an excellent example of the sustained mood of intelligent playfulness that so often buoyed and enriched that semester's iteration of our regularly offered course, "Introduction to Psychoanalysis: History, Theory, Practice"—not least because it was an opportunity to reflect on the inevitable transferences and projections that occur in the classroom itself, as Ari himself, on some level, clearly recognized. Because it satisfies a college-wide undergraduate humanities requirement—and because it's the "core" course in our six-course minor in psychoanalytic studies—our students come from all sorts of majors and programs, including biology, fine arts, history, literature, neuroscience, nursing, political science, and even a few brave souls from psychology.

This disciplinary heterogeneity turns out to be a powerful advantage— not least, because it helps us make the point that psychoanalysis is already in conversation with all of these disciplines and consequently that each student has some special interest or expertise of their own to contribute to our discussions of what is, to almost all of them, a brand-new field. Susan and I help them get acquainted with psychoanalysis, and they, in turn, teach us a thing or two. For example, Ari (the neurochemistry major) helped us understand the amygdala's role in the experience of anxiety. Another student explained how Japanese pronouns reflect a cultural understanding of subjectivity and social relationships that cuts against the grain of many (Western) psychoanalytic assumptions. A literature major shared a quote from Kate Chopin's 1899 novel, *The Awakening*, that seemed to anticipate Winnicott's concept of the "false self." And one of our history majors provided some helpful context when we discussed Freud's escape from Vienna after the Anschluss.

Indeed, Freud's Jewishness has been an important point of connection for several students who've taken our course, and this has led to discussions of other students' religious backgrounds. Not only is there a mix of Jewish, Christian, Muslim, and Buddhist students, but also a great diversity of classes, ethnicities, second (and third, and fourth!) languages, nationalities, races, genders, and sexualities. When Susan and I wrote the initial version of the syllabus, years ago, we included psychoanalytic readings on topics such as gender transition, comparative religion, African American psychoanalysts, teen suicide, lesbian autobiography, and the global practice of psychotherapy from urban US Latinx communities to the western provinces of China. But, before we met our new course's enrollees on the first day of class, we had no way of predicting just how relevant the politics of identity would be to our remarkably heterogeneous group of students—or how gratified they would be to learn that (most) contemporary psychoanalysts take their post-adolescent, real-world struggles and questions very seriously.

Unfortunately, students at US colleges and universities—private and public, rich and poor—have few opportunities to study psychoanalysis, even for a semester. With a small number of exceptions, writes Brahm Norwich, "psychoanalysis is ignored and dismissed from the Academy." And it's precisely in those parts of the university—departments of psychology and psychiatry—where psychoanalysis should presumably find itself most at home that "psychoanalytic ideas and approaches have been displaced by other areas of study and practice" (2013, 680). In 2007, the *New York Times* reported that, "if you want to learn about psychoanalysis at the nation's top universities, one of the last places to look may be the psychology department" (Cohen 2007, C6). In the US, the UK, Canada, France, Israel, and many other countries, academic psychology, especially, has become more rigidly empiricist and behaviorally oriented than ever before. Once again, hard data are difficult to assemble. But all available evidence strongly suggests that students are unlikely to learn anything about psychoanalysis in departments of psychology (Redmond and Shulman 2008, 398). Indeed, in their "Epilogue" to a 2019 special-issue of *Psychoanalytic Inquiry* on "The Future of Psychoanalysis in Undergraduate Education," Marcia Dobson and John Riker emphasize the extent to which psychoanalysis "has been attacked and dismissed … by psychology departments in American universities and colleges" (2019, 469). Similar concerns are expressed by the authors of a recent article about the Psychoanalytic and Psychodynamic Teachers' Academy sponsored by APsA: "Psychology textbooks are often peppered with caricatures of, and outright misinformation about, psychodynamic theories and treatments" (Tasso et al. 2022, 28).

Yet, unlike most of their psychology professors, many of the undergraduates in our introductory course on psychoanalysis already know a great deal about phenomena like dopaminergic seeking systems, infantile recognition memories, oxytocin-driven attachments, the frontal lobe's role in secondary process thinking, and the limbic system's role in dreaming. In other words, their study of the brain—in our astonishing contemporary moment of neuroscientific breakthroughs (advances that Freud, as a trained neurologist, not only predicted but longed for)—has already equipped them with a sophisticated understanding of the physiological dimensions of some of the psychic processes for which psychoanalysis still offers the richest and most accurate descriptions. The readings we assign by neuropsychoanalysts like Antonio Damasio and Mark Solms tend to make perfect sense to them, and many of them ask us the same question Paul Bloom reported hearing from students at the University of Toronto: "Why don't we ever hear about this stuff in our psychology courses?"

They should, of course. But Susan and I have different ways of answering this sort of question, when and as it arises. More will be said about the psychodynamics of pedagogy in Chapter 4. But here is an example of how this sort of team-teaching can work in the classroom. When we teach Freud's *Three Essays*, we try to whet their appetites for reading the book by telling them in advance that it's about how, in the early twentieth century, Sigmund Freud declared war on childhood. Once we've assembled for class, we can begin to speak to them less hyperbolically about how Freud set out to dismantle the widespread and tenacious nineteenth-century myth of children's "innocence" that was so prevalent at the time in most of Europe and North America. We explain that infants and prepubertal children, in particular, were commonly idealized as "pure" beings, not yet tainted by erotic impulses. And we remind them that things hadn't always been that way—that, in fact, earlier, Calvinistic beliefs about children as little devils, steeped in "original sin," had been largely displaced by images of little angels bathed in the refracted sunbeams of Romantic sentiment. (At this point, in one iteration of the course, an English major offered some supporting evidence from her own area of expertise by citing William Wordsworth's famous "Intimations Ode," in which he writes that "Heaven lies about us in our infancy" [1981, 525]).

In *Three Essays*, Freud insists that this is nonsense and argues that, although they have no adult understanding of sexuality, infants are, from the get-go, squirmy bundles of erotogenic zones and undifferentiated libido. This "polymorphously perverse disposition" (1953, 191), as Freud puts it, is every adult's inheritance from the child they once were. Does everyone notice how consistent Freud is in making such assertions in the most matter-of-fact way? We tell our students that, in conversation with one of his colleagues, Freud insisted that this "polymorphously perverse disposition" wasn't a startling discovery at all. On the contrary, the fact that even the youngest children have sexual feelings was something adults simply didn't want to admit. Freud told his friend that "it seems to be my fate to discover only the obvious." These were things, after all, that "every nursemaid knows" (Jones 1957, 1: 350). We want our students to understand, first and foremost, that Freud had been very brave, not just in pointing out the obvious, but also in pursuing his study of the obvious to its most surprising conclusions—brave enough to share his radical, non-judgmental story of human sexuality in all its variegated muckiness and splendor, and to withstand the shocked and ignominious reactions of his contemporaries. We ask them to appreciate what a consequential achievement it was—Freud's modesty notwithstanding—to finally, fully, and forever join children's history to the history of sexuality.

There are always some students who signal their skepticism in various, often subverbal, ways (e.g., grimacing, eyerolling, tooth-sucking, etc.). But instead of ignoring or feeling hurt by such responses, we encourage them to try to articulate their skepticism—to give words to their displays of negative affect. If things feel right, we might invite students to talk about how those sorts of subverbal responses could indicate a kind of defensive regression on their part and thus open up the challenging topic of classroom transference. Other students rightly point out the egregious aspects of Freud's remarks on sexual difference, and we applaud those observations, acknowledging that a lot has changed over the past century—including the correction and expansion of Freud's earliest theories, as well as the many dramatic transformations in our society's sexual and gender-related norms, practices, and identities. As teachers, Susan and I make sure we keep in mind the fact that Freud's *Three Essays* can still be unsettling reading, even for some of today's most precocious-seeming late-adolescents. Asking students who are (most of them) not yet out of their teens—and thus still figuring out what sorts of sexual beings they might be—to discuss *Three Essays* means leading them, as gently as we can, toward potentially risky forms of self-discovery and self-exposure. The questions they raise tend to skirt the explicitly autobiographical but are nevertheless clearly "about" themselves and their peers: "Why does Freud think that sexual object-choices can change, even later in life?" "Why does Freud think girls want to be boys?" "How can his use of the word 'perversion' really be non-judgmental?" "Is it true that everyone is bisexual?" "Do you believe what Freud says about sex and cruelty being connected?"

Asking us what we, their teachers, believe is one way of letting us know they need a certain amount of reassurance regarding their sense of implication in what Freud says—for example, what he says about the link between sexuality and "cruelty," or aggression, and the dimensions of "mastery" related to both. After all, our students include young men who don't yet know exactly how to manage their suddenly much larger, stronger bodies, or who might go to the gym to build up muscular armature as a defense against their own or others' suspicions that they're insufficiently "manly," or something other than heterosexual. Our students also include young women who are still socially conditioned not to appear aggressive, but who, just like their male counterparts, feel powerful and sometimes frightening impulses, and who also, sadly, know how much more vulnerable they are than most of their male peers to common forms of sexual assault, including date-rape, on their own campus. It's easy for teachers (especially as we get older) to forget the extent to which students in their late teens and early twenties are preoccupied with frequently and sometimes disturbingly intrusive psycho-somato-sexual thoughts and feelings—thoughts and feelings often experienced as unconscious conflicts and manifested in defensive and transferential projections that can be difficult for teachers to ignore or know what to do with.

In *Three Essays*, Freud himself has some advice for teachers of children, including late-adolescents: "The behavior of children at school, which confronts a teacher with plenty of puzzles, deserves in general to be brought into relation with their budding sexuality" (1953, 203). Easily said—but the challenge teachers continue to face is how best to help our students see this relation *for themselves* and, moreover, consciously to reflect, in ways that are both informed and unabashed, on *the erotic dimensions of their own physical, emotional, and intellectual experience of learning as such*— including the role played by what Freud calls the "instinct for knowledge," or "epistemophilia" (1953, 194). Susan and I sometimes ask our students to meditate on this quotation from *Three Essays* and to share their views on what it might mean for them to bring their classroom comportment "into relation with their budding sexuality." In their responses, many students talk about "sublimation," venturing that, at a fiercely competitive school like Penn, students are having sex less frequently, or not at all, in order to "divert" their libido into academic and professional pursuits. Others point out how the vagaries of our legal system dramatize the contingency of childhood as a social construction—reminding us that, in Pennsylvania, they're old enough to consent to sex but too young to purchase alcohol. We learned that in one student's home-state fourteen-year-olds can be legally married, but that if a nineteen-year-old male has sex with a sixteen-year-old female he can be tried for statutory rape. We've also heard students speak about finally being free, as young adults living away from home, to experiment with long-suppressed sexual urges and gender identities.

There are also plenty of students who have a hard time letting go of their skepticism about Freud's universalizing pronouncements on infant and early childhood sexuality. Some of them remain not just unconvinced but quite resistant, and we have to consider carefully whether to address their resistance directly, as part of our pedagogy. What are the potential risks and rewards, for example, of suggesting that their defensiveness might indicate that the idealization of early childhood and of the purity of child-parent relationships remains a powerful personal conviction for them? We don't want to push *too* hard against their resistance, but we also want them learn more frequently to question their as yet unexamined reactions. At the end of our work with *Three Essays*, we might ask them, for example, to consider again Freud's frank, solicitous, and de-idealized erotic iconography of mother-and-child:

A child's intercourse with anyone responsible for his care affords him an unending source of sexual excitation and satisfaction from his erotogenic zones. This is especially so since the person in charge of him, who, after all, is as a rule his mother, herself regards him with feelings that are derived from her own sexual life: she strokes him, kisses him, rocks him and quite clearly treats him as a substitute for a complete sexual object. A mother would probably be horrified if she were made aware that all her marks of affection were rousing her child's sexual instinct and preparing for its later intensity. She regards what she does as asexual, "pure" love, since, after all, she carefully avoids applying more excitations to the child's genitals than are unavoidable in nursery care. As we know, however, the sexual instinct is not aroused only by direct excitation of the genital zone .... Moreover, if the mother understood more of the high importance of the part played by instincts in mental life as a whole—in all its ethical and psychical achievements—she would spare herself any self-reproaches even after her enlightenment. She is only fulfilling her task in teaching the child to love.

(1953, 223)

As the semester progresses, we hope that they'll remember such passages and notice how Freud's early theories—including their male-centric bias—continue to be modified and corrected by others. But we also hope that passages like this one will continue to resonate for them as one of Freud's still vital contributions to our ongoing appreciation of the very real, very rich, and very human "perversity" of our entire erotic lives.

We've observed that, for most students, the notion that everyone has an innate curiosity about the world—indeed, that this curiosity is likely one of our species' most vital evolutionary achievements—isn't at all controversial. After all, we're born helpless, knowing nothing, which makes learning about the world essential to our survival. Newborns are natural investigators, and, at one point or another, most of our students have observed how much time and energy babies spend seeking, touching, manipulating, and reaching for the objects around them. Yet the psychoanalytic insight that cognitive development remains grounded in intensely felt libidinal and aggressive drives is often perceived as more troubling, even threatening— chiefly, perhaps, because it goes against deeply ingrained beliefs about ostensive opposites like "reason" and "emotion," "rational" and "irrational," "objective" and "subjective."

Entire societies and their systems of education, after all, continue to depend upon reassuring illusions about "a trustworthy, conscious, rational mind, grounded in objective reality, and confident in reasoned and bias- and affect-free thought" (D'Amour 2020, 60). One can grow giddy (or frustrated) with such reassurances, delight (or despair) in the pursuit of truth, savor the pleasures (or fear the challenges) of problem-solving, swell with pride in academic achievement (or shrivel with shame at academic failure). Nevertheless, we're still heavily conditioned to hide those feelings themselves, subjecting them to what D'Amour calls "dissociative disregard" (2020, 60). Even when the curricular content is human emotionality (in, say, a course on affective neuroscience or literary sentimentalism),

> feelings, and more generally affect of any sort and strength, are the unrecognized presences at the cultural conference table. Everyone in the room senses their presence, but with few exceptions no one talks to them. They are not addressed by name.
>
> (Damasio 2018, 16)

Even a psychoanalytic (or neuropsychoanalytic) curriculum is no guarantee that, in the lecture hall or around the seminar table, these affective presences will themselves be engaged ("talked to," "addressed by name," etc.). Intellectualization remains the readily available and widely encouraged defense against emotional spillovers or unreflective enactments of emotional entanglements, which might (however interestingly) interfere with the rational linearity upon which traditional education (and even the word "curriculum") insist. Rarely in any classroom setting does anyone "talk to" feelings—chiefly, perhaps, because so many of these feelings are bound to be, as cultural critic Sianne Ngai would say, "ugly." A feeling is "ugly," in Ngai's sense, when it threatens to reveal or betray certain "predicaments posed by a general state of obstructed agency with respect to other human actors or to the social as such" (2005, 3). The "agenda" of Ngai's study of these deeply equivocal and equivocated feelings is at least partly psychoanalytic, inasmuch as it seeks to identify and to "recuperate" them (in a non-idealizing way) "for their *critical* productivity" (2005, 3)—much as, in the consulting room, a persistent enactment can be consciously worked through, rather than allowed unconsciously to persist in its numbing "stuckness."

Classrooms are hothouses for enactments, because teacher-student relationships are strongly prone to projective identifications. Powerful feelings are mutually and unconsciously stimulated between teacher and student. Such feelings are often associated with early traumas, and while the specific traumatic association is, of course, different for each person, the denied and split-off feeling is often similar enough to bind the two of them together in an unanticipated, mutually reinforcing, unconscious repetition of some past dynamic or pattern. For example, many years ago, a student speaking to me privately in office-hours asked me if I disliked one of the other students in our seminar. The student she referred to was a young man I (consciously) considered to be one of the smartest in the course, so I felt especially taken aback. I asked her if she could describe what she'd observed going on between myself and the other student, and I was amazed to hear—and even more amazed to recognize, for the first time—that I was in the habit of interrupting and correcting him much more frequently than any of the other students, and in a manner that my office-hour student, at least, not only noticed but also sensed was a reciprocated hostility. I was startled and abashed. But, in light of what she said, I was able to call up my own memories of previous class meetings and, in this way, observe and verify the behavior myself. When had it begun? What might have triggered it? And, most importantly, what should I do about it (beyond making a conscious effort to interrupt him less frequently)? Ultimately, I was able to have a conversation with the student himself, during which we talked about the pedagogical purposes of class discussion and about different styles of dialogue and debate. (Regular participation in class-discussion was a course requirement on which each student would be graded.) Talking with him about talking— for example, about his eagerness not just to be heard but to be understood, about his interest in the course material, and about his desire (of which I'd been completely unaware) to become a teacher himself—made me, at first, unaccountably angry. But now, at least, I was conscious of this anger and able to contain it, cultivating, instead, a new sense of identification with him that was based, I believe, on some spontaneous memories of being his age. I shared only a few of these details with him, but I did refer once or twice to my undergraduate studies, which seemed to have a relaxing effect on him, and by the end of our meeting, we were happily scheduling our next office-hour session.

I imagine this description of a teacher-student enactment and the beginnings of its resolution strikes a familiar chord in other teachers. I myself could recount many such enactments from my twenty-five years of teaching, some of which were never resolved. And I'm sure there were many more of which I was never even aware. In any case, it's much harder to resolve such an enactment in the classroom itself—even though multiple students can get caught up in it, too. Would a more psychodynamic pedagogy make it easier to resolve? Would that be advisable from an academic point of view? Would its advisability depend upon the course's subject matter? That is, would it make a difference if the course were about psychoanalysis—with a syllabus including readings about projective identification, childhood trauma, Oedipal striving, and neurotic defense mechanisms—rather than, say, ethnomusicology, or calculus, or modern Chinese history? Teacher-student enactments are just as likely to occur in one course as in any another. The ugly feelings are just as ugly, and our desirous relation to knowledge is always in play.

But would some of the more puzzling behaviors of students in, say, the modern Chinese history course "deserve … to be brought into relation with their budding sexuality"? Would "talking to" the libidinal and aggressive expressions of epistemophilia be understood as a universalizing assault on the specificity of Chinese attitudes toward love, anger, and their expression? Would any Chinese students in the course feel threatened in their ethnic or racial identities? Would generational traumas be more or less likely to be triggered? Would the study of the Cultural Revolution's suppression of neo-Confucianism be reduced to sexual allegory, or would it be enhanced by being brought into relation with the students' own aggression? Posing comparable questions about the calculus course might seem even more risky or impertinent. Or could it be that our conventional curricula are too limited to engage them? Calculus, after all, is the mathematical study of change. And psychoanalysis is a calculus for the vicissitudes of desire.

Ψ

Imagining new pedagogical possibilities for a world—and a corporate, neo-colonial system of higher education—increasingly riven by extreme inequality, Columbia professor of comparative literature Gayatri Chakravorty Spivak writes that "education in the Humanities attempts to be an uncoercive rearrangement of desires" and an "uncoercive undermining of the class habit of obedience" (2004, 526, 562). One point of interest here is that Spivak's optative mood hinges on a disciplinary distinction between "the Humanities" (writ large) and the other disciplines—presumably including the STEM disciplines as well as the paraprofessional disciplines such as law, business, and communication. Moreover, Spivak adverts to the personal challenges she faces as a professor of literature in a city (New York) that she imagines might be something other than "necessarily the capital of the world," vowing to "continue to insist that the problem with US education is that it teaches (corporatist) benevolence while trivializing the teaching of the Humanities" (2004, 532). One striking feature of her polemic is that it engages in a defensive strategy—splitting—that she also, quite rightly, attributes to "US education."

In the psychoanalytic sense introduced by Klein to describe the most "primitive" type of defense against anxiety, the simultaneously loved and hated object—here, the University or *alma mater* (Lat.: "nourishing mother")—is split into a good part ("the Humanities") and a bad part (the non-humanities disciplines). At the same time, the university splits itself so as to create a bad or "trivialized" part ("the Humanities"), presumably at the behest of a coercive administration that is itself controlled by interests of the ruling class. In the specious zero-sum game the university is forced to play, one part must suffer (or give in to coercion) so that the other part can thrive. Psychodynamically, there will be a corresponding split in the ego—a split that might manifest itself in, say, the humanities professor's claim, "I'm no good at math," or in the humanities student's internalization of a parent's disparagement of their insufficiently lucrative or socially respected choice of major. Not to put too diagnostic a point on it, but Spivak herself rhetorically negates her home (and Columbia's) as "the capital of the world" in order successfully to introject "the global South" as that other part of the world to which she pledges a "Humanities to come" (2004, 526).

Within the university, as the principal locus of the desire to know, disciplinarity often manifests, both administratively and intellectually, in forms of psychic splitting. As James Shulman observes, "academic departments have their own norms that can be distinct from the overall institution's" (2023, 75–76). Faculty members may perceive such distinctions to be quite extreme and perhaps unfavorable to the department to which they belong and with which they identify. Real or perceived disparities between departments (with regard, say, to resource allocation or administrative favor) frequently generate tensions that exacerbate pre-existing conflicts over academic boundaries and areas of specialization or collaboration. As disciplinary formations, academic departments sometimes become internally riven by intellectual or ideological disputes that render them dysfunctional and subject to administrative restructuring, or worse.

Historically, both the word "discipline" and its practice are linked not only to divisions of knowledge, teaching, rules of conduct, and self-control, but also to what have often been their violent mechanisms of enforcement. As Foucault has shown, education is at the heart of the revaluation of discipline as a problematics of power in the modern era. From something largely negative to something in many ways quite positive, discipline comes to be reflected in such liberal aims as self-improvement and vocational preparation—though it never loses its association with the power that keeps the subject of such aims (the one who is to be improved or prepared) in their proper place. At the same time, Foucault would have us recognize that the modern academic discipline of "Education" helps to "discipline" its own object of study—the social institution of education—by producing knowledge about it that, in turn, influences its administration. Among the factors perpetuating education's seemingly interminable "crisis" is the ongoing defensive splitting of education's intellectual and affective dimensions. Thus, the broad inability to tolerate ambivalence about desire and the desiring body's ineluctable relation to knowledge continues almost everywhere to promote the idealization of counter-erotic pedagogies and the Foucaultian "docile bodies" they require (Foucault 1979, 135–69; see also, Ball 2013).

Few teachers have articulated their own experience of the ironies and dangers of this defensive splitting as publicly and as powerfully as Jane Gallop, who describes in her book, *Feminist Accused of Sexual Harassment*, the consequences of her refusal to "respect the line between the intellectual and the sexual" (1997, 12). Gallop begins her narrative by describing her college-age participation in the feminist "wave" of the early 1970s, and she credits her intellectual and sexual awakenings, not as two concurrent but separate phenomena, but as an effect of the necessary co-implication of desire and knowledge. Having been "deeply alienated from her own desire for knowledge," Gallop "gained access simultaneously to real learning and active sexuality. One achievement cannot be separated from the other" (1997, 5). The same desire that drove her intellectual growth led to "new kinds of pedagogical relations" (1997, 18)—relations of libidinally charged collaboration and disciplinary disruption and reconfiguration.

A quarter-century later—having become a senior scholar in an institutionally secure field—Gallop sees those "new kinds of pedagogical relations" everywhere in abeyance. Her efforts to revive them in her own teaching notwithstanding, Gallop finds herself in the grimly ironic position of being accused by two of her students of "sexual harassment." According to Gallop,

> the university's affirmative-action office conducted a lengthy investigation which resulted in a pretty accurate picture of my relations with these students. I had not tried to sleep with them, and all my professional decisions regarding them seemed clearly based in recognizable and consistent professional standards. No evidence of either "sexual advances" or "retaliations" was to be found.
>
> (1997, 32–33)

Nonetheless, the investigators found that Gallop had

> indulged in so-called sexual behavior that was generally matched by similar behavior directed toward me on the part of the students. Not only did they participate in sexual banter with me, but they were just as likely to initiate it as I was.
>
> (1997, 33)

The case of one student was dismissed. However,

> because my relationship with the other complainant was much more elaborate, it was determined that this mutual relationship of flirtatious banter and frank sexual discussion violated the [university's] consensual relations policy.
>
> (1997, 33)

Ultimately, the determination of the lawyer heading the affirmative-action office was that, although Gallop was not guilty of sexual harassment, she was in violation of university policy "because I had engaged with one of my students in a 'consensual amorous relation,'" which meant, more specifically, that the relation "was *'sexual' but did not involve sex acts*" (1997, 34). In Gallop's thoughtful analysis of the finding, she had, in effect, been found guilty of not respecting "the boundary between the sexual and the intellectual" (1997, 35).

Of course, policing "the boundary between the sexual and the intellectual"—in effect, seeking to de-libidinize the experience of education—is precisely what Gallop and her peers had been fighting against ever since the early 1970s and throughout their academic careers. Critiquing and dismantling the specious barricade between desire and knowledge was for them (and remains for us) one of the most important goals of any psychoanalytically informed education. Unless and until this is achieved, both students and teachers are effectively denied recognition as desiring subjects. Various forms of attachment, identification, and idealization are endemic to the teacher-student relationship, whether or not "sex acts" occur or are even consciously imagined. As Gallop tried to explain to her university's officials in the simplest terms, the phenomenon of transference/countertransference is endemic to teacher-student relationships. But these academic administrators not only failed to understand this basic concept, but went so far as to recommend "in the official report on my case … that in the future I should stop working with any student who has such a transference onto me" (1997, 56). Gallop's alarmed response is well-warranted: "If schools decide to prohibit not only sex but 'amorous relations' between teacher and student, the 'consensual amorous relation' that will be banned from our campuses might just be teaching itself" (1997, 57). University policies that penalize any and all transgressions of "the boundary between the sexual and the intellectual" can, as in Gallop's case, wrongly target and even dehumanize those whose discovery of the radical link between desire and knowledge enabled them to become scholars and teachers in the first place.

In Gallop's case, the misapplication of crucial safeguards against serious abuses of power led to her university's failure to safeguard the pedagogical relation as such by (ludicrously) requiring teachers not only to police but also to punish ("stop working with") their students *for having an unconscious*. In doing so, the university also failed to recognize itself as what Johnson calls a "wobbly, volatile space of intersubjective desire that defines the pedagogic enterprise" (2014, 8). Such an enterprise can't and won't survive the deterministic reductivism of the neoliberal fantasies of autonomy and self-awareness that, increasingly, govern higher education—fantasies in which the student unconscious is mistaken for ignorance and the teacher unconscious is mistaken for prurience. Only a psychoanalytically informed pedagogy can help teachers avoid becoming mere merchants of these fantasies and also help them take better advantage of unconscious desire as the precondition of education.

Ψ

As early as 1915, Freud's modifications to his theory of infantile sexuality stressed the formative consequences of what he called the "sexual researches of childhood" (1953, 194ff.). These "researches"—for example, children's autoerotic exploration of their own bodies and their efforts to investigate their parents' sexual anatomies and behaviors—are strongly motivated, in Freud's view, by an instinctual appetite or "drive" for knowledge, an *epistemophilia*, of which the products are both precocious and distorted, largely repressed yet—as such—destined to influence one's sexual development and one's ongoing relation to knowledge itself. Epistemophilia may be either inhibited or encouraged, punished or rewarded, in ways that are potentially of tremendous consequence for children's future intellectual lives. From his treatment of obsessional and melancholic patients, Freud also knew that epistemophilia could easily be perverted by the super-ego's punitive subjugation of the ego (1955e, 245), which is why so many early theorists of psychopedagogy stressed the importance of permissiveness and disinhibition (see Chapter 1).

Freud's understanding of epistemophilia—of the radical link between knowledge (Gr. *episteme*: "knowledge") and love (Gr. *philia*: "love")—is also central to Melanie Klein's revision of Freud's drive theory, with its emphasis on early object relations:

> The infant, still undeveloped intellectually, is exposed to an onrush of problems and questions. One of the most bitter grievances which we come upon in the unconscious is that these many overwhelming questions, which are apparently only partly conscious and even when conscious cannot yet be expressed in words, remain unanswered. Another reproach follows hard upon this, namely, that the child could not understand words and speech ... The early feeling of *not knowing* has manifold connections. It unites with the feeling of being incapable, impotent, which soon results from the Oedipus situation. The child also feels this frustration the more acutely because he knows nothing definite about sexual processes.
>
> (1975c, 188)

The infant's utter dependence on its earliest objects—usually mother and father—engenders experiences of both care and deprivation that, confusingly, enragingly, set off a struggle between love and hate that gets played out in Klein's version of the Oedipal scenario and, in various ways, throughout our lives, in all of our object relations, including self-object relations and the stakes of recognition.

Epistemophilia, in Klein's view, entails not only the desire to know but also the desire to *be known*, to be recognized. That is, we want to be recognized as the knowing subjects we're striving to become. Even more than Freud and Klein, Bion considered the drive to know as vital to the life of the individual as the libidinal and aggressive drives, and he conceived of thinking, with its origins in the infant's earliest object relations, as inherently tied to the vicissitudes of emotion. Knowing and feeling, in other words, are not opposed but conjoined, in Bion's influential view. Following Klein's position that the primary object of curiosity (the desire to know) is the mother, including the mother's body and the possibility of harming or destroying that body, Bion concluded that it would be impossible for cognitive functioning to emerge free of emotional influence. The capacity to think (to reason), then, requires what Michael Rustin calls "an experience of nurture in emotionally rich relationships" and "a configuration of the mind within which aggression and anxiety are contained and limited. Where this does not happen, the capacities of the mind are liable to be fragmented or inhibited" (2018, 695; see also, Rudberg 1996).

Epistemophilia—the desire for the pleasures associated with curiosity, recognition, and understanding—turns on a narcissistic position that is also imbued with libidinal and aggressive drives. Thus, certain kinds of knowledge may arouse intense anxiety and corresponding defenses against it. As a context for epistemophilic satisfaction, the school is also one of the places most likely to generate epistemic anxiety—for example, over the disciplining of the more intrusive and destructive forms of curiosity. The object of curiosity may be loved or hated in ways that pedagogical requirements, expectations, and evaluations tend to frustrate and inhibit. Curiosity may be aroused by jealousy, rivalry, and envy, along with unconscious anxieties concerning potential retaliation or loss of approval and recognition.

Into today's college classrooms, students bring unprecedented demands for recognition—chiefly in the register of identity (e.g., gender, sexuality, race, class, ethnicity, religion, disability, etc.). Previous generations were more likely to worry about their identities being "spoiled" in Erving Goffman's sense, which has chiefly to do with stigmatization (1963). Many identities remain widely stigmatized, of course. But the contemporary student's greater concern often seems to be with the destabilization or loss of a cherished or hard-won identity. Yet while that identity needs to be recognized and reinforced in other parts of their lives, it can be a perilous expectation to bring to the scene of education, where students' conscious and unconscious attempts to elicit and control recognition are necessarily challenged by new ideas and perspectives as well as by sustained contact with diverse classroom communities.

Consequently, instructors and others involved in curricular design feel significant pressure to accede to learning theories and teaching techniques that prioritize students' ability to recognize themselves in, or to experience some personal connection with, the material being taught. In the absence of such affirmative curricular mirroring, vestiges of the unavoidable deprivations of childhood and the necessary ambivalence of our early object relations are all the more likely to provoke destructive impulses as well, impulses that can become forces of envy and even sadism—including attacks on recognition. As David McIvor explains, Klein sees such envy as being, to at least some degree, unavoidable, while also concluding that it

> *can* be mitigated through a reflective process of working through combined with experiences of recognition. The subject's desire for truth is not only posited within its use of language but within the intersubjective medium of care, without which the individual could not survive. Yet this desire must compete with envy because between the passions of love and hate 'there is the closest union and interaction … at every point' [Klein 1975b, 253].
>
> (2015, 413)

All students take to learning with varying degrees of eagerness. But the emphasis on curricular mirroring begs the question: Can (or should) students only be taught what they already (desire to) know?

Adam Phillips identifies two Freudian models of education. The first follows the pattern of early-childhood "sexual researches," in which children learn what they *want* to know about sex, despite the enigmatic messages of adults, rather than because of them. The second is modelled on what Phillips calls "the dreaming self—with its dreamwork and its idiosyncratic desire" (1998, 58). Phillips concludes his essay on "The Beast in the Nursery" by interpolating a question he says Freud confronts us with: "What would education look like if we took dreaming and children's sexual curiosity as the model for teaching and learning?" (1998, 59). In Phillips view, Freud is the principal "beast" in the nursery—the one who declares war on cherished illusions of childhood innocence, most notably in his *Three Essays*. However, for Klein (and ultimately for Freud as well), the beast is the child him- or herself: the child whose destructive impulses are always competing with the desire to know, the desire to see and be seen. As the beast in the nursery becomes the beast in the classroom, children and adolescents manifest these destructive impulses in various forms of defense, resistance, and inhibition.

Sometimes, as Britzman observes, students may "act out" or cultivate "habits of avoidance" and "inhibitions of curiosity" as defenses against formal education's "structures of authority, dependency, and interference" (2003, 4–5). Against Freud's concept of epistemophilia or "desire to know," Marshall Alcorn goes so far as to posit a "desire-not-to-know," which he associates primarily with the neurobiology of emotions (2013, 77). Because knowledge-acquisition is heavily associational, Alcorn also relates this "desire-not-to-know" to Bion's analytic concept of "attacks on linking." According to Bion, attacks on linking are "destructive attacks which the patient makes on anything which is felt to have the function of linking one object with another" (1959, 308). These destructive attacks, Bion writes, "originate in what Melanie Klein calls the paranoid-schizoid phase … dominated by part-object relationships" (1959, 311). In the classroom as well as the consulting room, attacks on linking often present as splitting (a Manichean rejection of nuance or compromise) and excessive projective identification (e.g., projecting extreme defensiveness onto a teacher).

For Freud, the working-through of resistances is to be accomplished by the patient "with the help of [the analyst's] suggestion operating in an *educative* sense. For that reason psycho-analytic treatment has justly been described as a kind of *after-education* [*Nacherziehung*]" (Freud 1963, 451). Analogies to education are pervasive in Freud's writings, yet he also consistently maintains that the analyst must not fall into the role of an educator as such—that is, primarily, the sort of educator who seeks to make education what Petry and Hernández call a merely "technical affair in which a teacher with the right pedagogical methods could transform a student's knowledge according to the teacher's objectives" (2010, 64). In contrast, teaching in the "educative sense" to which Freud refers would do its best to acknowledge and facilitate the workings of desire in the teacher-student relationship.

Indeed, as illustrated by the circuitous history of dissatisfaction sketched in Chapter 1, psychoanalysis keeps trying to return to education *as its own object of desire*. In other words, education remains a problem for psychoanalysis because, from the start, it rejects what Lacan mocks as the "cretinizing" effect of conventional schooling (Lacan 2008, 74)—the kind of instruction that relies on "informing people in a certain way to make them do things in a certain way" (Phillips 2004, 781). Lacan's writings on education are neither sustained nor programmatic, and his own teaching style was flamboyantly idiosyncratic. However, he clearly emphasizes the central place of desire in learning and gestures toward what should be regarded as the centrality of the workings of desire in the teacher-student relationship:

> What is important is to teach the subject to name, to articulate, to bring desire into existence. The subject should come to recognize and to name her/his desire. But it isn't a question of recognizing something that could be entirely given. In naming it, the subject creates, brings forth, a new presence in the world.
>
> (1988, 228–29)

Teaching and learning, in this sense, would proceed metonymically with respect to desire—not by trying "to make oneself understood," but by giving language to "what one doesn't understand" (Miller 1990, xxiv).[2]

Of course, giving language to what one doesn't understand is what many students fear most. They don't want to hear themselves think out loud or risk "sounding dumb." And the lack of formal emphasis on interlocutory performance in contemporary higher education only exacerbates this problem. Few teachers are asked or equipped to prioritize interlocutory performance as a set of skills to be learned and as a kind of work that's just as important as rhetoric, literacy, and numeracy. The disciplines of "composition studies" and "rhetoric and composition studies" emerged in the 1970s as a response both to radically new theories of the nature of written discourse as well as to a perceived national crisis in writing skills. Despite the recovery of "rhetoric" within composition studies, reading and writing remained the overwhelming focus, and, over the next couple of decades, two profound changes occurred in US higher education: 1) the hiving-off of writing instruction from the study of literature, often through the creation of entirely separate departments, and 2) the virtual disappearance of oratory from the meaning of "rhetoric." A famous 1983 *Newsweek* cover story, "Why Johnny Can't Write," sounded the alarm about America's failing schools (Sheils 1975). But in the hullabaloo over the pedagogy of the written word, few people bothered to ask why Johnny couldn't speak either—speak, that is, extemporaneously with deliberation, precision, and style to a range of different addressees. Of course, class "discussion" is still valued highly on US campuses (often to the amazement of exchange students from other countries). But direct and systematic (non-remedial, non-therapeutic) instruction in speaking one's own language has been almost entirely marginalized within the liberal arts curriculum—relegated, almost exclusively, to paraprofessional departments of "communication."

Freud's early insistence that analysands be highly verbal didn't mean they had to speak with fussy Quintilian precision. It meant that for "the talking cure" to work, patients needed to be able and willing to speak intelligibly about what was unfolding in the present moment, even when that meant trying to find words for something as amorphous as a childhood memory or as potentially embarrassing as a sexual fetish or as turbulent as transferential affect. Once Anna Freud, Klein, and others had begun their analytic work with children, it became clear that there were many other forms of analytic communication, and Freud himself insists that the unconscious can never be superseded by conscious articulacy. Yet the process of striving for what Marie Cardinal (1975) calls "the words to say it" remains essential to analytic self-observation and discovery, just as the attempt to give spoken shape to thought, as it begins to emerge in the classroom, can be invaluable to understanding new kinds of knowledge.

Contemporary educators could do much more to teach students how "to name, to articulate, to bring desire into existence," to use Lacan's words—to find spoken language for that which can't be "entirely given." Freud wrote that if someone asked him what happens in the psychoanalytic consulting room, he would say: "Nothing takes place between them except that they talk to each other" (1959c, 187). Or, in Ana-María Rizzuto's elaboration of this flat statement,

> psychoanalysis recruits the power of the spoken word to modify the subject's relationship with his or her own unconscious psychic processes. It helps the analysand to reclaim for his or her words the psychic integrity that was lost or never achieved due to the power of defensive dissociation and repression. The psychoanalytic dialogue and the working through mediated by it lead to the elaboration of self-narratives and interpretive understandings, which contribute to the transformation of the subject's self-experience.
>
> (2003, 287)

Lacan, too, expresses the simple hope for his patients that their symptoms can be "well-spoken" (1990, 45). Any "interpretive understandings" could only come from what he calls "the rhetoric of the discourse the analysand actually utters" (2006, 433). In the patient's speech, Lacan hears rhetorical figures that operate like dream work or like mechanisms of defense:

> Ellipsis and pleonasm, hyperbaton or syllepsis, regression, repetition, apposition—these are the syntactical displacements; metaphor, catachresis, antonomasia, allegory, metonymy, and synecdoche—these are the semantic condensations; Freud teaches us to read in them the intentions—whether ostentatious or demonstrative, dissimulating or persuasive, retaliatory or seductive—with which the subject modulates his oneiric discourse.
>
> (2006, 221–22)

Needless to say, the attempt to replicate the conditions and goals of a "psychoanalytic dialogue" in the classroom would be neither possible nor advisable. Nor would imposing the rarified lexicon of classical rhetoric, or reviving nineteenth-century standards of oratorical eloquence. Yet the rhetoricity of affect upon which the "course" of that special type of dialogue called psychoanalysis depends is also a general feature of the pragmatics of spoken discourse in the classroom. Unfortunately, however, the methodologies and pedagogies of contemporary academic disciplines continue largely to ignore the importance of spoken discourse—especially when it "does not intend to instruct," as Nietzsche puts it, "but to convey to others a subjective emotion and its apprehension" (1983, 107; translation modified).

Attending to such "conveyances" was essential to Freud's earliest insights into the power of spoken words to produce changes in the minds of subjects who speak them and to his (and to Lacan's) understanding of the transferential dynamics of the analytic dyad. Well beyond and far apart from that dyad, however, in the university classroom, this nonetheless highly adaptable way of speaking and listening has only rarely (and never systematically) been implemented. Some reliable testimony as to its pedagogical (as distinct from psychotherapeutic) utility comes from literature professor Emma Lieber, who is also a practicing psychoanalyst:

> My teaching is psychoanalytic not only in its content, but because I'm always listening very carefully to the form of my students' articulations

as well as the group process as it coheres around a certain text, with the understanding that the speech that gets produced by a text speaks to the workings of the text itself, and that to begin to track those mechanisms is itself a form of education: an education in psychoanalysis but also an education proper, that is, a way of learning to speak. To me, the aim of education is the same as what Lacan identifies as the aim of an analysis: that is, to become "well-spoken." Obviously, this analogy works best in the humanities, but I think there's an analogy to be made for [disciplines] outside the humanities as well.

(2024)

It's significant that Lieber refers to the importance of attending not just to the speech of individual students but also to "the group process." For the complexity of group dynamics is something often ignored or regarded warily in the psychopedagogical literature.

For example, in one of his essays on psychoanalysis and the university, Laplanche worries about teachers turning classrooms into "analytical" groups, if "the relationship to a specific object of study is removed and the teacher systematically takes an interpretive attitude in relation to group processes" (1975a, 658). Laplanche identifies other group-related pedagogical dangers as well:

> fixation on imaginary and specular relationships; non-resolution of a transference that is unwieldy because it is not very specific; degraded caricatures of the analytical situation, in which the generality of processes or collective patterns of behavior (even if they are formulated in Oedipal or phallic terms) come to obscure the specificity of a singular desire that is part of a journey [*parcours*] that cannot be superimposed on other journeys.
>
> (Laplanche 1975a, 659)

In his book on group psychology, Freud gives only marginally attention to educational settings (1955c, 120). Bion, however, devoted extensive attention both to "experiences in groups" and to the phenomena of thinking and learning—including their inherently affective dimensions—and has strongly influenced contemporary psychoanalytic theorists of education. Deborah Britzman, for example, is especially fascinated with Bion's notion that there is, among established groups, a "hatred of learning by experience" (2004, 86). In Britzman's reading of Bion, this hatred arises from a shared fear of existential threats to the group's security and to the fundamental assumptions about the world the group maintains as ostensive props to that security. Learning from experience requires a tolerance for feelings of frustration in the face of insecurity and the need to modify or reject fundamental assumptions. But instead of seeing group learning as a necessary liability to psychoanalytic pedagogy, Britzman concludes that it can be advantageous—that "one learns *with others* to tolerate the frustration of having to learn from experience" (39–40; italics added).

In this more optimistic light, academic disciplines might be thought of as a set of fundamental assumptions that secure the disciplinary identity of affiliated teachers and students, whose *shared* task is to manage the hatred of learning from experience, and thus that at least some of these assumptions will be overturned and displaced by feelings of uncertainty, conflict, and frustration—feelings that, in turn, will be worked through collectively. How that thinking proceeds will always be determined to some extent—both unconsciously and consciously—by the particular methodologies and epistemologies of the discipline in question, as well as by the various emotions and defenses that being part of a group tends to provoke and reproduce. I take Lieber's "group process" to mean something along these lines: a psychoanalytically informed and guided process that makes ample room for the rhetoricity of affect in order to pursue (primarily) hermeneutic rather than therapeutic aims. Yet while the therapeutic (or pastoral) aims can be subordinated, they can't be done away with entirely—not without recklessly ignoring the emotional and behavioral vicissitudes of group experience. The following chapter takes a closer look at what it means to be the subject of such a pedagogy.

Notes

1 Of the "new form of discourse" that Freud invented," Forrester writes that it has become "even more vital and fundamental insofar as other disciplines … have looked to a general theory of discourse. The specific theory of psychoanalytic discourse pre-exists all the other post-modern general theories of discourse; it challenges them to justify the very project of their generality, it offers them an example, maybe even a template, and it incites the question that is antecedent to any possible treatment of discourse" (1991, 3).

2 These remarks are from Jacques-Alain Miller's introduction to Lacan's *Télévision* (1974), which is a partially re-written transcription of the filmed dialogue between Miller and Lacan in Benoît Jacquot's film *Psychanalyse*, first aired on French broadcast TV in 1973. The film can be viewed on YouTube: https://www.youtube.com/watch?v=EF-SElmdOY4.

Chapter 4

Psychoanalysis and Pedagogy

Teaching is more than just a subject, you know. It's a person, too.
You can't get away from that, even if you want to.[1]
—MAY SARTON, *The Small Room* (1961)

Perhaps pedagogy is the scholar's unconscious.
—T. R. JOHNSON, *The Other Side of Pedagogy* (2014)

"*The child*," Lee Edelman observes, "is the exemplary object of education, lending even adults engaged in 'formal' or 'higher' education an implicit association with something that is not—or not yet fully—formed" (2022, 1). Students—both children and adults—remain engaged with their teachers in asymmetrical, shifting, but always reciprocal educative (formative) relationships. Whatever knowledge or doctrine is meant to be transmitted in any classroom is always to some degree occulted (Edelman would say ironized) by the incessant exchange of unconscious communications—as well as by the underexamined and underutilized rhetoricity of affect discussed in the previous chapter.

From Edelman's Lacanian perspective, this ironization of knowledge makes both education and psychoanalysis what Freud so famously called "impossible professions" (1961c, 273):

> Irony hystericizes knowledge, generating ever-expanding circles of irony instead .... Escaping one's grasp, precluding comprehension: such an irony approaches madness. So, too, does psychoanalysis, according to Lacan, by engaging in an analytic act "all the madder for being unteachable." This leads him to insist on "the antagonism ... between education [*l'enseignement*] and knowledge [*le savoir*]."
>
> (2022, 40)

DOI: 10.4324/9781003540588-5

For Lacan, in the "Address on Teaching" Edelman cites here, knowledge isn't a truth that can be spoken (e.g., by a teacher to a student), but rather "the truth of our speech" (2001a, 302). In other words, Lacan asks us to think of the classroom's discursive exchange as the epistemological foundation of whatever emerges—and often, crucially, *doesn't* emerge and remains *unknown*—in the situation of teaching. Elsewhere, echoing Nietzsche, Lacan insists that "for centuries, knowledge has been pursued as a defense against truth" (qtd. in Fink 2017, 33).

Lacan's annual "seminars" were attended by both students and faculty from multiple disciplines, the very diversity (and frequent confusion) of which highlighted the improbability of meaningful and systematic "applications" of psychoanalysis to their respective academic domains—including its possible application to the field of "education" itself, which emerged, like psychoanalysis, at the end of the nineteenth century. Indeed, it was G. Stanley Hall, orchestrator of Freud's 1909 American debut at Clark University, who developed the first college course *about* education in 1893. Hall and his associate William H. Burnham "designed a higher education concentration in his pedagogical 'subdepartment,' which was housed in the psychology department," and by 1900 Clark University was conferring "doctoral degrees with topics on higher education" (Goodchild 1991, 17).

As seen in Chapter 1, many foundational writings on psychoanalysis and education by Sigmund and Anna Freud, Wilfrid Lay, August Aichhorn, Alice Bálint, Wilhelm Reich, George Green, Isador Coriat, Erik Erikson, and others are addressed to both parents and teachers. Teachers—especially of the youngest children—were already expected to serve *in loco parentis*, extending and adapting for the classroom and schoolyard various aspects of the emotional and behavioral, as well as cognitive, instruction that children begin receiving at home. The early psychopedagogues sought to amplify and instrumentalize teachers' pastoral role by encouraging their cultivation and use of students' transferential attachments. As students move through and beyond the secondary school level, both the necessity and the pedagogical value of such pastoral care inevitably diminish. Yet, no matter what the level, teacher-student relationships always have at least some pastoral dimension and continue to be informed by transferential and countertransferential vicissitudes (see Basch 1989, 772).[2]

Oddly, the language of psychoanalysis still has no single, satisfactory term for the interactional phenomenon of "transference and countertransference." Not only is "transference and countertransference" a mouthful, but neither can exist without the other. Moreover, the word "countertransference" obscures, as psychoanalyst Lewis Aron writes, "the recognition that the analyst is often the initiator of the interactional sequences, and therefore the term minimizes the impact of the analyst's behavior on the transference" (1991, 33). Despite the special emphasis that psychoanalysis accords to transference and countertransference, the same sorts of "interactional sequences" characterize every relationship—including teacher-student relationships. Any intersubjective experience, in which two people recognize one another, is going to be an open-ended process of shared conscious and unconscious transmission, projection, absorption, desire, fantasy, identification, aggression, dissociation, excess, and paradox. Despite the enormous difference between the analyst-patient relationship and the teacher-student relationship, both occur as interactional sequences—shared, always, by both parties to the encounter, who meet both in and as a shared space that Winnicott calls a "potential" or "intermediate" space (1971, 104–10). And, like the analyst, the teacher has the greater responsibility for keeping track of what's going on in this intermediate space and for deciding how to make use of it.

Unlike the analyst, however, the teacher bears this responsibility not only in interactions with individual students but also in the classroom, facing multiple students simultaneously. On one hand, the sheer complexity of groups mitigates the teacher's ability, and therefore responsibility, to remain attuned to any one student in particular. On the other hand, the students' numerousness compounds the difficulty without simply eliminating the teacher's responsibility for their asymmetrical relationship with each student—and with the group of students as such. Like the analyst, the teacher is bound to experience this responsibility as anxiogenic, and anxiety can make the teacher the "initiator" of an "interactional sequence" that one or more students might consciously or unconsciously experience. This can be daunting, as Derrida describes, in one of his many essays on education, in anticipation of such a scene:

> Before preparing the text of a lecture, I find I must prepare myself for the scene I shall encounter as I speak. That is always a painful experience, an occasion for silent, paralytic deliberation. I feel like a hunted animal, looking in darkness for a way out where none is to be found. Every exit is blocked.
>
> (1983, 5)

Derrida's hyperbole notwithstanding, even the most authoritative and experienced teachers have no special immunity from such feelings.

Moreover, anxiety is only one of a wide range of feelings and affective states that can influence—in ways both salutary and disruptive—teachers' experiences of their students. Teachers' own needs, ambitions, insecurities, preoccupations, resentments, attachments, and fantasies can precipitate various reactions *in* students and can also be activated unwittingly *by* students, who are left to guess at the teacher's disposition toward themselves and toward the class group. It's often particularly challenging for teachers to distinguish between affective disruptions that pertain to the course material and those that exceed and may undermine the goals of the course. Like the psychoanalyst, the teacher must remain attune to their own affective responses, while observing those of their students, and make difficult decisions about whether to make pedagogical use of affective intrusions. Few teachers are taught how to make such decisions—certainly not in the contemporary field of education in the US. Even in the much smaller field of curriculum studies, which has a history of engagement with psychoanalysis, "psychoanalytic theory moved to the sidelines during the 1980s canon wars [to] focus on identity politics" (Taubman 2012, 132). The shift away from psychoanalysis, according to Taubman, is

> particularly glaring in teacher education and in educational policy, where the learning sciences, neoliberal agendas, and business models determine the dominant approaches to education and provide the terms to describe teaching and curriculum [displacing] the inner lives of teachers and students with behavioral techniques and quantifiable outcomes. Ignored or disparaged are the very theories constitutive of psychoanalysis, theories that work on the border between the socio/cultural and the intrapsychic, that explore the mysteries of subjectivity, and that can illuminate the dreams, desires, ideals, and terrors that shape our understanding of education.
>
> (2012, 1–2)

Thus the conceptual tools most likely to help teachers manage the transferential/countertransferential interactional sequences inherent to scenes of teaching and learning are ignored or dismissed in most teacher-training contexts—including modeling, upon which pedagogical instruction heavily relies.

Anna Freud anticipated this problem long ago: "So many teachers judge themselves by what they get children to learn. But teaching is not only presentation of facts; it is persuading students to be interested in the world—a state of mind" (qtd. in Coles 1991, 31). And her contemporary Hans Zulliger posited numerous pedagogical advantages to teachers being analyzed as part of their training, including: the loosening of ingrained character traits and libidinal fixations; greater tolerance of student aggression; diminished professional narcissism, freeing them from distortions of guilt; greater tolerance for their own and their students' failures; and reduced susceptibility to students' libidinal demands (2018, 71–72). Yet there has never been sufficient incentive for the comprehensive training of teachers in even the fundamentals of psychoanalytic theory—and certainly not for making analysis a prerequisite for teaching.

Much of the resistance has come from members of the psychoanalytic profession itself, who have expressed concerns, for example, about the academic "dilution" of concepts and theories and also about the potential "damage" that teaching teachers "about" psychoanalysis could do. As Laplanche describes it, this condemnation "invokes the well-known mechanisms of rationalization and intellectualization" and the defensive workings of "denegation" (1975a, 655). Yet Laplanche can't avoid a fundamental paradox in maintaining, as did for decades, "that the presence of psychoanalysis at the University was one guarantee among others of the rigorous confrontation of positions, of argumentation, of taking an enlightened position, even of refutation" (2004, 10). Here, Laplanche emphasizes the hermeneutic dimension of psychoanalytic discourse, which has remained intrinsic to critical theory for almost a century (see Allen 2021). But not even Laplanche can keep from striking the perennial false note. For "the presence of psychoanalysis at the University" also means the *avowal of the unconscious* at the university, and the unconscious does not traffic in "refutation." This paradox is also a stumbling point for pedagogical theorists like Britzman: How, she asks, can the academic teaching of psychoanalysis avoid "the need for tidiness and simplicity [that is] tied to the dream of mastery, prediction, management and control, all of which are features of institutional life"? "The problem," Britzman continues, "is that if the unconscious cannot be left out of this picture, the very qualities of the unconscious resist its own unveiling: it knows no time, no negation, and tolerates contradiction" (1999, 314). Even in some fanciful world, where not only teachers but all of their students, too, had spent time in psychoanalysis, the classroom work of analyzing the unconscious dynamics of transference and countertransference would still, by definition, be unable to follow any pre-arranged curricular program or neatly conclude in some "enlightened position."

Another reason why the classroom is such a fecund petri dish for transferential dynamics is that, for teachers, it's an overwhelmingly familiar place, endlessly evocative of their earlier classroom experiences as both students and teachers (Britzman and Pitt 1996, 117). Their students, too—by the time they've reached university—have spent almost twenty years in classrooms, adoring, fearing, resisting, idealizing, crushing on, gossiping about, and critically comparing dozens of teachers. An analogy could be drawn here with Freud's understanding of the sexual couple's phantasmatic multiplication of erotic partners and fantasies (see, e.g., Bersani 1998, 10–11): for the student, the teacher in their classroom is never the only teacher in their classroom, just as each student is superimposed upon by various objects of the teacher's desiring positions. Yet the transferential relation isn't one of mere regression, remembrance, and repetition, doomed to a kind of autistic closure. It's also a new and uncertain relation, the prospect of a novel and unexpected encounter, thanks to the very qualities that Britzman identifies with the unconscious. Each "interactional sequence" is an invention to which both parties—or all parties—contribute. The curriculum, too, is "the invention of both teacher and students .... Each one projects distillates of his own inner perceptions and experiences, past and present, onto the subject under study, be it mathematics[,] history, or literature" (Field 1989, 853). Any such "subject under study" has a past, transmitted as accumulated knowledge to the students by the teacher, and it also has a future, transferentially renewed in ways that are always different, thanks to the singularity of each subject's desire and to the eternal cycle of semesters.

Of course, plenty of teacher-student relationships extend over many years. Undergraduate and graduate students often take multiple courses with the same professor, who might also become their academic advisor or thesis supervisor. But most teacher-student relationships begin and end with a single three- or four-month-long semester, during which students in larger courses might have very little direct contact with their teacher or with one another. (The austerity economics of higher education in the US and especially in the UK continues to swell student-faculty ratios in most courses and to eliminate courses that don't meet jacked-up enrollment minimums.) Yet, as Isca Salzberger-Wittenberg points out, a student's transferential feelings may emerge and be observed even in the absence of intimate, long-term relationships:

> We do not need to unravel a person's past history in order to understand him. If we are observant, we can gain insight into his assumptions and beliefs from his behaviour and reactions to ourselves and others in the here and now. Awareness of the transference elements enables us to have some space to think about the nature of the relationship, to take a more objective view of it. Thus we may be able to resist being carried away by the flattering adulation of an adolescent, recognising instead that we are merely at the moment the embodiment of a longed-for dream-figure and are being seen through rose-tinted spectacles in order to maintain a desired illusion. It may also make us modestly aware that the love and trust with which a child comes to school is likely to be in a large measure due to his own loving impulses, strengthened by good relations at home, rather than attributable to ourselves.
>
> (1993, 36)

According to Kernberg (drawing on Winnicott's theories of holding and transitional space), a teacher's identity should be characterized by what he calls

> a parental attitude of holding or containing the conflictual and chaotic nature of intrapsychic conflict. Holding or containing has cognitive and affective components and includes a basic attitude of concern for oneself and the [student] and a psychological openness to the unknown in others as well as in oneself.
>
> (2016, 5–6; see also Elson 1989, 801)

Of course, the parameters, goals, and circumstances of the teacher-student relationship are vastly different from those of the analyst-patient relationship. Yet the "attitude of holding," with its "cognitive and affective components," is common to both and need not constitute, in the case of the teacher, a transgression of roles or a violation of professional ethics. To the contrary, such an "attitude of holding" is essential to the ethics of teaching.

Although Freud mused about psychoanalysis and higher education in various writings throughout his career, he never did so in a sustained or practical way. Like his contemporaries, he considered the potential benefits of replacing authoritarian styles of teaching with a more liberated and lib-erating pedagogy grounded in psychoanalytic principles and techniques. But ultimately his understanding of the nature of the psyche (not to mention his increasingly pessimistic view of the world, in which the imperatives of the drives were forever battling the fierce demands of civilization) tended to defeat such notions. While many fellow analysts, including his own daughter, devoted much more attention—and in some cases extensive experimentation—to the development of psychoanalytically informed education, it seemed impossible for any of them to move beyond the push-me-pull-yous of license and constraint, liberation and adjustment, prophy-laxis and cultivation, whether in the kindergarten or the university.

Like them, many recent theorists of the fully constituted fields of educa-tion and curriculum studies have made fundamental errors of judgment with regard to the *application* of psychoanalytic principles. That is, like their early-twentieth-century precursors, many contemporary theorists of educa-tion have tried in vain to apply that which cannot *consciously* be applied. As psychotherapist and professor of education Stephen Appel concedes, one can't "engage with the actual processes of educational socialization" precisely because "these processes are largely *unconscious*" (1995, 167). Lacanian analyst Catherine Millot (also a professor of psychoanalysis at Paris VIII) has argued that "the action of the educator and that of the analyst are precisely contrary." The typical educator, Millot explains, inevitably aligns herself with the superego against the id and seeks to manipulate the pleasure-unpleasure dynamic in the interest of knowledge-transmission, whereas the analyst relies upon the id and the aspirations of repressed knowledge and feeling to manifest themselves against the narcissistic prior-ities of the pleasure principle (1979, 139). What *can* be deduced from "psy-choanalytic experience," Millot argues, is "an ethics from which pedagogy could draw inspiration—an ethics based on demystification of the function of the ideal as fundamentally false and opposed to a lucid apprehension of reality" (Millot 1979, 168). More pithily, Appel calls on his peers not to try to apply psychoanalysis *to* education but, instead, to acknowledge the cen-tral place of the unconscious *in* the educational setting (1995, 169).

With help from Lacan, later psychopedagogues like Millot and Appel have carried forward Freud's early distinction between learning "something *about* psycho-analysis" and learning "something *from* it" and developed a pedagogically minded appreciation of psychoanalysis as a revolution-ary theory of epistemology—of how we know what we know. Indeed, the very possibility of knowing, in the positivist sense, is a central problem for Freud and for every school of psychoanalytic thought up to the present day. For educators, awareness of the unconscious dimensions of human experience throws knowledge—self-knowledge, in particular—into an especially problematic, but also potentially fortuitous light.

Problematic, because it's difficult for some students even to entertain the notion of unconscious determinism. Fortuitous, because instead of holding fast to the notion of a "subject supposed to know" (Lacan 1998), psychoanalysis makes locating, defining, and representing the "subject of *uncertainty*" its unending epistemological project. This project depends, not on a discourse of rational mastery, but on exploring the sustained transferential dynamics of self and other. Thus, the pedagogical value of psychoanalysis— which in this sense is *not* antithetical to its therapeutic value—inheres in a sustained willingness, on the part of both teachers and students, to persevere collaboratively in searching for what Phillips calls "good ways of bearing our incompleteness."

Needless to say, this sort of sustained willingness is tough to achieve— not least, because it calls for everyone's tolerance of a very different temporality than the linear, cumulative temporality of traditional pedagogical practice. Proceeding, as Shoshana Felman puts it,

> through breakthroughs, leaps, discontinuities, regressions, and deferred action, the [transferential] learning-process puts [into] question the traditional pedagogical belief in intellectual perfectibility, the progressistic view of learning as a simple one-way road from ignorance to knowledge.
>
> (1982, 27)

This very different temporality, or way of experiencing time, can't be achieved only, or even primarily, through conscious effort. It's chiefly the temporality of unconscious experience. Even for advanced undergraduates and graduate students, the emotional and intellectual demands of this sort of work can be daunting, depending on their developmental level and on whether the course introduces students explicitly to the psychoanalytic concepts of transference, identification, and defense. In some cases, it may be wiser

> to use psychoanalysis subtly and not always to offer it labeled as such. The core ideas—the processes of questioning and going deeper,

of observing and monitoring transferences, and of noting subtle recurrences in symbolic function and behavior—can be utilized and made conscious even when [psychoanalysis] is not the ostensible subject, nor [its] texts per se on the table.

(Spitz 2018, 83)

Either way, the classroom, like the consulting room, is first and foremost a space of human relationship and therefore strongly characterized—whether we like it or not—by various forms of resistance, defense, idealization, projection, aggression, desire, identification … in short, by many unconscious as well as conscious communications.

This is why teaching and learning make us nervous: the classroom's transferential dynamics are always pulling us toward that very different temporality of "breakthroughs, leaps, discontinuities, regressions, and deferred action"—that very different experience of learning in which all sorts of narcissistic investments are challenged and might be undone. Indeed, any form of education that seeks to do more than induce intellectual compliance or go beyond the rote delivery and assimilation of "information" is likely to threaten our libidinal attachments to any number of cherished people, ideas, and beliefs—whether we're teachers struggling with anxieties about authority, competence, and the love of our students, or students struggling with anxieties about autonomy, worthiness, and the love of our teachers.

Britzman rightly observes that, with the recognition of the transferential dynamics of pedagogy, what we're used to calling "education" endures a salutary delay: "Learning is delayed because we feel before we know and learn before we understand, akin to Freud's notion of 'remembering, repeating, and working through'" (2015, 44). The immediate—often hollow and transient—satisfactions of knowledge-acquisition are deferred. And, in that space of deferral, frustrations arise.

Teaching students, primarily through our own example, how to tolerate such frustrations, while at the same time helping them to cope with affective disturbances and runaway meanings is perhaps the greatest potential value of introducing psychoanalysis into the university classroom, whatever the content of the particular course might be. In courses on anthropology, economics, law, literature, medicine, neuroscience, philosophy, political science, psychology, or what you will, teachers and students who attend to the classroom's transferential dynamics are more likely to recognize their implication in both the *content* of the course and in the *ways* that content is presented and handled:

> To implicate oneself in one's own narratives of learning and teaching means turning habituated knowledge back upon itself and examining its most unflattering, indeed, for many, its most devastating features. It also means exploring how even this most unflattering moment may offer insight into making significance.
>
> (Britzman 2021, 26)

This isn't to say that content—the specifics of "habituated knowledge"— doesn't matter. On the contrary, there are dangers lurking in the specificities.

Presumably, this is why many instructors in recent years (often at students' behest) have taken to adding "trigger warnings" to course materials and even to entire courses. These warnings are supposed to alert students to especially fraught matters (e.g., torture, rape, racism, child abuse, and suicide) that are discussed or depicted in lectures or in assigned readings and recordings. The idea is that "warning" students what to expect will reduce the risk of "triggering" post-traumatic responses. In effect, trigger warnings are imagined to bolster or work in place of what Freud calls "signal anxiety," a phenomenon that draws on our recollection of a past event and seeks to prepare us for its recurrence in the present. As Avgi Saketopoulou puts it, "if trauma is injury, signal anxiety is preparedness anticipating that more injury is to come." But this is an insufficient characterization, as Saketopoulou herself explains:

> The phenomenology of signal anxiety is not that of a benign warning sign but it is, oftentimes, a paralyzing, overwhelming cascade of emotional and physiological responses commensurate *not with the anticipation of danger but with the experience of the danger itself.* It can lead to symptom formation (e.g., anxiety attacks, phobias, psychosomatic phenomena) whose links to the traumatic experience are neither linear nor easily detectable because by nature signal anxiety is unconscious .... We are often surprised by what it is that arouses our traumatic response .... What will be triggering or not is impossible to predict.
>
> (2014)

Calls for trigger warnings are expressions of the understandable wish to avoid pain. Trigger warnings themselves, however, are far more likely to promote avoidance and feelings of helplessness and can have the unintended effect of metastasizing into a generally fearful and aversive stance toward the new.

No matter how dedicated teachers are to their pastoral role, they can't promise not to hurt their students. As Robert French puts it, "all learning occurs in relationship, with all that this implies in terms of 'danger to the ego'" (1997, 484). Gregory Jay goes so far as to say that "the teacher's task is to make the student ill"—or, in more temperate terms, "to unsettle the complacency and conceptual identities of the student" (1987, 790). Certainly, a teacher's role is not to swaddle or shield students, but rather to serve as a model and a guide to help them find their own best means of accommodating a hard truth: knowledge does not exist for their protection. No matter what the course, this might be the most difficult lesson of all to teach well.

At most institutions, the call for trigger warnings comes from students themselves. For example, in 2023 Cornell University's Student Assembly passed a resolution urging the university to require faculty members to "provide content warnings on the syllabus for any traumatic content that may be discussed, including but not limited to: sexual assault, domestic violence, self-harm, suicide, child abuse, racial hate crimes, transphobic violence, homophobic harassment, [and] xenophobia" and to ensure that "students who choose to opt-out of exposure to triggering content will not be penalized, contingent on their responsibility to make up any missed content" (Cornell University Student Assembly 2023). Ultimately, the resolution was rejected as a clear violation of Cornell's academic and free-speech policies.

Among the many other problems with mandatory trigger warnings are the potentially distressing effects of the warnings themselves, as well as the fact that, for a student (or anyone) suffering from PTSD after, say, a sexual assault, "what will be triggering or not is impossible to predict." It could be an explicit depiction of rape. But it could also be the appearance of the first name of one's rapist in a book, a reminder of the location or setting where the rape occurred, a combination of otherwise benign-seeming words, a certain color or sound in a film, or the manifestation of a particular scent in the classroom itself. Moreover, such triggers are just one of the ways in which a whole range of resistances to knowledge (including self-knowledge) can be activated—especially in the libidinal context of teaching and learning.

As early as the mid-1930s, child psychiatrist Edward Liss was studying what in one of his articles he calls "the phenomenon of learning as an erotic, sensuous experience" (1941, 520). Like Liss, Klein allots a substantial role to infantile anxiety in learning and development, but, more like Freud, she perceives the inhibitions and disinhibitions of epistemophilia to be very broad and complex phenomena, however closely they might be associated with infantile erotic conflict. Klein's contemporary Otto Fenichel similarly observes that, in school-age children, the psychosexual mechanisms of intellectual inhibition and disinhibition are innumerable and often inscrutably "triggered":

> Studies have been made of a number of specific disturbances of intelligence, such as the failure of children in certain subjects at school, or their inability or unwillingness to study certain things .... The particular subject, or something associated with the first instruction in this subject, or the personality of the teacher and his way of teaching, or an accidental feature that essentially has nothing to do with the subject proper, like a particular number in mathematics or a particular letter in reading and writing, proved to be associated with fundamental conflicts around infantile sexuality.
>
> (1945, 181)

Klein's work also led Bion to conclude that the epistemophilic drive should be accorded the same importance as the libidinal and aggressive drives (see, e.g., Bion 1994, 99). And as recently as 2002, psychotherapist Duncan Barford proposed that further

> exploration of the bodily "enjoyment" associated with, triggering or triggered by intellectual effort, may offer a means to theorise which kinds of intellectual engagement generate excitement and anxiety; where and under what conditions we recoil from ideas that are too wayward or disturbing; how ideas and our unconscious enjoyment of them are played out, in and through the body; and what the parameters of these processes are.
>
> (Barford 2002, 40)

Bodily sensations of displeasure as well as pleasure, of course, can trigger or be triggered by intellectual effort, and while school-age children often need substantial help from their teachers to anticipate, limit, recognize, manage, and (if possible) understand such sensations, college-age-and-over students are, as maturing adults, pedagogically ill-served by similar attempts to limit or avoid such sensations—especially by such scattershot methods as trigger warnings and curricular censorship. This is in no way to minimize the substantial emotional discomfort and even psychological harm to which both students and their teachers may be susceptible. Nor is it to suggest that teachers aren't responsible for their curricular choices and pedagogical practices. The stakes of teaching and learning are always high. But their watchword should be humility, not fear.

The mind simply can't accommodate everything it wants to, even in the best of circumstances. And even the canniest teachers and students will always be tempted to inhibit or ignore intrusions of what Christopher Bollas calls "the unthought known" (1987). Unconscious thoughts, feelings, memories, and fantasies are always ready and waiting to make learning unruly. They have the potential to disrupt accustomed patterns of gratification-seeking, "spoil" cherished identifications, and unmask our carefully constructed alibis for resistance, indulgence, sympathy, discipline, and denial. They unleash desires that seem "out of place." But that's only because the place of desire at the heart of epistemology is so thoroughly unfamiliar to traditional pedagogy.

Teaching *with* as well as *about* psychoanalysis can open up possibilities for education that make this inconvenience not just tolerable but (so to speak) desirable. Teaching with psychoanalysis can help illuminate and ultimately transform the "objects of knowledge" that all of our academic disciplines are "supposed to know." Having broken through at least some of the methodological barriers discussed in the previous chapter, psychoanalytic concepts and techniques can be used to enhance pedagogy itself, *whatever the subject being taught*. Phenomena including identification, transference/countertransference, projection, projective identification, and idealization inevitably occur between teachers and students, just as they do in all human relationships. But teachers and their students can learn to recognize these phenomena when they manifest themselves and to use them in positive ways both to facilitate learning and to enhance meaningful student-teacher relationships. And teachers can learn to incorporate various techniques from the consulting room into their pedagogical styles and practices without lapsing into an inappropriately "therapeutic" mode.[3]

Ψ

Of course, there are many different modes of psychoanalytic psycho-therapy, just as there is a wide variety of psychoanalytic metapsycholo-gies. Freud may have invented psychoanalysis, but it has been re-invented time and again—by Freud himself and by many others, from his era to our own. They proliferate as numerous, sometimes divergent, sometimes over-lapping "schools" of theory and practice: for example, object relational, self-psychological, Jungian, ego psychological, developmental, Lacanian, interpersonal, relational, intersubjective, neuropsychoanalytic, etc. It's impossible in a book of this length to attend adequately to each school's potential implications for higher education. Nevertheless, they share in common a number of basic principles: the existence of a dynamic uncon-scious, the conviction that most of human experience happens apart from our conscious awareness, and an appreciation of the formative and lasting influence on psychic functioning of early-childhood experience. They also share several highly adaptable therapeutic techniques: dream interpretation, free association, and transference analysis. Among these three psychoan-alytic techniques, the first two can readily be used in many educational contexts. The third—transference analysis—is both the most potentially transformative and also the most problematic.

In psychoanalytic treatment, transference is the phenomenon whereby the patient unconsciously displaces feelings, memories, attitudes, desires, or fantasies about someone in their lives onto the analyst. For example, a patient whose childhood was plagued by the erratic and mendacious behav-ior of his nonetheless beloved father might displace onto his analyst disa-vowed feelings of distrust. Such a patient might have a more difficult time accepting the analyst as reliable and honest. Another patient, due perhaps to the early childhood loss of their father, might displace onto their analyst disavowed feelings of longing and insecurity and be especially eager to win the analyst's love and approval.

Such transferential feelings aren't pathological. They occur in some form in every patient's experience. But, left unrecognized and unavowed, they can substantially compromise and even spoil the treatment. The analyst does their best to recognize the patient's transference, in part by remaining alert to signs of their own unconscious reactions to the patient's transfer-ences. The analyst, too, will inevitably displace feelings, memories, atti-tudes, desires, or fantasies about someone in their lives onto the patient. A patient might, for example, remind their analyst of his own child, conceivably generating unconscious feelings of frustration or guilt at his patient's failure to thrive, which the patient, in turn, could experience unconsciously as the analyst's disappointment or dislike.

Comparably complex transferential dynamics occur in every relationship, and it's easy to imagine other ways they might play out between teacher and student. A teacher might, for instance, have a student who reminds her of herself as a young person, which could generate unconscious envy of the student's superior intellect, which the student could experience unconsciously as the teacher's hostility. Most residential college students are living apart from their parents for the first time and trying to cope with that separation through persistent unconscious efforts to satisfy the long-familiar parental desires they now project onto unsuspecting teachers. In such cases of "positive" transference, as Constance Penley puts it, "the student, like the child with the parent, is almost *clairvoyant* when it comes to understanding the desire of the Other and how best narcissistically to mirror what the Other desires" (1989, 169). In cases of "negative" transference, the student may have an equally "clairvoyant" understanding of how to frustrate or shame the desire of the teacher/Other.

Whether positive or negative, the transferential dynamics between teachers and students seldom become objects of conscious acknowledgment, much less active pedagogical use, whereas in the psychoanalytic consulting room the analyst's observation and exploration of transference/countertransference is usually deemed therapeutically essential. Yet there is a longstanding debate in the psychoanalytic profession concerning whether and how the analyst should make use of disclosure. Traditional Freudian analysis dictates that the analyst's ideal demeanor toward the patient should be one of "evenly suspended attention," as Freud put it—a kind of freely wandering, non-judgmental alertness to whatever transpires in the patient's speech and comportment (1958c, 110-11). If, in the patient, intense feelings arise and are directed at the analyst, this isn't to be taken "personally," since these feelings aren't "really" about the analyst. Instead, they represent the re-emergence of early, repressed feelings toward figures from the patient's childhood—feelings that have simply been "transferred" or displaced onto the analyst, who is there to take note of them as potential keys to the patient's treatment. The analyst's feelings toward the patient, however, are regarded as intrusions that compromise their "evenly suspended attention" to what's going on with the patient. Freud and other analysts who work in this traditional mode understand, of course, that people always evoke various conscious and unconscious reactions in one another. But the more traditional analysts try to hold those feelings apart and to work through them on their own time, either through self-analysis or with the help of a supervising analyst.

But for analysts with a more interpersonal, or "two-way" understanding of the analytic relationship, the thoughts and feelings evoked in them can't and shouldn't be held apart. Instead, with caution and circumspection, the analyst's internal responses are sometimes disclosed to the patient in the interest of their treatment. The analyst's associations, reveries, thoughts, and emotional responses, when shared judiciously with the patient, can help illuminate the patient's own circumstances. Indeed, many interpersonalists consider the relationship between analyst and patient—the "interactional field"—to be the focus of the treatment. And the relational school of psy-choanalysis—which emerged in the 1980s from both the interpersonal and object relational traditions—considers relationship itself to be the matrix of subjectivity. Both the patient's actual relationship with the analyst and the patient's internal object relationships (relationships with psychic repre-sentations—"objects" or "imagoes"—of other people) constitute the chief focus of the analytic work in the "here and now" of relational psychoanaly-sis. Stephen Mitchell writes that,

> for Freud, the relationship with the analyst was a re-creation of past relationships, a new version struck from the original "stereotype plate." The here-and-now relationship was crucial—but as a replication, as a vehicle for the recovery of memories or the filling in of amnesias, and it was this function that was understood to cure the patient. Contemporary relational-model views tend to put more emphasis on what is new in the analytic relationship. The past is still important—but as a vehicle for comprehending the meaning of the present relationship with the analyst, and it is in the working through of that relationship that cure resides.
>
> (1988, 151)

Building on Mitchell's work, clinicians and theorists continue to observe and conceptualize what Freud considered largely a distraction: the patient's experience of the analyst's subjectivity.

For Freud, the intrapsychic and interpersonal forces at play in any rela-tionship are heavily determined by what he calls "drives": innate libidinal and aggressive impulses at the core of the psyche-soma. Freud certainly understood (and wrote a great deal about) the consequential role of environmental factors in human development throughout the life-cycle. But the intrapsychic need to discharge the energy of the drives is, for him, the *sine qua non* of human experience. For contemporary relationalists, on the other hand, the drive model has been supplanted by a radically different understanding of human beings as fundamentally attachment-oriented. Still, this is no mere either/or dilemma. Indeed, affective neuroscience and the emergent field of neuropsychoanalysis strongly suggest that innate drives and attachment formations are intimately linked aspects of neurophysiological and neurochemical processes, such as dopaminergic seeking systems. We now know for instance that

> the drive to seek information can come from diverse motives, fulfilling different biological and neurological functions, and producing disparate outcomes when paired in opposition to other drives, such as toward reward or avoidance of pain. Acquiring new information serves the crucial functions of making sense of reality, improving our internal representations of the world, and driving the development of our skills and intellect .... Yet we do not only desire useful or relevant knowledge; rather, new information and novel sensations seem to be enjoyed for their own sake. Information thus seems to have hedonic value and can induce sadness, joy, or fear. Our drive for knowledge is therefore tangled up in the regulation of emotions and affective states.
>
> (Dezza et al. 2022, xvi)

Ψ

The notion that "we do not only desire useful or relevant knowledge" is anathema to the contemporary legislative and corporate masters of higher education, whose comprehensive push for the instrumentalization of knowledge is one of the chief factors in the ongoing destruction of the US university system. Fueled in large part by anxiety over the country's massive post-Cold War failure to preserve the connection between research and manufacturing, even President Obama urged college students in 2014 to steer clear of fields like art history and to consider foregoing altogether "a four-year college education as long as you get the skills and the training that you need" (Obama 2014). Terrified of China's pre-eminence in optimizing the research-manufacturing nexus, US education policy makers, corporate donors, and university trustees have continued to project their fears onto students and parents, in order to pacify their unease at the closing of humanities departments and skyrocketing tuition costs for increasingly vocational degree programs. A recent unsigned article in *The Economist*, called "Universities Are Failing to Boost Economic Growth," begins with the assertion that "too often they generate ideas that no one knows how to use"—meaning, knows how to *make profitable*. "In a world of weak economic growth, lavish public support for universities may come to seem an unjustifiable luxury" (*Economist* 2024).

This argument's foreclosure of understanding is especially benighted (even for *The Economist*). And it's nothing new. In 1939 (the year of Freud's death), Abraham Flexner published the definitive rejoinder to such arguments in *The Usefulness of Useless Knowledge*. Flexner—founding director of the Institute for Advanced Study, where intellectuals like Albert Einstein, George Kennan, Erwin Panofsky, Hetty Goldman, and Clifford Geertz have been producing "useless" knowledge since 1933—wrote that "curiosity, which may or may not eventuate in something useful, is probably the outstanding characteristic of modern thinking" and that the most "useful" discoveries in human history were made by people "driven not by the desire to be useful but merely the desire to satisfy their curiosity" (2017, 56–57). Flexner also understood that the "desire to satisfy their curiosity" included the desire to understand their desire—to understand themselves and their relation to the world and its unforeseeable changes. Almost a century later, universities in the US and elsewhere continue their dangerous descent into what Oscar Wilde calls "careless habits of accuracy" (2007, 77)—habits including the naïve empiricism and neo-positivism that are as inimical to the national economy as they have been to academic departments of psychology, from which the "useless knowledge" of psychoanalysis has been excluded.[4]

Of course, anything that can't easily be "known" through isolation and quantification can become a source of anxiety and frustration for both students and teachers, who may then respond defensively against such displeasure. If a teacher, for example, feels anxious about their own knowledge or competence and anticipates feelings of guilt or shame, they might engage defensively in unconscious splitting, rejecting certain materials as "unteachable" (e.g., inappropriate, prurient, "triggering," beyond the scope of the curriculum, etc.) or assessing certain students as "unteachable" (e.g., incurious, unruly or disobedient, prone to acting out, insufficiently intelligent, inadequately prepared, etc.). Similarly, if a student feels anxious about their competence or ability to understand some course material, they might react with a defensive rationalization about that material's "uselessness" or "irrelevance." Other common defenses include undoing, projection, sublimation, repression, and regression, and it's worth asking how pedagogically "useful" it would be to regard such defensive reactions, not as mere obstacles to learning to be ignored or "corrected," but as further material to be examined and understood from a psychoanalytic perspective.

But this is too frightening a question for the masters of the corporate university and their servants among the professoriate, who would like everyone to believe—unquestioningly—that universities should toe the line of rationalist humanism and encourage only dispassionate intellectual engagement with the subject at hand. Indeed, Alan Bainbridge and Linden West point to some "strident criticism of what is called 'therapeutic education,' for which, at least in part, psychoanalysis is seen as responsible" and which is characterized by some as "a pernicious subjectivism and an obsession with fragile selves." As Bainbridge and West make clear, however, the problem with such criticisms of psychoanalytic pedagogy is that they mistake "analytic" for "therapeutic"—as if its goal were merely to bolster students' self-esteem and to protect their "fragile" egos from emotional upset, at the expense of intellectual rigor (2012, 8–9). They fail to see how the inherently affective dimensions of learning, including Ngai's "ugly feelings" (see Chapter 3) and all the other positive and negative emotional traffic that occurs in the classroom—whether or not it is acknowledged or addressed—can often be recuperated for the work of learning and knowing.

A case in point is something that occurred in a course I co-taught with psychoanalyst Susan Adelman, who wrote about it eloquently in her blog post, "Recovering Race" (2019). We were teaching our hybrid lecture-discussion course, "Introduction to Psychoanalysis: History, Theory, Practice," in an auditorium-style classroom to about 45 students. It was late in the semester, and, as Susan narrates,

> we were discussing the final pages of Avgi Saketopoulou's wonderful essay, "Minding the Gap" (2011), about her rageful, wonderful, and gender-variant preadolescent African American patient, DeShawn—a

child struggling mightily with her and even more profoundly with his own gender and racial identities. From DeShawn, Avgi comes to learn that "for black boys racial identification trumps gender anytime."

For the author, Saketopoulou, and many of her readers, this insight feels revelatory. But as Susan read the passage aloud in class, one of our students—a Black woman—interjected: "I could have told you that!"

Like most of our students, Jamila (a pseudonym) was smart, attentive, and, as Susan writes, "polite and level in her intonation" of this remark. But, beneath Jamila's words, Susan perceived "a piercing 'Duh!'…. What was already obvious to her was not already obvious to me—and had not been even to Saketopoulou." In her long clinical and teaching career, Susan—a child of Holocaust survivors—has done more than most of her white colleagues to understand her own racial privilege and learn about the realities of Black experience in the US Yet she suddenly felt taken aback by Jamila's remark: "I clearly remained insufficiently sensitive and informed. Whereas Avgi's words had struck me like a revelation, they had struck Jamila as a mere restatement of the obvious." As our discussion continued, several other students asked if

there was some sort of racial exploitation going on between the Greek Cypriot psychotherapist [Saketopoulou was raised in Greece when it was still largely monoracial] and her African American patient …. Avgi had been brave and committed in her work with DeShawn, who, at their initial meeting, had pulled out two handfuls of her hair and continued to act out, often in violent ways.

"Despite this unpromising beginning," Susan points out, "Avgi persevered and was ultimately able to work well with DeShawn—something I wasn't at all sure I could have done under similar circumstances."

To me, this seemed like a reasonable rejoinder. But, at home after class, Susan started to worry that she'd been overly defensive and had perhaps shut down an important line of discussion regarding racial privilege. She emailed me that night saying she "felt awful," and I encouraged her inclination to do something about it—that is, not to ignore but to recuperate and try to work with this "ugly feeling" collaboratively, with our students. Before our next class meeting, Susan emailed them about her discomfort at what she saw as her "belated recognition that I had been over-identifying with

Avgi and that, as DeShawn says to Avgi at one point, I should have "shut up" and listened to what was being said by others in the class."

That same night, I emailed Avgi herself, asking for some follow-up information about DeShawn that she would feel comfortable sharing with our students. We began the next class by reading aloud from Avgi response and then had what Susan calls an "extremely animated and engaged [discussion], with a great deal of participation. Everyone was relieved to hear that DeShawn—now in late adolescence—was doing relatively well." Susan, though, still felt "unhappily aware of my ignorance" and, much to her credit, made full pedagogical use of it, sharing

> with our students my sense of how my own slip and recovery pertained to what we were teaching them about psychoanalysis as well as to its contemporary practice. If such a central component of identity as gender is, in some circumstances, less overdetermined than race, then how might we—as analysts as well as teachers—pay more adequate attention to race as well as to gender? Too many clinicians, alas, still indulge themselves in thinking that "social" factors are relatively superficial to their more traditional understanding of deep, unconscious dynamics. We wanted our students to understand that the "social," including race and many other dimensions of identity as well, is a profound part of everyone's conscious and unconscious functioning. But just how well did we ourselves really understand that?

Susan made clear to the class that she wasn't "finished"; she would continue to reflect on her defensiveness, and she and I would find ways of returning to these questions by slightly modifying the syllabus. Our students had clearly appreciated her email and understood that Susan wasn't merely apologizing but trying to make use of an uncomfortable feeling in order to extend and enhance important aspects of the emotional *and* intellectual work of the course. In her post, Susan recounts how that work unfolded:

> We made room for a separate class that paired Winnicott's 1949 article, "Hate in the Counter-Transference," with Kathleen Pogue White's searing 2002 essay, "Surviving Hating and Being Hated"....We hoped, by pairing these essays, to deepen everyone's psychoanalytic understanding of the inter- as well as intra-subjective consequences of societal racism.

This, in turn, "helped us to revisit Jamila's implicit challenge" and to show ourselves to the class as people with a responsibility both to teach them what we could and to learn from them when we were able, "to be humble about all that we don't know or fully appreciate about" one another's lives. Susan was then able to offer a very different response to Jamila's remark than she had during the previous class meeting. She told the class that she had been uncomfortably reminded

> that any relevant psychoanalytic teaching (or treatment) requires a willingness 1) to learn from students (and patients), who always have forms of knowledge and experience that differ—sometimes radically—from our own and 2) to participate with them in a basic truth of psychoanalytic engagement: that what psychoanalysts and teachers don't know may create opportunities (if we can muster the honesty and courage to pursue them) for mutual teaching and learning—and that the candor of mutual engagement, with all its many forms of discomfort and awkwardness, is the best route to intimacy and understanding.
>
> (Adelman 2019)

By sharing her discomfort, Susan facilitated an explicit discussion of what might have become a forgotten—or repressed—question, a question that even Jamila might not have known she was asking. Instead of letting the comment "I could have told you that!" serve an exclusively defensive purpose, Susan showed the class how, by working through her reciprocal defensiveness, she could "bring out" the implicit question without staging it as a struggle of authority between herself and Jamila.

Susan didn't say so to our students, but it seemed to me at the time that part of her defensiveness must have had to do with her countertransferential feeling (most likely a consequence of students' projective identifications) that her own Jewish identity was being "collapsed into the imperatives of whiteness" (Britzman 1998, 104). This is an all-too-common form of tension between Blacks and Jews in the US and part of the unreconciled history of psychoanalysis itself—that is, between its early vilification as "a Jewish science" and its own lingering remissness in attending to matters of racism and racial identity in both theory and practice. Because the psychic fallout of state-sponsored violence—including racially motivated police brutality and the extrajudicial murder of BIPOC people—has scarcely begun to be calculated, much less adequately addressed, by the psychoanalytic community,

Susan and I had, in designing our syllabus, done our best to include material about the interwoven histories of psychoanalysis, Judaism, and antisemitism and about the longstanding racial disparities in access both to psychoanalytic training and treatment. We included exemplary readings from the belated but burgeoning clinical and theoretical literature on race and psychoanalysis (see, e.g., Eng and Han 2019, Gherovici and Christian 2019, Leary 2000, Powell 2018, Saketopoulou 2011, Suchet 2004), and we screened two particularly illuminating films: Basia Winograd's groundbreaking documentaries, *Black Psychoanalysts Speak* (2014) and *Psychoanalysis in El Barrio* (2016).

Both of these very "teachable" films dramatize the damaging consequences of the still prevalent clinical view that psychoanalytic treatment should remain aloof from sociopolitical issues—despite the fact that, from its inception, psychoanalytic theory and practice have so often sought to engage with progressive political thought and to promote social justice. Psychoanalytic institutes still focus chiefly on training and treating a comparatively privileged and overwhelmingly white clientele. The medical establishment continues to link certain mental disorders to ethnicity and race, rather than to the societal harms that cause them. Racialist thinking continues to impede mourning for past and present victims of American slavery and its traumatic sequelae. And white supremacism continues in forms both subtle and brazen to impede the decolonization of American minds. We know that these and other failures are not irremediable. Nor do they devalue the extraordinary efforts of past and present educators, clinicians, and theorists, who've helped psychoanalysis increase the pace and quality of its contributions to building a more just and unfettered world. But if there were ever a time to bring more of this work into our undergraduate classrooms, where psychoanalytic ideas and their progressive potentials are so rarely even discussed, that time would be now.

However, while a race-centered psychoanalytic curriculum is no longer difficult to design, the pedagogical challenges to be anticipated remain substantial—and potentially overwhelming. Some teachers, Stuart Hall observes, "try to sidestep the explosive nature of the subject itself and walk around it, to catch it unawares (except that it usually catches you unawares)" (2021, 123). Thus, many often unbidden, suppressed questions become inescapable: To what extent should individuals' racial identities be discussed in the classroom? What sort of authority will be allotted to race-based experience? How will the inescapability of the institutionalization of white privilege be addressed? To what extent might a course's content be adapted to a particular class group's racial and ethnic demographics? Will it be necessary for students and teachers to read or listen to racist discourse in order to study its intrapsychic and intersubjective effects? To what extent might racial dissonance, disidentification, and even antagonism find an adequate "holding environment" in the classroom? What mechanisms would help students and teachers recognize self-censorship and facilitate disclosure? How will embodiment as a psychoanalytic concern intersect with racial or racialized embodiment? How does an explicit focus on race change the psychoanalytic discussion of trauma (individual, collective, and historical/generational), with its potential for both minimization and competition? How do race and ethnicity intersect with other visible and non-visible markers of identity? Does psychoanalysis make adequate room for an ontology of race? What about psychoanalytic ethics and questions of responsibility for one's own or another's suffering? Are psychoanalytic theory and technique sufficiently adaptable to ethnocultural differences, and to what extent do their universalizing tendencies erase or distort racial, ethnic, and cultural differences?

In any course that sets out to face such questions, "you have to create an atmosphere which allows people to say unpopular things .... [because] what you don't hear you don't engage with" (Hall 2021, 124). Primary responsibility for creating such an atmosphere is the teacher's, but no teacher can unilaterally impose it upon a group of students, each of whom, like the teacher, will have their own particular beliefs, prejudices, fantasies, ideological commitments, and identifications—all strongly "felt," perhaps, but nonetheless frequently very difficult to articulate, whatever the atmosphere might be like. Students help create the atmosphere, not just by being who they are, but also by communicating their desires (i.e., what they want, and also what they don't want). It may be particularly difficult for them to explain what many students "will be most sensitive to, i.e., the interplay of feelings between the groups which are structured around the awareness of racial difference" (Hall 2021, 126).

As in Hall's UK, in the US it's impossible for the members of a classroom group not to be aware of 1) everyone's awareness of perceived markers of racial difference and 2) everyone's ignorance of what assumptions and associations those perceived markers call up in the other members of the group. A frequent inclination, therefore, is to tread as if on the thinnest of ice—to fear and therefore steer clear of the affectively charged thoughts pressing hardest for utterance. When teachers do so, students know it, even if they're not consciously aware of knowing it. And, because they know it, they will often feel unrecognized or misunderstood, or they'll push away their own most pressing thoughts and feelings, or feel guilty, as if they'd caused the impasse themselves. In an already challenging situation, a teacher's reluctance or refusal to reflect upon and, at least sometimes, to make use of their countertransference will almost inevitably generate lots of conscious awkwardness and tumultuous unconscious communication. Such conditions are signaled by the whole paralinguistic range of sighs, snorts, grunts, scoffs, winces, eyerolls, startles, laughter, scowls, and the like, which may be deliberately performative but which also erupt spontaneously as traumatic abreactions.

Dissociation is a common refuge for both teachers and students who, for whatever reason, don't want to be identified with racial forms of privilege, isolation, anger, or degradation. And projective identification is a powerful mechanism for offloading one's unwanted or vulnerable self-states onto someone else. Some teachers might manifest a blunt insensitivity in a reaction-formation against their own ambivalent urge to protect certain students from traumatization. And any late-adolescent college student might, under the pressure of such discomfort, regress to some earlier psychic position of frustrated hostility or fantasy of escape. All such defense mechanisms can lead to enactments that lock teachers and students into unwanted, disruptive, and even violent patterns of behavior. Indeed, in what the authors of a recent volume on *Teaching Race* call our "perilous times" (Cohen et al. 2021), interactions among members of courses with race-centered curricula will hardly be able to avoid aggravating such defenses and thereby provoking what Bion (after Klein) calls the "inborn disposition to excessive destructiveness, hatred, and envy" (1959, 313).[5]

It's entirely understandable that accepting such an atmosphere might seem defeatist or worse to many teachers. Yet teachers who are able to recognize signs of anxiety, discomfort, frustration, and disengagement in themselves might also be able to sustain a pedagogical "holding environment" for their safe (but not *too* safe) acknowledgment and exploration. Doing so would begin with a commonsensical and pre-psychoanalytic ethos—described here in a non-psychoanalytic article about teaching mathematics:

> Teaching is not only about teaching what is conventionally called content. It is also teaching students what a lesson is and how to

participate in it. From the activities the teacher sets for them, students learn what counts as knowledge and what kind of activities constitute legitimate academic tasks. Face-to-face interaction between students and their teacher follows context-specific rules, and cues within these contexts signal how what anyone says is to be understood in relation to the task everyone is assembled to accomplish. The teacher has more power over how acts and utterances get interpreted ... but these interpretations are finally the result of negotiation with students.

(Lampert 1990, 34–35)

A psychoanalytically informed teaching practice would augment this already appealing model of classroom culture by including the unconscious in "what a lesson is and how to participate in it" and in "what counts as knowledge and what kind of activities constitute legitimate academic tasks." Such a practice would introduce students to the existence of unconscious communication and the various "cues" that "signal how what anyone says [might] be understood in relation to the task everyone is assembled to accomplish." It would acknowledge the asymmetry of "power" between teacher and student, and it would help accustom students to the affective as well as "social and intellectual" aspects of interpretive "negotiation."

Crucially, it would also include discussion and negotiation of the consequences of working psychodynamically for conventional learning expectations and standardized assessment outcomes. Students in first-year calculus, after all, need to learn, among other things, how to estimate derivatives and interpret the behavior of accumulation functions. Their implication as students of calculus in, say, the racialized psychic structures that help determine their place in a capitalist social order isn't something they're going to be asked about on the final exam. But it can only help them to do better in the course—and thus on the final exam—if they also develop a greater self-awareness of the workings of desire and resistance *in their study of*, say, derivatives and accumulation functions. This comes down to what it means to teach *with*, rather than *about*, psychoanalysis.

But does one have to be qualified to do the latter in order to do the former? If a teacher—a math teacher, for example, or an art history teacher—of any sort of course without explicitly psychoanalytic content—wants to implement a psychoanalytic approach to pedagogy, should they have had analytic clinical training? If not, should psychoanalysis be one of their areas of academic expertise? Do they need to have been analyzed themselves? These would all be advantageous, and it's hard to imagine someone without any of these qualifications having the desire, much less the ability, to develop such a pedagogy. At the same time, it's hard to imagine someone—a calculus professor, for example—with at least one of these qualifications who wouldn't find themselves incorporating at least some of that psychoanalytic knowledge into their style of teaching (i.e., their style of relating to others).

Mathematical thought, after all, is conducted by intellectuals who, like the rest of us, are saturated with beliefs and fantasies—including beliefs and fantasies about race. In psychoanalytic terms, these beliefs and fantasies are no less "real" to them than derivatives and accumulation functions, even though the rejection of race as "real" (that is, as a biologically determined phenomenon) is now settled knowledge throughout most quarters of higher education. "The truth," writes philosopher Kwame Anthony Appiah, "is that there are no races ... The evil that is done is done by the concept and by easy—yet impossible—assumptions as to its application. What we miss through our obsession with the structure of relations of concepts is, simply, reality" (1985, 35–36). Similarly, sociologist Robert Miles asserts that

> there are no "races" and therefore no "race relations." There is only the belief that there are such things, a belief which is used by some social groups to construct an Other (and therefore the Self) in thought as a prelude to exclusion and domination, and by other social groups to define Self (and so to construct an Other) as a means of resisting that exclusion. Hence, if it is used at all ... "race" should be used only to refer descriptively to such uses.
>
> (1993, 42)

As a social construct and fluid analytical category, race tends to be regarded as the intellectual province of the humanities and social sciences and irrelevant to the STEM disciplines. This distinction is now commonly taken for granted, even though the ostensibly "pure" sciences are just as thoroughly committed to politico-economic ends (e.g., through funding, application, ideological motivation, etc.). It's taken for granted, for example, in Susan Giroux's otherwise rigorous critique of the contemporary university's

> intellectual complicity with a new "post-racial" politics that parallels the ascendancy of the latest phase of world capitalist development, or global neoliberalism .... Aware of it or not, willing or not, intellectuals

who devote their lives to studying, teaching, and writing about the human condition regardless of disciplinary location are acting with moral consequence [and] political effect. Hence it is imperative to ask: What pressures will intellectuals in the academy bring to bear on the issues of our time? Which values and whose interests will they reflect in the identification of problems said to require scholarly attention, in the formulation of key concepts, in the choice of methodologies, and in the staging of solutions? And what pressures, in turn, will be brought to bear on them? The task at hand is, then, to assess critically the last forty years of academic allegiance to colorblindness and to theorize the possibilities for a much-needed reconciliation with a social reality that is highly and historically raced, as well as a rehabilitation of critical and creative thought.

(Giroux 2010, 4, 6)

It's easy for "scientific thought" to be forgotten in such a peroration, just as negative racial stereotypes are easier to overlook in large, ostensibly "colorblind" STEM lecture courses. But of what use would a psychoanalytic pedagogy be to anyone in, say, a 400-student calculus course?

Ψ

Such large STEM lecture courses (as well as much smaller, seminar-style courses with fewer than 15 or 20 students) are examples of what Bion calls "experiences in groups" (2004). Psychodynamically, the experiences that distinguish smaller groups from larger ones include regular face-to-face interactions involving speaking and listening; personal accountability for one's own speech and behavior; and development of small-group skills like cooperation and temporary leadership. The larger the class size, the more challenging it becomes for teachers to attune themselves to the unconscious experience of individual students and to register and assess their own targeting by students' projective identifications, without becoming overwhelmed by feelings of disorientation or inauthenticity. For individual students in larger classes, the challenges have chiefly to do with their relation to the group and its "collective" consciousness: regression to unruliness or passivity; splitting and defensive exclusion; narcissistic self-encapsulation; defense against merger stemming from anxiety over identity loss; wrestling with the desire to be seen and the desire not to be seen; changes to attention and memory; etc.

The unconscious experience of an individual BIPOC student in a very large and overwhelmingly white calculus course is unlikely to be reached, even by a highly psychoanalytically inclined teacher. But such a teacher could, at a minimum, apply their psychodynamic knowledge of group experience to elicit what organizational psychologist Michael Diamond calls "valuable preconscious data—the unexamined, undiscussed, avoided, and denied issues of [group] experience" (1993, 35). Racism is a *group* enmity and practice of defensive exclusion shared by individuals who might or might not care a great deal more about their group *identity* than about the perceived racial differences or racializations that subtend it. In any case, from the complex psychology of race, it might be inferred that the interpersonal relations that precipitate into such groups stem from what Frantz Fanon theorized as a historically damaged "doing of the self."

Indeed, as an educational project, Fanon's work points toward a new iteration of humanism—one that would be "constituted," as sociologist of education Marlon Simmons puts it (paraphrasing Adolf Reinach), "through a particular doing of the self that is not limited to the essentializing properties of colonial epistemes of color" (2023, 3). Fanon experienced directly how colonialism undermines and ultimately destroys the cultural foundations of colonized peoples by using education as a weapon of domination: "I came into the world imbued with the will to find a meaning in things, my spirit filled with the desire to attain to the source of the world, and then I found that I was an object in the midst of other objects" (1967, 109). But, as a psychoanalytic psychiatrist, he also knew that a mere displacement of colonialist ontologies couldn't satisfy his fundamental, epistemophilic "desire to know." As Simmons writes,

> Fanon is notably interested in determining how experiences of marginalization, racism, resistance, and disenfranchisement become voiced through relational ontologies and how they provide different pathways to think about making sense of the world through interpretive practices, to be curious about our relationship with the known, with knowing, and coming to know.
>
> (2023, 11)

Fanon's own striking characterization of this curiosity as the condition of being "imbued with the will to find a meaning in things, my spirit filled with the desire to attain to the source of the world" resounds with the psychoanalytic insight that grounds the pursuit of knowledge of the world and of oneself in the desiring subject (see Chapter 3).

Threatened by oppressive and utilitarian doctrines of education that would have him remain "an object in the midst of other objects," Fanon turns, with the help of psychoanalytic theories of the subject, toward critique, which is always, as anthropologist Didier Fassin writes, "a response to a certain state of the world being developed within a certain configuration of power and knowledge in the academic and public sphere" (2019, 14). Fanon's work on education attends to the present conditions of both the desire for and the production of knowledge, while also attempting to write a different account of the present and its possible future. It also acknowledges an important difference between the desire to know and the desire for a critique of knowing that has become all the more salient in the current "post-truth" era of education, in which there is such pervasive mistrust of critique as, at best, mere relativism and, worse, an ideological attempt to undermine conditions for the operation of reason and rationality. The resurgence of naïve empiricism in the humanities and the economic and political power of STEM fields enjoy a mutually reinforcing relation with quantitative assessment and skill-centered curricula—based, as Claudia Ruitenberg puts it, "on the conceit that all educationally relevant human qualities or attributes can be understood as competencies" (2021, 64).

Ruitenberg argues that, unlike the desire for knowledge, desire for critique

> is not a given. In fact, educators may encounter students who have little desire for critique, for being vigilant to deconstructive potential— especially if they have already been socialized into expecting a practical pay-off in education …. The desire for critique is not a competency and cannot be taught or assessed as such. It cannot be trained or instructed, but must be awakened, lit, aroused.
>
> (2021, 64)

Let's say our hypothetical BIPOC student in a very large and overwhelmingly white calculus course has just as powerful a desire for knowledge as anyone else in the room. Like other students, she may also be experiencing tremendous pressure from both without and within to channel that desire toward those areas of knowledge she's been socialized into expecting will provide ample paternal/institutional approval and the greatest practical pay-off. When Gayatri Spivak, for instance, refers to education as the "uncoercive rearrangement of desires," she means education *in the humanities* (2004, 526). Moreover, as Ruitenberg points out, Spivak is referring "to a particular rearrangement of desires in the context of global inequality and common mechanisms of human rights activism that leave in place the assumption of superiority on the part of those in a position to help, and the assumption of subalternity on the part of those receiving the help" (2021, 63). Ruitenberg's concern is that this is a specific political goal, rather than an effective argument for the university-wide revaluation of competency-based education.

But there is a more radical argument to be made for the "uncoercive rearrangement of desires" that would avoid the disciplinary splitting Spivak takes for granted (see Chapter 3)—one that would extend to the large calculus course as well—by making a more vital and comprehensive place for psychoanalysis in higher education. It's an argument not primarily about concentrated curricula or disciplinary authority, but about pedagogy and the longstanding need for pedagogical reform. It's an argument for the recalibration of relationships among teachers and students throughout the university, in light of their inescapably unconscious as well as conscious dimensions. It's less an argument for the instrumentalization of localized psychoanalytic knowledge than for a broader awareness of and more complete engagement with the full subjectivity of teachers and students engaged in learning.

The steadily diminishing returns of higher education are due in part to the failure to adapt our pedagogies to our changing understanding of psychic reality—a reality we've known for decades to include the not-yet-complete neurological and psychological development of the late-adolescents and early-adults who constitute the vast majority of college and university students. Indeed, in a recent plea for pedagogical reform at the most elite US universities, former Harvard president Derek Bok stresses the fact that

> various important behaviors and capabilities, such as creativity, empathy, resilience, and conscientiousness, which were long thought to become largely immutable during childhood, continue to be malleable, and hence potentially teachable, at least through early adulthood. Since these capabilities are of great value to students and, in the form of so-called soft skills, to employers as well, concerted effort by leading universities to explore ways to teach them could eventually enhance the benefits of undergraduate education significantly.
>
> (2024, 201)

Like Spivak, Bok is ultimately concerned with specific political and civic goals. But, also like Spivak, he is calling necessary attention to learning's affective dimension as something not only overlooked and underutilized in most campus classrooms, but also actively (if unconsciously) resisted by faculty and administrators. Bok argues that under escalating budgetary pressures and the shrinking of the professoriate,

> the incentives for experimenting with new and better methods of teaching are very weak. Students are not clamoring for reform. Nor are there any financial benefits for universities from introducing more effective methods of teaching. As a result, the process of improving teaching and learning is sluggish at best. The most obvious example of this tendency is the snail-like transition from relying heavily on lecturing to a passive student audience to a pedagogy emphasizing active discussion and problem solving.
>
> (2024, 139)

What's missing from Bok's argument is any consideration of the extent to which "active discussion and problem solving" could be dramatically enhanced through reflexive attention to the unconscious dimensions of group discussion and problem solving as such. The success of such a pedagogy could help incentivize the push toward smaller class sizes. And even in large lecture courses, a psychodynamic approach to group behavior could make the experience less "passive" and more likely to precipitate "the unexamined, undiscussed, avoided, and denied issues of [group] experience" that, if ignored, can make such settings unduly challenging for those who experience forms of non-alignment with the group's collective consciousness and who might end up as subjects of its unconscious fantasies and projections—including the pervasive fantasy of the deracialization of the subject of pedagogy.

Notes

1 Reprinted by the permission of Russell & Volkening as agents for the author. Copyright © 1961 by May Sarton.
2 Due to the current crisis in campus mental healthcare, more and more faculty members are struggling, according to a recent article in *The Chronicle of Higher Education*, "to tend to students' mental health" (Field 2023, 6).
3 On students' own anxieties about being "seen through," see Eifermann (1993, 1009).

4 Ironically, Flexner's highly influential 1910 report on *Medical Education in the United States and Canada*—a blueprint for the radical overhauling of American medical education and practice, with its call for strict adherence to mainstream scientific principles and protocols—helped justify the restriction of eligibility for psychoanalytic training and practice to those who had completed medical school and a psychiatric residency under Flexner's own more stringently scientific standards. My thanks to Jack Drescher for reminding me of this fact.

5 While this is not to say that either students or teachers in such classroom situations commonly lash out like enraged children, on rare occasions enactments that involve verbal and even physical violence can lead to a course's outright cancelation (see, e.g., Thornton 2018).

Chapter 5

Psychoanalysis, the University, and the Professions

> A scheme of training for analysts has still to be created. It must include elements from the mental sciences, from psychology, the history of civilization and sociology, as well as from anatomy, biology and the study of evolution .... It is easy to meet this suggestion by objecting that analytic colleges of this kind do not exist and that I am merely setting up an ideal. An ideal, no doubt. But an ideal which can and must be realized.
> —SIGMUND FREUD, "The Question of Lay Analysis" [1926]

Psychoanalytic education can yield enormous benefits to pre- and para-professional students in many fields: premed, prelaw, nursing, business, teaching, and the mental health professions, including both cognitive and psychodynamic psychotherapies, counselling, art and play therapies, mindfulness training, community-based therapies, and of course psychoanalysis itself. Moreover, students training for careers in mental health face robust hiring prospects. News outlets, especially in the post-Covid era, continue to report that the demand for therapists and other mental health professionals greatly surpasses the supply, and the psychoanalytic and psychotherapeutic professions, in particular, are not only stretched thin but also suffering from superannuation due to insufficient numbers of younger trainees.[1] Expanding and enriching psychoanalytic education in colleges and universities would enhance countless students' lives and careers. It would also help increase the number of younger analytic candidates, thereby both rejuvenating the profession and adding to the number of much-needed mental healthcare providers generally. Arguably, the best way to achieve these humanistic, academic, professional, and clinical goals would be to make universities the principal centers of psychoanalytic education, research, and training.

In a 2009 article in the *International Journal of Psychoanalysis*, analyst Robert Wallerstein argued that Freud's 1926 vision of an ideal institution

DOI: 10.4324/9781003540588-6

for the training of analysts "can be realized fully *only* within the academic university structure" (2009, 1109; italics added). Freud himself had already rejected the notion that medical schools could, on their own, meet the necessary requirements (1959c, 246–48), and he would surely have been appalled by APsA's longstanding mandate that accredited US analytic training institutes could only admit candidates who had completed a medical degree. From 1938 until 1989, only medically trained psychiatrists could become candidates or members of APsA, with limited exceptions made for certain émigrés and for a small number of US psychological researchers. Moreover, the IPA denied membership to any US analyst or institute not already a member of APsaA. Thus, while many non-physician analysts in other parts of the world could join the IPA, almost all US-based psychologists, social workers, and other non-physician mental health professionals were barred from joining either organization and could train only at non-accredited analytic institutes. Indeed, for several decades, New York's William Alanson White Institute was the only nationally prominent analytic training institute that admitted non-physician psychologists as candidates. It wasn't until 1985 that US psychologists organized to file civil and class-action lawsuits against APsA, the IPA, and two of the leading analytic training institutes (the New York Psychoanalytic Institute and the Columbia University Center for Psychoanalytic Training), charging them with restraint of trade under the Sherman Anti-Trust Act. The case was settled out of court in 1988, and by 1989 the doors to accredited institutes were effectively flung open.[2]

Ironically, however, the major success of this campaign coincided with what Nathan G. Hale has called "the decline of psychoanalysis in psychiatry." "Between 1960 and 1985," Hale writes, "nearly all the factors that had contributed to the rise of psychoanalytic psychiatry were in part reversed" (1995, 300; see also Paris 2005). Waning confidence in its scientific validity and therapeutic efficacy, the explosion of behavioral therapies and psychopharmacology, and the shrinking of public and private funding for psychoanalytic training and research led to the diminished authority of psychoanalysis in departments of psychiatry and clinical psychology all over the country. Before the 1960s, most of these departments were run by psychoanalysts. Today, virtually none of them are, and it's almost impossible to complete one's psychoanalytic training at a US university; one can do so only at one of the very small number of university-based analytic institutes, which include Adelphi University's Postgraduate

Program in Psychoanalysis and Psychotherapy, the Columbia University Center for Psychoanalytic Training and Research, the Emory University Psychoanalytic Institute, New York University's Postdoctoral Program in Psychotherapy and Psychoanalysis, and the independently accredited Boston Graduate School of Psychoanalysis.

In an article on the Columbia program (the first psychoanalytic institute affiliated with the American Psychoanalytic Association to be established in a university medical school), George Daniels and Lawrence Kolb express the commonly held mid-century view that it is the "medical setting" of a psychiatry department within a medical school attached to a teaching hospital—and not the university setting as such—that make such programs the most effective means of promoting psychoanalytic training, research, theory, and practice within the larger "universe" of the sciences (1960, 170). Yet within the psychoanalytic community there was always a great deal of opposition to the *de facto* status of psychoanalysis in the US as a "medical specialty." For one thing, there was a rich and enduring tradition of lay (non-physician) analysis practiced by many of the great European analysts who fled to the US in the 1930s, 40s, and 50s. And it wasn't only refugees from totalitarianism who mistrusted what Kurt Eissler called "the conspicuous accumulation of power in the national association [i.e., APsA]" (1965, 102). With that power, he wrote, came

> the organization of psychoanalysis as a medical specialty—or worse still, as a subdivision of psychiatry. In no other country has the representative psychoanalytic association committed itself so solidly and irrevocably as in the United States in favor of medically applied psychoanalysis.
>
> (1965, 91)

By the time APsA agreed to "de-medicalize" accredited psychoanalytic training, both the social and scientific prestige enjoyed by the profession during the postwar period had all but disappeared—as had the institutional circumstances that inspired Daniels and Kolb's confidence in the medical-school model. The corporatization of both the university and the healthcare industry have made most US medical schools virtually independent—financially, administratively, and intellectually—while the persistent extramural influence of the training-analyst system still tends, quasi-cabalistically, to promote ideological splitting and professional and scientific/intellectual isolation, as Kernberg (2016, 264–67) and others have repeatedly argued. Indeed, in his recent call for better models for university-based psychoanalytic education and training, Kernberg praises Columbia's Psychoanalytic Center because "in recent years" it has distinguished itself through "its encouragement of scientific dialogue within its department of psychiatry, with Columbia University, and its development of interdisciplinary symposia and conferences" (2016, 70).

Beginning in the 1960s and 70s, as psychoanalysis continued to lose scientific prestige and academic authority, its cultural capital was also declining in value. Smelling weakness, the vultures circled, and it became fashionable, almost to the point of necessity, for any antagonist with a mouthpiece to gloat—often in the most egregious terms. For example, in 1975, the renowned medical researcher Peter Medawar declared in the *New York Review of Books* that

the opinion is gaining ground that doctrinaire psychoanalytic theory is the most stupendous intellectual confidence trick of the twentieth century: and a terminal product as well—something akin to a dinosaur or a zeppelin in the history of ideas, a vast structure of radically unsound design and with no posterity.

(1975, 17)

In the mid-1990s, in the same publication, the distinguished Freudian literary critic Frederick Crews did a complete *volte face* in a series of articles on what was then the highly controversial subject of "recovered" memories. His disavowal of psychoanalysis matches Medawar's in its florid reactionism:

Freudian clichés are breeding promiscuously with those of religious zealots, self-help evangelists, sociopolitical ideologues, and outright charlatans who trade in the ever seductive currency of guilt and blame. So long as "Freud's permanent revolution"… retains any sway, the voodoo of "the repressed" can be counted upon to return in newly energetic and pernicious forms.

(1994, 58)

Thanks in part to such caricatures, the discrediting of psychoanalysis has become *de rigueur* in popular culture. For example, several prominent portrayals of psychiatrists in major television series either minimize their association with psychoanalysis, like the character Dr. Jennifer Melfi in HBO's *The Sopranos* (1999–2007), or reject that association completely, as in the NBC series *Hannibal* (2013–15), in which the cannibalistic psychiatrist Dr. Lecter refers to psychoanalysis as a "dead religion."

Both within and beyond the scientific community, the field of psychoanalysis has not just been put on the defensive, but has consistently been impugned in terms of *discredited belief* (e.g., Medawar's "confidence trick," Crews's "voodoo," and Lecter's "dead religion"). Douglas Kirsner suggests that, from the start, psychoanalysts have left themselves open to such treatment by choosing to remain "domiciled in autonomous, freestanding institutes and societies" and by keeping away from "universities and other public institutions, preferring to lord over psychoanalysis themselves. In this respect, psychoanalysis bears a structural resemblance to a political movement or a religion" (2009, 234). Another discrediting factor over the past several decades, according to analyst Carlo Strenger (2015), is the seemingly boundless exaltation of faith in numeracy and quantification. And the neoempiricist trend in the social sciences, and even the humanities, exerts further pressure on psychoanalysis to quantify its theories and its therapeutic results. Of course, the quantifying doctrine of the healthcare industrial complex has continued to chip away at insurance coverage for psychodynamic treatments, not only in the US but also, increasingly, in European countries like Germany (Wurmser 2006, 229). Psychoanalysis is a favorite target of contemporary apostles of scientism and a flashpoint for quasi-religious controversies over "objectivity," "verifiability," and the nature of the "real" (see, e.g., Clarke 2017; Cole 2012; Hanly 2014; Hoffman 2010; Mills 2015; Tuckett 2008).

The psychoanalytic field has continued to defend itself in a variety of ways. Joel Paris identifies four of these defenses as "fundamentalism," "revisionism," "demedicalization," and something he calls "the flight from treatment," by which he means the shift in focus by some analysts and their patients from diagnostics to hermeneutics—that is, the shift from concentrating on types of illness and cure to addressing nonpathological forms of impasse and resolution (2005, 153). Of course, these are not incompatible or inconsistent ways of practicing psychoanalysis, and patients both with and without serious mental illness have always sought and often found relief and revitalization in psychoanalytic treatment. Yet, like many other would-be eulogists of psychoanalysis, Paris's understanding of the contemporary field (his book appeared in 2005) and its rapprochement with the neurosciences is minimal at best.

Almost two decades later, psychoanalysis remains in many ways a conservative, slow-moving field, with a disinclination for public discussion and debate. In 2020, analyst Alexander Stein published a polemical essay in the journal *Psychoanalytic Perspectives* that challenged his peers to help the psychoanalytic profession overcome its "perplexingly self-abnegating relationship with the outside world" (2020, 149), chiefly by endeavoring to:

(1) Mitigate the peripheralization and decline of psychoanalysis; (2) help advance greater public awareness and more accurate understanding of what psychoanalysis is and what psychoanalysts are capable of doing; and (3) deliver actionable insight and practical assistance to leaders and decision-makers.

(2020, 144)

But how? Stein's particular emphasis is on the need to extend the reach of psychoanalytic writing by adapting it for different audiences and by exploiting short, popular forms like the op-ed, the news article, and the magazine column—as Stein himself (who is also a business consultant) has done for venues including the *New York Times*, *Fortune Small Business*, and *Forbes*. "Writing psychoanalytically—psychoanalysis itself—can and should be used," Stein urges, "in more muscular, actionable, and outward facing ways" (2020, 159).

Stein insists that there are many further opportunities "for psychoanalysis to be used more expansively in ways that will only enhance, not replace it, none of which derogate its essentialness as a science of the mind or efficacy as a treatment method" (2020, 154), and he recognizes that one of the chief amongst them is higher education:

Though psychiatrists with medical school appointments and psychologists in academic posts can also train and become licensed to practice as psychoanalysts, psychoanalysis itself has never established footholds in numbers as a stand-alone department in teaching hospitals, universities, and research centers. In fact, the norm today is that undergraduates interested in psychoanalysis will not be attending psychology classes but studying literary critical theory. Psychoanalytic thought and work have over time become eclipsed by empirical research in cognitive and behavioral psychology and neuroscience. Its influence is circumscribed, and its functionality frequently questioned. Psychoanalysis has failed to adequately address any of this.

(2020, 150)

This exhortation is hardly original. Indeed, Chapter 1 makes clear that different versions of it have continued to be expressed (and often implemented) throughout the history of psychoanalysis. Yet, in our own era, the triumphs of cognitive psychology and psychopharmacology, the massive encroachments of neoempiricism, and the exponentiating campus mental health crisis, along with the dire circumstances of higher education itself, make it hard to overestimate the importance of 1) introducing psychoanalysis into the standard college and university curriculum and 2) relocating the centers of professional psychoanalytic education, training, and research to the university system.

Both of these objectives have strong advocates within the fields of psychoanalytic practice and research, including Stephen Frosh, Otto Kernberg, Stephen Sonnenberg, and Robert Wallerstein. Frosh, for example, has been advocating for the university teaching of psychoanalysis for over forty years, during which time he's also been practicing what he preaches:

Much of my academic career has been devoted to working out what psychoanalysis might have to say to students who want their studies to challenge them and also speak directly to their experience of the world. This has fuelled my own allegiance to the development of "Psychosocial Studies," by which I mean an approach to understanding the human subject as a kind of meeting-point for "external" (or social) and "internal" (or subjective) forces—though of course this internal/ external distinction is an oversimplification .... What I try to show my students at Birkbeck, University of London, is that psychoanalysis promotes an openness to otherness by helping us to map the complexity of psychic life, including the ways in which it's both conditioned and disrupted by affective, often conflictual, engagements with those to whom and for whom we are responsible. I try to show them how the pursuit of clarity and rationality is always conditioned by the murk and mystery of our relations with others and by our own largely unconscious experience.

(2022)

In this 2022 post, written for the blog I edit, *Psyche on Campus*, Frosh expresses his principal hope that his students, regardless of what profession they enter, "can use their psychoanalytic education to help them link the immediacy and delicacy of their sense of 'inner' selfhood with the aspects of social and political life they see around them" (2022).[3]

Unfortunately, Frosh's experience as a professor in an official, university-based psychoanalytic studies program is exceptionally uncommon (see Chapter 2 above), and even some university-based clinicians seem unaware of the substantial obstacles to the goals they advocate. For example, as a clinician and professor of psychiatry at the Dell Medical School of the University of Texas, Austin, Sonnenberg has written that "in the United States the time has come for psychoanalysts to enter the world of higher education as humanities scholars. Doors are now opening for clinical psychoanalysts with non-quantitative research interests to find a home in the humanities in major research universities" (2011, 641). Sadly, while a certain number of "doors" may be open to temporary fellowships and visiting appointments, the prospects for anyone seeking "to find a home in the humanities" as a psychoanalytic teacher-researcher are virtually nil. Even at R1 research universities, humanities departments are shrinking, and at less wealthy and prestigious schools they are being eliminated entirely. The rare humanities faculty positions that occasionally open up are almost always entry-level. Moreover, Sonnenberg seems to have based his impression that "psychoanalysis is seen in the university as an important branch of the humanities" almost exclusively on his own singular experience as a very senior, one-year, non-teaching Faculty Fellow at his own university's Humanities Institute (2011, 657). Sonnenberg mentions neither the ongoing employment crisis in the humanities nor the extremely marginal contemporary status of psychoanalysis as an academic discipline.

The psychoanalytic community should, of course, put more collective effort into training and supporting psychoanalytic researchers. But that would hardly begin to address the much more radical—and potentially transformational—schema outlined by Frosh, Kernberg, Wallerstein, and others. Only concerted collaborative efforts by psychoanalytic institutes and societies and university leaders can bring about such large-scale institutional changes—changes that would be of enormous benefit to the futures of both psychoanalysis and higher education. Their implementation would not be cost-prohibitive; it would in fact be comparatively inexpensive: existing infrastructure could be used, faculty appointments or "lines" could be combined, accreditation and licensing would be largely bureaucratic matters, and numerous students with tuition dollars would flock to such institutions from all over the world. The two chief obstacles are 1) intra- and extramural misunderstanding and resistance to psychoanalytic educa- tion, and 2) the conservatism and resistance to change that universities and psychoanalytic institutions have always shared in abundance. The fact that both of these obstacles are highly susceptible to internal and external criti- cism and collective action gives us reason not merely to hope but to act. Shall we begin?

Notes

1 "According to the International Psychoanalytic Association (IPA)," writes Sarah Goldberg, "the average age of a psychoanalytic member is sixty-five, and the average age of a training analyst is seventy-three" (2022). Goldberg also reports that "the average age for members of the American Psychoanalytic Association is 66" (2021, 72).

2 For a monumental account of the history of the lawsuits and of the question of lay analysis in the US, see Wallerstein (1998).

3 See also Frosh's book *Psychoanalysis Outside the Clinic* (2010), which explores the real and potential impact of what is often derogatively referred to as "applied" psychoanalysis for broad realms of intellectual, social, and political life.

Appendix: Resources

Syllabus archive

The "Syllabus Archive" feature of the blog *Psyche on Campus* gathers together syllabi from courses taught at several research universities and colleges in the US and the UK. They range from introductory undergraduate courses to courses for graduate and professional students. The "Syllabus Archive" can be accessed from https://web.sas.upenn.edu/psycheoncampus/syllabus-archive/. Instructors of psychoanalytically oriented courses are encouraged to contribute syllabi of their own, which can be sent to: cavitch@upenn.edu.

Programs and institutional resources

psychoanalytic organizations with commitments to higher education

Academics for the Advancement of Psychodynamic Psychology (A^2P^2)
https://ambitious-asquaredpsquared.wordpress.com/
This recently formed organization—founded by Nancy McWilliams and Leora Traub—had its first meeting on June 2, 2024. A^2P^2's chief goal is to address the contemporary crisis in psychodynamic psychology, as awareness and knowledge of psychodynamic and other depth-oriented thought, training, and research continue rapidly to be attenuated. For further information, contact Leora Traub at asquarepsquared@gmail.com.

American Psychoanalytic Association (APsA)
Education and Research: https://apsa.org/education-research/
"Explore psychoanalytic career paths, including training for adult psychoanalysis, child and adolescent psychoanalysis, psychoanalytic psychotherapy, as well as research and academic psychoanalytic education. APsA

and affiliated institutes and societies also offer several educational fellowships and programs to support researchers and trainees."

American Psychological Association (APA)
Education and Career: https://www.apa.org/education-career
"Resources for students, teachers and psychologists at all levels to
explore career growth in psychology."

Center for Psychoanalysis and Technology (CPT)
https://centerforpsychoanalysisandtech.com/
Founded by Nicolle Zapien in 2022, CPT engages psychoanalysts in
conversations about the reciprocal influences of consumer technology and
the psyche, fostering discussions of technological change and individual
and group unconscious processes.

Division 39 (Society for Psychoanalysis and Psychoanalytic Psychology
of the APA)
Psychoanalytic-Friendly Universities and Programs: https://div39members.
wildapricot.org/Psychoanalytic-Friendly-Universities
"Beginning in October 2009, a survey was distributed to Universities
with graduate programs in psychology to determine if they were psychoanalytically friendly. The results of this survey have been compiled and
included in this website by state."

International Psychoanalytic Association (IPA)
Resources: https://www.ipa.world/ipa/en/Resources/en/Resources/
Resources.aspx?hkey=1c5857db-a8d3-47de-aa75-c19e26e81e1d

Suggested readings not included in the bibliography

Ackerman, Sarah. 2018. "Reading Beyond *The Interpretation of Dreams.*" *American Imago*
    75.2: 303–06.
Adler, Alfred. 1930. *The Education of Children.* Tr. Eleanor and Friedrich Jensen. New
    York: Greenberg.
Appel, Stephen. 1996. *Positioning Subjects: Psychoanalysis and Critical Educational
    Studies.* Westport: Bergin and Garvey.
Appel, Stephen, ed. 1999. *Psychoanalysis and Pedagogy.* Westport: Bergin and Garvey.
Bibby, Tamara. 2011. *Education, an 'Impossible Profession'? Psychoanalytic Explorations
    of Learning and Classrooms.* Abingdon: Routledge.
Bibby, Tamara. 2018. *The Creative Self: Psychoanalysis, Teaching and Learning in the
    Classroom.* Abingdon: Routledge.
Blanchard-Laville, Claudine. 2013. *Au risque d'enseigner: Pour une clinique du travail
    enseignant.* Paris: Presses Universitaires de France.

Blum, Lawrence. 2018. "Teaching Freud, Teaching Psychoanalysis: From College Students to Professionals." *American Imago* 75.2: 307–17.

Blum, Lawrence D., Richard F. Summers, and Greg Urban. 2016. "Lunch; or, How to Develop an Undergraduate Minor in Psychoanalytic Studies." *American Psychoanalyst* 50.1: 18–19.

Bracher, Mark. 2006. *Radical Pedagogy: Identity, Generativity, and Social Transformation.* New York: Palgrave Macmillan.

Braddock, Louise, and Michael Lacewing, ed. 2007. *The Academic Face of Psychoanalysis: Papers in Philosophy, the Humanities and the British Clinical Tradition.* London: Routledge.

Brandell, Jerrold R. 2002. "The Marginalization of Psychoanalysis in Academic Social Work." *Psychoanalytic Social Work* 9.2: 41–50.

Britzman, Deborah P. 2009. *The Very Thought of Education: Psychoanalysis and the Impossible Professions.* Albany: SUNY Press.

Britzman, Deborah P. 2011. *Freud and Education.* New York: Routledge.

Burston, Daniel. 2020. *Psychoanalysis, Politics and the Postmodern University.* Cham: Palgrave Macmillan.

Chimbganda, Tapo. 2017. *The Classroom as Privileged Space: Psychoanalytic Paradigms for Social Justice in Pedagogy.* Blue Ridge Summit: Lexington.

Cho, K. Daniel. 2009. *Psychopedagogy: Freud, Lacan, and the Psychoanalytic Theory of Education.* London: Palgrave Macmillan.

Cifali, Mireille. 1982. *Freud pédagogue? Psychanalyse et éducation.* Paris: InterÉditions.

Cifali, Mireille, and Francis Imbert. 1998. *Freud et la pédagogie.* Paris: Presses Universitaires de France.

Clarke, Matthew. 2022. *Education and the Fantasies of Neoliberalism: Policy, Politics and Psychoanalysis.* London: Routledge.

Dunn, Jonathan. 2013. "Toward a Psychoanalytic Way of Teaching Psychoanalysis." *Psychoanalytic Review* 100.6: 947–71.

Eifermann, Rivka R. 1984. "Teaching Psycho-analysis to Non-psychoanalytic Students through Work on Their Own Dreams." *Psychoanalysis in Europe* 22: 38–45.

Ekstein, Rudolf, and Rocco L. Motto, ed. 1969. *From Learning for Love to Love of Learning: Essays on Psychoanalysis and Education.* New York: Brunner/Mazel.

Fradenburg, Aranye. 2011. "The Liberal Arts of Psychoanalysis." *Journal of the American Academy of Psychoanalysis and Dynamic Psychiatry* 39.4: 589–610.

Gallop, Jane, ed. 1995. *Pedagogy: The Question of Impersonation.* Bloomington: Indiana University Press.

Gourguechon, Prudy. 2005. "Reaching Out to Undergraduates: The 10,000 Minds Project." *American Psychoanalyst* 39.2: 15–17.

Granger, Collette A. 2011. *Silent Moments in Education: An Autoethnography of Learning, Teaching, and Learning to Teach.* Toronto: University of Toronto Press.

Imbert, Francis. 1997. *L'inconscient dans la classe, transferts et contre-transfert.* Paris: ESF.

Jenness, Katherine. 2015. "The Flattened Self: Generation Y Reads Freud." *Psychoanalysis, Culture and Society* 20.3: 284–302.

Jersild, Arthur T., and Eve Allina Lazar. 1962. *The Meaning of Psychotherapy in the Teacher's Life and Work.* New York: Teachers College.

Johnson, T.R. 2014. *The Other Side of Pedagogy: Lacan's Four Discourses and the Development of the Student Writer.* Albany: SUNY Press.

Jones, Richard M. 1968. *Fantasy and Feeling in Education.* New York: New York University Press.

Jurist, Elliott L., ed. 2016. "Special Issue: Psychoanalysis and the Humanities." *Psychoanalytic Psychology* 33.Suppl. 1: 1–225.

Kernberg, Otto F. 2006. "The Coming Changes in Psychoanalytic Education: Part I." *International Journal of Psychoanalysis* 87: 1649–73.

Kernberg, Otto F. 2007. "The Coming Changes in Psychoanalytic Education: Part II." *International Journal of Psychoanalysis* 88: 183–202.

Kernberg, Otto F. 2010. "A New Organization of Psychoanalytic Education."

Kernberg, Otto F. 2014. "The Twilight of the Training Analysis System." *Psychoanalytic Review* 101.2: 151–74.

Laplanche, Jean. 2004. "Pour la psychanalyse à l'Université." *Recherches en psychanalyse* 1: 9–13.

Lippi, Silvia. 2020. *The Decision of Desire [La décision du désir, 2013].* Tr. Peter Skafish. Minneapolis: University of Minnesota Press.

Luxon, Nancy. 2013. "Risk and Resistance: The Ethical Education of Psychoanalysis." *Political Theory* 41.3: 380–408.

Mayes, Clifford. 2020. *Archetype, Culture, and the Individual in Education: The Three Pedagogical Narratives.* London: Routledge.

Milhaud-Cappe. 2007. *Freud et le mouvement de pédagogie psychanalytique, 1908-1937: A. Aichhorn, H. Zulliger, O. Pfister.*

O'Loughlin, Michael, ed. 2013. *Psychodynamic Perspectives on Working with Children, Families, and Schools.* Lanham: Lexington Books.

Paul, Robert A. 2018. "Teaching Freud's 'Project.'" *American Imago* 75.2: 318–23.

Pearson, Gerald H. J. 1954. *Psychoanalysis and the Education of the Child.* New York: W. W. Norton.

Pitt, Alice J. 2003. *The Play of the Personal: Psychoanalytic Narratives of Feminist Education.* New York: Peter Lang.

Razinsky, Liran. 2016. "On the Need for Openness to the Humanities in Psychoanalysis." *Psychoanalytic Psychology* 33.1: S56–S74.

Roth, Philip. 1977. *The Professor of Desire.* New York: Farrar, Straus and Giroux.

Salecl, Renata. 1994. "Deference to the Great Other: The Discourse of Education." In Bracher et al., ed. *Lacanian Theory of Discourse: Subject, Structure, and Society.* New York: New York University Press, 163–75.

Shulman, Michael. 2018. "Teaching Freud's 'On Narcissism.'" *American Imago* 75.2: 297–302.

Stuart, Jennifer. 2018. "Teaching Freud Today?" *American Imago* 75.2: 287–96.

Terral, M. Hervé. 1994. "La psychopédagogie: une discipline vagabonde." *Revue française de pédagogie* 107: 109–21.

Thomä, Helmut. 2015. "Remarks on the First Century of the International Psychoanalytic Association and a Utopian Vision of Its Future." *International Forum of Psychoanalysis* 24.2: 109–32.

Todd, Sharon, ed. 1997. *Learning Desire: Perspectives on Pedagogy, Culture, and the Unsaid.* New York: Routledge.

Wallerstein, Robert S. 2007. "The Optimal Structure for Psychoanalytic Education Today: A Feasible Proposal?" *JAPA* 55.3: 953–84.

Wallerstein. Robert S. 2011. "Psychoanalysis in the University: The Natural Home for Education and Research." *International Journal of Psychoanalysis* 92.3: 623–39

Wallerstein. Robert S. 2012. "Will Psychoanalysis Fulfill Its Promise?" *International Journal of Psychoanalysis* 93.2: 377–99.

Winter, Sarah. 1999. *Freud and the Institution of Psychoanalytic Knowledge.* Stanford: Stanford University Press.

Youell, Biddy. 2006. *The Learning Relationship: Psychoanalytic Thinking in Education.* London: Karnac.

Bibliography

Adelman, Susan. 2019. "Recovering Race." *Psyche on Campus* (blog). University of Pennsylvania. November 8, 2019. https://web.sas.upenn.edu/psycheoncampus/2019/11/08/recovering-race/.

Adler, Alfred. 1930. *The Education of Children* [*Kindererziehung,* 1930]. Tr. Eleanore Jensen and Friedrich Jensen. New York: Greenberg.

Adler, Alfred. 1930. *Guiding the Child: On the Principles of Individual Psychology* [*Individualpsychologie in der Schule: Vorlesungen für Lehrer und Erzieher,* 1929]. London: Routledge.

Aichhorn, August. 1935. *Wayward Youth* [*Verwahrloster Jugend,* 1925]. London: Imago.

Akhtar, Salman, ed. 2005. *Freud along the Ganges: Psychoanalytic Reflections on the People and Culture of India.* New York: Other Press.

Alcorn, Marshall Wise. 2013. *Resistance to Learning: Overcoming the Desire Not to Know in Classroom Teaching.* London: Palgrave Macmillan.

Aldridge, Jerry, Jennifer L. Kilgo, and Grace Jepkemboi. 2014. "Before and Beyond Psychoanalysis: Anna Freud as Educator." *International Journal of Case Studies* 3.3: 16–20.

Alexander, Franz. 1960. *The Western Mind in Transition: An Eyewitness Story.* New York: Random House.

Allen, Amy. 2021. *Critique on the Couch: Why Critical Theory Needs Psychoanalysis.* New York: Columbia University Press.

Allison, Elizabeth. 2017. "Observing the Observer: Freud and the Limits of Empiricism." *British Journal of Psychotherapy* 33: 93–104.

Álvares, Cristina. 2019. "L'impromptu de Vincennes: Lacan et le discours unis-vers-cythère au lendemain de mai 68." *Carnets* 16 (second series): 1–12.

Ambrose, Charles M., and Michael T. Nietzel. 2023. *Colleges on the Brink: The Case for Financial Exigency.* Lanham: Rowman and Littlefield.

Anderson, Amanda, and Joseph Valente, ed. 2002. *Disciplinarity at the Fin de Siècle.* Princeton: Princeton University Press.

Appel, Stephen. 1995. "The Unconscious Subject of Education." *Discourse* 16.2: 167–89.

Appiah, Kwame Anthony. 1985. "The Uncompleted Argument: Du Bois and the Illusion of Race." *Critical Inquiry* 12: 21–37.

Aron, Lewis. 1991. "The Patient's Experience of the Analyst's Subjectivity." *Psychoanalytic Dialogues* 1: 29–51.

Auden, Wystan Hugh. 1991. *Collected Poems.* Ed. Edward Mendelson. New York: Vintage.

Augustine, Saint. 1961. *Confessions.* Tr. Richard Sidney Pine-Coffin. Harmondsworth: Penguin.

Bainbridge, Alan, and Linden West, ed. *Psychoanalysis and Education: Minding a Gap*. London: Karnac.

Balaci, Gabriel. 2013. "Psychoanalysis in the University." *Euromentor Journal* 4.3: 112–20.

Bálint, Alice. 1931. *A gyermekszoba pszichológiája: Pszichoanalitikai tanulmány* [*The Psychology of the Nursery: A Psychoanalytic Study*]. Budapest: *Pantheon Kiadás*.

Bálint, Alice. 1953. *The Psychoanalysis of the Nursery*. London: Routledge and Kegan Paul.

Bálint, Michael. 1965. "Strength of the Ego and Its Education [1938]." In *Primary Love and Psycho-Analytic Technique*. Rev. ed. New York: Liveright, 189–200.

Ball, Stephen J. 2013. *Foucault, Power, and Education*. New York: Routledge.

Barford, Duncan. 2002. "Psychoanalytic Research on Learning: An Appraisal and Some Suggestions." In *The Ship of Thought: Essays on Psychoanalysis and Learning*. Ed. Duncan Barford. London: Karnac, 17–40.

Bargal, David. 1998. "Kurt Lewin and the First Attempts to Establish a Department of Psychology at the Hebrew University." *Minerva* 36.1: 49–68.

Bar-Haim, Shaul. 2017. "The Liberal Playground: Susan Isaacs, Psychoanalysis and Progressive Education in the Interwar Era." *History of the Human Sciences* 30.1: 94–117.

Barnard-Naudé, Jaco. 2022. *Decolonising the Neoliberal University: Law, Psychoanalysis and the Politics of Student Protest*. Abingdon: Birkbeck Law Press.

Barratt, Barnaby B. 2013. *What Is Psychoanalysis?* London: Routledge.

Barrett, Denia G. 2018. "So You Want to Start a Psychoanalytic School? Succumbing to an Almost 'Irresistible Temptation.'" *The Psychoanalytic Study of the Child* 71.1: 130–36.

Barzin, Nader. 2010. "La psychanalyse en Iran." *Topique* 1.110: 157–71.

Basch, Michael Franz. 1989. "The Teacher, the Transference, and Development." In *Learning and Education: Psychoanalytic Perspectives*. Ed. Kay Field, Bertram J. Cohler, and Glorye Wool. Madison: International Universities Press, 771–87.

Basseches, Harriet. 2003. "Chair of Psychoanalysis, Uncommon or Not?" *American Psychoanalyst* 37.4: 9–10.

Benjamin, Jessica. 2018. *Beyond Doer and Done To: Recognition Theory, Intersubjectivity and the Third*. New York: Routledge.

Berlant, Lauren. 2022. *On the Inconvenience of Other People*. Durham: Duke University Press.

Bernfeld, Siegfried. 1921. *Kinderheim Baumgarten: Bericht über einen ernsthaften Versuch mit neuer Erziehung*. Berlin: Jüdischer Verlag.

Bernfeld, Siegfried. 1973. *Sisyphus; or, The Limits of Education* [*Sisyphos oder die Grenzen der Erziehung*, 1925]. Tr. Frederic Lilge. Berkeley: University of California Press.

Bersani, Leo. 1998. "Against Monogamy." *Oxford Literary Review* 20.1/2: 3–21.

Bettelheim, Bruno. 1969. "Psychoanalysis and Education." *The School Review* 77.2: 73–86.

Bion, Wilfred R. 1959. "Attacks on Linking." *International Journal of Psychoanalysis* 40: 308–15.

Bion, Wilfred R. 1994. *Cogitations: New Extended Edition*. London: Karnac.

Bion, Wilfred R. 2004. *Experiences in Groups and Other Essays*. New York: Taylor and Francis.

Birmingham, Kevin. 2017. "'The Great Shame of Our Profession': How the Humanities Survive on Exploitation." *Chronicle of Higher Education* 63.24: B6–B9.

Bleger, José. 1962. "Clase Inaugural de la Cátedra de Psicoanálisis." *Acta Psiquiátrica y Psicológica Argentina* 8.1: 56–60.

Bloom, Paul. 2023a. "Why We Should Keep Reading Freud." Wall Street Journal February 25, 2023: C3.

Bloom, Paul. 2023b. *Psych: The Story of the Human Mind*. New York: HarperCollins.

Blum, Lawrence D., Richard F. Summers, and Greg Urban. 2016. "Lunch; or, How to Develop an Undergraduate Minor in Psychoanalytic Studies." *The American Psychoanalyst* 50.1: 18–19.

Bok, Derek. 2024. *Attacking the Elites: What Critics Get Wrong—and Right—About America's Leading Universities*. New Haven: Yale University Press.

Bollas, Christopher. 1987. *The Shadow of the Object: Psychoanalysis of the Unthought Known*. New York: Columbia University Press.

Borgos, Anna. 2021. *Women in the Budapest School of Psychoanalysis: Girls of Tomorrow*. London: Routledge.

Bornstein, Robert F. 2001. "The Impending Death of Psychoanalysis." *Psychoanalytic Psychology* 18.1: 3–20.

Bornstein, Robert F. 2002. "The Impending Death of Psychoanalysis: From Destructive Obfuscation to Constructive Dialogue." *Psychoanalytic Psychology* 19.3: 580–90.

Britzman, Deborah P. 1998. *Lost Subjects, Contested Objects: Toward a Psychoanalytic Inquiry of Learning*. Albany: SUNY Press.

Britzman, Deborah P. 1999. "'Thoughts Awaiting Thinkers': Group Psychology and Educational Life." *International Journal of Leadership in Education* 2.4: 313–35.

Britzman, Deborah P. 2003. *After-Education: Anna Freud, Melanie Klein, and Psychoanalytic Histories of Learning*. Albany: SUNY Press.

Britzman, Deborah P. 2015. *A Psychoanalyst in the Classroom: On the Human Condition in Education*. Buffalo: SUNY Press.

Britzman, Deborah P. 2021. *Anticipating Education: Concepts for Imagining Pedagogy with Psychoanalysis*. Gorham: Myers Education Press.

Britzman, Deborah P., and Alice J. Pitt. 1996. "Pedagogy and Transference: Casting the Past of Learning Into the Presence of Teaching." *Theory Into Practice* 35.2: 117–23.

Brooks, Peter. 1987. "The Idea of a Psychoanalytic Literary Criticism." *Critical Inquiry* 13: 334–48.

Burnham, John, ed. 2012. *After Freud Left: A Century of Psychoanalysis in America*. Chicago: University of Chicago Press.

Cardinal, Marie. 1975. *Les mots pour le dire*. Paris: Grasset and Fasquelle.

Chen, Patricia. 2007. "Freud Is Widely Taught at Universities, Except in the Psychology Department." *New York Times*, November 25, 2007: C6.

Chiesa, Lorenzo. 2008. "Of Teaching and the University Discourse." In *Psychoanalytic Practice and State Regulation*. Ed. Ian Parker and Simona Revelli. London: Routledge, 75–84.

Childress, Herb. 2019. *The Adjunct Underclass: How America's Colleges Betrayed Their Faculty, Their Students, and Their Mission*. Chicago: University of Chicago Press.

Chopin, Kate. 1889. *The Awakening*. Chicago: Herbert S. Stone.

Clarke, Brett H. 2017. "The Epistemology Behind the Curtain: Thoughts on the Science of Psychoanalysis." *Psychoanalytic Quarterly* 86.3: 575–608.

Clemens, Justin. 2013. *Psychoanalysis is an Antiphilosophy*. Edinburgh: Edinburgh University Press.

Cohen, Jason E., Sharon D. Raynor, and Dwayne A. Mack. 2021. *Teaching Race in Perilous Times*. Albany: SUNY Press.

Cohen, Jonathan. 2018. "Education." In *Textbook of Applied Psychoanalysis*. Ed. Salman Akhtar and Stuart W. Twemlow. London: Routledge, 231–37.

Cohen, Patricia. 2007. "Freud Is Widely Taught at Universities, Except in the Psychology Department." *New York Times* 157.54139: C6.

Cohen, Sol. 1999. "In the Name of the Prevention of Neurosis: Psychoanalysis and Education in Europe, 1905–1938." *Counterpoints* 76: 157–83.

Cocks, Geoffrey. 1985. *Psychotherapy in the Third Reich: The Göring Institute*. New York: Oxford University Press.

Cole, Gilbert W. 2012. "On Answering Critiques of Psychoanalysis: Empiricism, Unified Theories, and Clinical Innovation." *Psychoanalytic Perspectives* 4.2: 108–21.

Coles, Robert. 1991. *Anna Freud: The Dream of Psychoanalysis*. Reading: Addison-Wesley.

Coriat, Isador H. 1919. *What Is Psychoanalysis?* London: Routledge, Trench, Trubner.

Coriat, Isador H. 1926. "The Psycho-Analytic Approach to Education." *Progressive Education* 3.1: 19–25.

Cornell University Student Assembly. 2023. "Resolution 31: Mandating Content Warnings for Traumatic Content in the Classroom." March 23, 2023. https://assembly.cornell.edu/sites/default/files/resolution_31_-_content_warnings.pdf.

Cory, Herbert Ellsworth. 1919. *The Intellectuals and the Wage Workers: A Study in Educational Psychoanalysis*. New York: Sunwise Turn.

Council of the Sociological Society. 1924. "Annual Report of the Sociological Society." *Sociological Review* a16.3: 262–64.

Crews, Frederick C. 1994. "The Revenge of the Repressed: Part II." *New York Review of Books* 41.20: 49–58.

Crichton-Miller, Hugh. 1922. *The New Psychology and the Teacher*. New York: Thomas Seltzer.

Croall, Jonathan. 1983. *Neill of Summerhill: The Permanent Rebel*. New York: Pantheon Books.

Culp, Julian, Johannes Drerup, and Douglas Yacek, ed. 2023. *The Cambridge Handbook of Democratic Education*. Cambridge: Cambridge University Press.

Dagfal, Alejandro A. 2018. "Psychology and Psychoanalysis in Argentina: Politics, French Thought, and the University Connection, 1955–1976." *History of Psychology* 21.3: 254–72.

Damasio, Antonio. 2018. *The Strange Order of Things: Life, Feeling, and the Making of Cultures*. New York: Pantheon.

D'Amour, Lissa. 2020. *Relational Psychoanalysis at the Heart of Teaching and Learning: How and Why It Matters*. Abingdon: Routledge.

Daniels, George E., and Lawrence C. Kolb. 1960. "The Columbia University Psychoanalytic Clinic: An Experiment in University Teaching in Psychoanalysis." *Journal of Medical Education* 35: 164–71.

Danto, Elizabeth Ann. 2012. "'Have You No Shame'—American Redbaiting of Europe's Psychoanalysts." In *Psychoanalysis and Politics: Histories of Psychoanalysis under Conditions of Restricted Political Freedom*. Ed. Joy Damousi and Mariano Ben Plotkin. Oxford: Oxford University Press, 213–32.

Danto, Elizabeth Ann. 2018. "The Hietzing Years." *Psychoanalytic Study of the Child* 71.1: 137–48.

Danto, Elizabeth Ann. 2023. "Anna Freud's Advances in Community Psychoanalysis." *Psychoanalytic Social Work* 30.2: 1–13.

Danto, Elizabeth Ann, and Alexandra Steiner-Strauss, ed. 2019. *Freud/Tiffany: Anna Freud, Dorothy Tiffany Burlingham and the "Best Possible School" 1920s Vienna and Beyond: An Illustrated Book of Memoir and History*. London: Routledge.

Derrida, Jacques. 1983. "The Principle of Reason: The University in the Eyes of Its Pupils." Tr. Catherine Porter and Edward P. Morris. *Diacritics* 13.3: 3–20.

Derrida, Jacques. 2002a. *Who's Afraid of Philosophy?: Right to Philosophy 1*. Tr. Jan Plug. Stanford: Stanford University Press.

Derrida, Jacques. 2002b. "The University without Condition." In *Without Alibi*. Tr. Peggy Kamuf. Stanford: Stanford University Press, 202–37.

Derrida, Jacques. 2004. *Eyes of the University: Right to Philosophy, 2*. Tr. Jan Plug et al. Stanford: Stanford University Press.

De Stefano, Cristina. 2022. *The Child Is the Teacher: A Life of Maria Montessori* [*Il bambino è il maestro: Vita di Maria Montessori, 2020*]. Tr. Gregory Conti. New York: Other Press.

Dezza, Irene Cogliati, Eric Schulz, and Charley M. Wu, ed. 2022. *The Drive for Knowledge: The Science of Human Information Seeking*. Cambridge: Cambridge University Press.

Diamond, Michael A. 1993. *The Unconscious Life of Organizations*. Westport: Quorum.

Dobson, Marcia D-S. 2023. "Building an Undergraduate Psychoanalytic Studies Program." *Psyche on Campus* (blog). University of Pennsylvania. June 21, 2023. https://web.sas. upenn.edu/psycheoncampus/2023/06/21/building-an-undergraduate-psychoanalytic-studies-program/.

Dobson, Marcia D.-S., and John Riker. 2019. "Epilogue: Psychoanalysis and Undergraduate Education: A National Picture and Hopes for the Future." *Psychoanalytic Inquiry* 39.6: 469–71.

Dosse, François. 1997. *History of Structuralism, Volume 2: The Sign Sets, 1967–Present* [1992]. Tr. Deborah Glassman. Minneapolis: University of Minnesota Press.

Dybel, Paweł. 2020. *Psychoanalysis—The Promised Land? The History of Psychoanalysis in Poland 1900–1989: Part I. The Sturm und Drang Period. Beginnings of Psychoanalysis in the Polish Lands during the Partitions 1900–1918*. Tr. Tomasz Bieroń. Berlin: Peter Lang.

Economist. 2024. "Universities Are Failing to Boost Economic Growth." *The Economist*. February 5, 2024. https://www-economist-com.proxy.library.upenn.edu/finance-and-economics/2024/02/05/universities-are-failing-to-boost-economic-growth.

Edelman, Lee. 2022. *Bad Education: Why Queer Theory Teaches Us Nothing*. Durham: Duke University Press.

Eifermann, Rivka R. 1993. "Teaching and Learning in an Analytic Mode—A Model for Studying Psychoanalysis at University." *International Journal of Psychoanalysis* 74: 1005–15.

Eissler, Kurt R. 1965. *Medical Orthodoxy and the Future of Psychoanalysis*. New York: International Universities Press.

Elia, Luciano da Fonseca. 2016. "A lógica da diferença irredutível: a formação do psicanalista não é tarefa da universidade." *Estudos e Pesquisas em Psicologia* 16.4: 1138–52.

Elliott, Anthony, and Jeffrey Prager, ed. 2016. *The Routledge Handbook of Psychoanalysis in the Social Sciences and Humanities*. London: Routledge.

Elson, Miriam. 1989. "The Teacher as Learner, the Learner as Teacher." In *Learning and Education: Psychoanalytic Perspectives*. Ed. Kay Field, Bertram J. Cohler, and Glorye Wool. Madison: International Universities Press, 789–808.

Emre, Merve. 2023. "Are You My Mother? Transference and the Contemporary Classroom." *The New Yorker*. 11 July 2023, online only. https://www.newyorker.com/culture/cultural-comment/are-you-my-mother.

Eng, David L., and Shinhee Han. 2019. *Racial Melancholia, Racial Dissociation: On the Social and Psychic Lives of Asian Americans*. Durham: Duke University Press.

Erikson [originally Homburger], Erik H. 1987a. "Dorothy Burlingham's School in Vienna [1980]. In *A Way of Looking at Things: Selected Papers from 1930 to 1980*. Ed. Stephen Schlein. New York: W. W. Norton, 3–13.

Erikson [originally Homburger], Erik H. 1987b. "The Fate of the Drives in School Compositions [1931]." In *A Way of Looking at Things: Selected Papers from 1930 to 1980*. Ed. Stephen Schlein. New York: W. W. Norton, 39–69.

Erikson [originally Homburger], Erik H. 1987c. "Psychoanalysis and the Future of Education [1930]." In *A Way of Looking at Things: Selected Papers from 1930 to 1980*. Ed. Stephen Schlein. New York: W. W. Norton, 14–30.

Erikson [originally Homburger], Erik H. 1987d. "Late Adolescence [1959]." In *A Way of Looking at Things: Selected Papers from 1930 to 1980*. Ed. Stephen Schlein. New York: W. W. Norton, 631–43.

Erikson, Erik H., and Joan Erikson. 1980. "Dorothy Burlingham's School in Vienna." *Bulletin of the Hampstead Clinic* 3: 91–94.

Erős, Ferenc. 2023. "The Problems of Education and Society in the Budapest School of Psychoanalysis." In *Michael Balint and His World: The Budapest Years*. Ed. Judit Szekacs-Weisz, Raluca Soreanu, and Ivan Ward. London: Routledge, 18–29.

Etezady, M. Hossein, Inga Blom, and Mary Davis, ed. 2018. *Psychoanalytic Trends in Theory and Practice: The Second Century of the Talking Cure*. Lanham: Lexington Books.

Etkind, Alexander. 1997. *Eros of the Impossible: The History of Psychoanalysis in Russia* [1993]. Tr. Noah and Maria Rubins. Boulder: Westview.

Fanon, Frantz. 1967. *Black Skin, White Masks* [*Peau Noire, Masques Blancs*, 1952]. Tr. Charles Lam Markmann. New York: Grove.

Fanon, Frantz. 2018. *Écrits sur l'aliénation et la liberté*. Paris: Éditions la Découverte.

Fassin, Didier. 2019. "How Is Critique?" In *A Time for Critique*. Ed. Didier Fassin and Bernard Harcourt. New York: Columbia University Press, 13–35.

Felman, Shoshana. 1982. "Psychoanalysis and Education: Teaching Terminable and Interminable." *Yale French Studies* 63: 21–44.

Fenichel, Otto. 1945. *The Psychoanalytic Theory of Neurosis*. New York: W. W. Norton.

Ferenczi, Sándor. 2002. "Psychoanalysis and Education [1908]." In *Final Contributions to the Problems and Methods of Psycho-Analysis*. London: Karnac, 280–90

Field, Kay. 1989. "Some Reflections on the Teacher-Student Dialogue: A Psychoanalytic Perspective." In *Learning and Education: Psychoanalytic Perspectives*. Ed. Kay Field, Bertram J. Cohler, and Glorye Wool. Madison: International Universities Press.

Field, Kelly. 2023. "Professors Struggle With Demands to Tend to Students' Mental Health." *Chronicle of Higher Education* 70.6: 6.

Fink, Bruce. 2017. "The Master Signifier and the Four Discourses." In *Key Concepts of Lacanian Psychoanalysis*. Ed. Dany Nobus. London: Karnac, 29–47.

Fisher, David James. 2008. *Bettelheim: Living and Dying*. Amsterdam: Rodopi.

Flexner, Abraham. 1910. *Medical Education in the United States and Canada*. New York: Carnegie Foundation.

Flexner, Abraham. 2017. *The Usefulness of Useless Knowledge* [1939]. Princeton: Princeton University Press.

Florence, Jean, ed. 2002. *La psychanalyse et l'université: L'expérience de Louvain*. Louvain-La-Neuve: Academia Bruylant.

Fonagy, Peter. 2015. "The Effectiveness of Psychodynamic Psychotherapies: An Update." *World Psychiatry* 14.2: 137–50.

Forrester, John. 1991. *The Seductions of Psychoanalysis: Freud, Lacan and Derrida*. Cambridge: Cambridge University Press.

Foucault, Michel. 1979. *Discipline and Punish: The Birth of the Prison* [*Surveiller et punir; naissance de la prison*, 1975]. Tr. Alan Sheridan. New York: Vintage.

Foucault, Michel. 1994. *The Order of Things: An Archaeology of the Human Sciences* [1966]. Tr. Alan Sheridan. New York: Vintage.

Foucault, Michel. 2006. *History of Madness* [1972]. Tr. Jonathan Murphy and Jean Khalfa. London: Routledge.

French, Robert B. 1997. "The Teacher as Container of Anxiety: Psychoanalysis and the Role of Teacher." *Journal of Management Education* 21.4: 483–95.

Freud, Anna. 1935. *Psycho-Analysis for Teachers and Parents: Introductory Lectures* [*Einführung in die Psychoanalyse für Pädagogen*, 1930]. Tr. Barbara Low. New York: Emerson

Freud, Anna. 1968a. *The Ego and the Mechanisms of Defense* [1939]. Rev. ed. London: Karnac.

Freud, Anna. 1968b. "Willie Hoffer, M.D., Ph.D." *The Psychoanalytic Study of the Child* 23.1: 7–11.

Freud, Anna. 1978. "Inaugural Lecture for the Sigmund Freud Chair at the Hebrew University, Jerusalem." *International Journal of Psychoanalysis* 59: 145–48.

Freud, Anna. 1989. *Normality and Pathology in Childhood: Assessments of Development* [1966]. London: Karnac.

Freud, Sigmund. 1912. Letter from Sigmund Freud to C. G. Jung, March 21, 1912. In *The Freud/Jung Letters: The Correspondence Between Sigmund Freud and C. G. Jung*. Ed. William McGuire. Princeton: Princeton University Press, 494–5.

Freud, Sigmund. 1953. *Three Essays on the Theory of Sexuality* [1905]. Tr. James Strachey. In *The Standard Edition of the Complete Psychological Works of Sigmund Freud*. London: Hogarth, 7: 123–245.

Freud, Sigmund. 1955a. "Analysis of a Phobia in a Five-Year-Old Boy [1909]." Tr. James Strachey. In *The Standard Edition of the Complete Psychological Works of Sigmund Freud*. London: Hogarth, 10: 1–149.

Freud, Sigmund. 1955b. "The Claims of Psycho-Analysis to Scientific Interest [1913]." Tr. James Strachey. In *The Standard Edition of the Complete Psychological Works of Sigmund Freud*. London: Hogarth, 13: 163–90.

Freud, Sigmund. 1955c. *Group Psychology and the Analysis of the Ego* [1920]. Tr. James Strachey. In *The Standard Edition of the Complete Psychological Works of Sigmund Freud*. London: Hogarth, 18: 65–143.

Freud, Sigmund. 1955d. "Lines of Advance in Psycho-Analytic Therapy [1919]." Tr. James Strachey. In *The Standard Edition of the Complete Psychological Works of Sigmund Freud*. London: Hogarth, 17: 157–68.

Freud, Sigmund. 1955e. "Notes Upon a Case of Obsessional Neurosis [1909]." Tr. James Strachey. In *The Standard Edition of the Complete Psychological Works of Sigmund Freud*. London: Hogarth Press, 10: 151–318.

Freud, Sigmund. 1955f. "On the Teaching of Psycho-Analysis in Universities." Tr. James Strachey. In *The Standard Edition of the Complete Psychological Works of Sigmund Freud*. London: Hogarth, 17: 169–73.

Freud, Sigmund. 1955g. "Preface to J. J. Putnam's *Addresses on Psycho-Analysis* [1921]." Tr. James Strachey. In *The Standard Edition of the Complete Psychological Works of Sigmund Freud*. London: Hogarth, 18: 269–70.

Freud, Sigmund. 1957a. Leonardo da Vinci and a Memory of His Childhood [1910]. Tr. James Strachey. In *The Standard Edition of the Complete Psychological Works of Sigmund Freud*. London: Hogarth, 11: 57–137.

Freud, Sigmund. 1957b. "On the History of the Psycho-Analytic Movement [1914]." Tr. James Strachey. In *The Standard Edition of the Complete Psychological Works of Sigmund Freud*. London: Hogarth, 14: 1–66.

Freud, Sigmund. 1958a. "Formulations on the Two Principles of Mental Functioning [1911]." Tr. James Strachey. In *The Standard Edition of the Complete Psychological Works of Sigmund Freud*. London: Hogarth, 12: 213–26.

Freud, Sigmund. 1958b. "Introduction to Pfister's *The Psycho-Analytic Method* [1913]." Tr. James Strachey. In *The Standard Edition of the Complete Psychological Works of Sigmund Freud*. London: Hogarth, 12: 327–31.

Freud, Sigmund. 1958c. "Recommendations to Physicians Practising Psycho-Analysis [1912]." Tr. James Strachey. In *The Standard Edition of the Complete Psychological Works of Sigmund Freud*. London: Hogarth, 12: 107–20.

Freud, Sigmund. 1958d. "Some Reflections on Schoolboy Psychology [1914]." Tr. James Strachey. *The Standard Edition of the Complete Psychological Works of Sigmund Freud*. London: Hogarth, 13: 239–44.

Freud, Sigmund. 1959a. "An Autobiographical Study [1925]." Tr. James Strachey. In *The Standard Edition of the Complete Psychological Works of Sigmund Freud*. London: Hogarth 20: 1–74.

Freud, Sigmund. 1959b. "Delusions and Dreams in Jensen's *Gradiva* [1907]." Tr. James Strachey. In *The Standard Edition of the Complete Psychological Works of Sigmund Freud*. London: Hogarth 9: 1–95.

Freud, Sigmund. 1959c. "The Question of Lay Analysis [1926]." Tr. James Strachey. In *The Standard Edition of the Complete Psychological Works of Sigmund Freud*. London: Hogarth, 20: 177–258.

Freud, Sigmund. 1960a. *Jokes and Their Relation to the Unconscious* [1905]. Tr. James Strachey. In *The Standard Edition of the Complete Psychological Works of Sigmund Freud*. London: Hogarth, 8: 1–258.

Freud, Sigmund. 1960b. *Letters of Sigmund Freud: 1873–1939*. Tr. Tania and James Stern. New York: Basic Books.

Freud, Sigmund. 1961a. *Civilization and Its Discontents* [1930]. Tr. James Strachey. In *The Standard Edition of the Complete Psychological Works of Sigmund Freud*. London: Hogarth, 21: 57–145.

Freud, Sigmund. 1961b. Letter from Sigmund Freud to Judah Magnes, December 5, 1933. In *Letters of Sigmund Freud, 1873–1939*. Tr. James and Tania Stern. London: Hogarth, 418–19.

Freud, Sigmund. 1961c. "Preface to Aichhorn's *Wayward Youth* ["Geleitwort," 1925]." Tr. James Strachey. In *The Standard Edition of the Complete Psychological Works of Sigmund Freud*. London: Hogarth, 19: 271–75.

Freud, Sigmund. 1963. *Introductory Lectures on Psycho-Analysis (Part III)* [1917]. Tr. James Strachey. In *The Standard Edition of the Complete Psychological Works of Sigmund Freud*. London: Hogarth, 1–496.

Freud, Sigmund. 1964a. "Analysis Terminable and Interminable [1937]." Tr. James Strachey. In *The Standard Edition of the Complete Psychological Works of Sigmund Freud*. London: Hogarth, 23: 209–53.

Freud, Sigmund. 1964b. *New Introductory Lectures on Psycho-Analysis* [1933]. Tr. James Strachey. In *The Standard Edition of the Complete Psychological Works of Sigmund Freud*. London: Hogarth, 22: 1–182.

Freud, Sigmund, and Sándor Ferenczi. 2000. *The Correspondence of Sigmund Freud and Sándor Ferenczi*. 3 vols. Tr. Peter T. Hoffer. Cambridge: Harvard University Press.

Frosh, Stephen. 2010. *Psychoanalysis Outside the Clinic: Interventions in Psychosocial Studies*. Houndmills: Palgrave Macmillan.

Frosh, Stephen. 2022. "Psychoanalysis through a Psychosocial Lens." *Psyche on Campus* (blog). University of Pennsylvania. July 13, 2022. https://web.sas.upenn.edu/psycheoncampus/2022/07/13/psychoanalysis-through-a-psychosocial-lens/#more-285.

Gallo, Rubén. 2010. *Freud's Mexico: Into the Wilds of Psychoanalysis*. Cambridge: MIT Press.

Gallop, Jane. 1997. *Feminist Accused of Sexual Harassment*. Durham: Duke University Press.

Gana, Nouri. 2023. *Melancholy Acts: Defeat and Cultural Critique in the Arab World*. New York: Fordham University Press.

Gardner, Dorothy E. M. 1969. *Susan Isaacs*. London: Methuen Educational.

Gaztambide, Daniel José. 2019. *A People's History of Psychoanalysis: From Freud to Liberation Psychology*. Lanham: Lexington Books.

Gay, Peter. 1998. *Freud: A Life for Our Time*. New York: W. W. Norton.

Gherovici, Patricia, and Christopher Christian, ed. 2019. *Psychoanalysis in the Barrios: Race, Class, and the Unconscious*. London: Routledge.

Gieryn, Thomas F. 1983. "Boundary-Work and the Demarcation of Science from Non-Science: Strains and Interests in Professional Ideologies of Scientists." *American Sociological Review* 48: 781–95.

Giffney, Noreen. 2023. "How Do We Teach Psychoanalytic Theory?" *New Associations* 39: 5.

Gilman, Sander. 2009. "Psychoanalysis and the University: The Clinical Dimension." *International Journal of Psychoanalysis* 90: 1103–05.

Ginsberg, Benjamin. 2013. *Fall of the Faculty: The Rise of the All-Administrative University and Why It Matters*. Oxford: Oxford University Press.

Giroux, Susan Searls. 2010. *Between Race and Reason: Violence, Intellectual Responsibility, and the University to Come*. Stanford: Stanford University Press.

Gitre, Edward J. K. 2010. "Importing Freud: First-Wave Psychoanalysis, Interwar Social Sciences, and the Interdisciplinary Foundations of an American Social Theory." *Journal of the History of the Behavioral Sciences* 46.3: 239–62.

Goffman, Erving. 1963. *Stigma: Notes on the Management of Spoiled Identity*. New York: Touchstone.

Goldberg, Sarah. 2021. "Fresh Sufferings: Psychoanalysts in the Retirement Phase." Ph.D. diss., Institute for Clinical Social Work.

Goldberg, Sarah. 2022. "Fresh Sufferings: On When Analysts Won't Terminate." *Parapraxis* 1 (December 2022), www.parapraxismagazine.com/articles/fresh-sufferings.

Goodchild, Lester F. 1991. "Higher Education as a Field of Study: Its Origins, Programs, and Purposes, 1893–1960." *New Directions for Higher Education* 76: 15–32.

Grady, Melissa. 2011. "Who Will Teach Psychodynamics in the Future?" *American Psychoanalyst* 45.2: 26–27.

Graham, Philip. 2008. "Susan Isaacs and the Malting House School." *Journal of Child Psychotherapy* 34.1: 5–22.

Graham, Philip. 2009. *Susan Isaacs: A Life Freeing the Minds of Children*. London: Karnac.

Green, George Herbert. 1922. *Psychanalysis* [sic] *in the Classroom*. New York: G. P. Putnam's Sons.

Gutkin, Len. 2023. "Triumph of the Therapeutic: Competing Perspectives on the Activist Classroom Now." *Chronicle of Higher Education* 69.24: 44.

Gyimesi, Júlia. 2010. "The Problem of Demarcation: Psychoanalysis and the Occult." *American Imago* 66.4: 457–70.

Habarth, Janice, James Hansell, and Tyler Grove. 2011. "How Accurately Do Introductory Psychology Textbooks Present Psychoanalytic Theory?" *Teaching of Psychology* 38.1: 16–21.

Hai, Alessandra Arce, Helen May, Kristen Nawrotzki, Larry Prochner, and Yordanka Valkanova. 2020. *Reimagining Teaching in Early 20th Century Experimental Schools.* Cham: Palgrave Macmillan.

Hale, Nathan G., Jr. 1971. *Freud and the Americans: The Beginnings of Psychoanalysis in the United States, 1876–1917.* New York: Oxford University Press.

Hale, Nathan G., Jr. 1995. *The Rise and Crisis of Psychoanalysis in United States: Freud and the Americans, 1917–1985.* New York: Oxford University Press.

Hall, G. Stanley. 1923. *Life and Confessions of a Psychologist.* New York: D. Appleton.

Hall, Stuart. 2021. "Teaching Race." In *Selected Writings on Race and Difference.* Ed. Paul Gilroy and Ruth Wilson Gilmore. Durham: Duke University Press, 123–35.

Hamilton, Laura T., and Kelly Nielsen, 2021. *Broke: The Racial Consequences of Underfunding Public Universities.* Chicago: University of Chicago Press.

Hanly, Charles. 2014. "The Interplay of Deductive and Inductive Reasoning in Psychoanalytic Theorizing." *Psychoanalytic Quarterly* 88.4: 897–915.

Heller, Peter, ed. 1992. *Anna Freud's letters to Eva Rosenfeld.* Tr. Mary Weigand. Madison: International Universities Press.

Herman, Ellen. 1995. *The Romance of American Psychology: Political Culture in the Age of Experts.* Berkeley: University of California Press.

Herzog, Dagmar. 2017. *Cold War Freud: Psychoanalysis in an Age of Catastrophes.* Cambridge: Cambridge University Press.

Hoffman, Leon. 2010. "The First Century of Psychoanalytic Ideas: Toward Greater Scientific Empiricism." *JAPA* 58.2: 349–57.

Holland, Norman. 1968. *The Dynamics of Literary Response.* Oxford: Oxford University Press.

Horkheimer, Max. 2007. *A Life in Letters: Selected Correspondence.* Tr. Manfred R. Jacobson and Evelyn M. Jacobson. Lincoln: University of Nebraska Press.

Houssier, Florian, and François Marty. 2009. "Drawing on Psychoanalytic Pedagogy: The Influence of August Aichhorn on the Psychotherapy of Adolescents." *Psychoanalytic Quarterly* 78.4: 1091–108.

Huertas-Maestro, Miguel, Silvia Lévy, and Rafael Huertas. 2022. "Psychoanalysis and Academia: The Case of Ángel Garma and the University of Buenos Aires." *International Journal of Psychoanalysis* 103.6: 1002–24.

Hunt, Joshua. 2018. *University of Nike: How Corporate Cash Bought American Higher Education.* New York: Melville House.

Isaacs, Susan. 1930. *The Intellectual Growth of Young Children.* London: Routledge and Kegan Paul.

Isaacs, Susan. 1933. *Social Development in Young Children: A Study of Beginnings.* London: Routledge and Kegan Paul.

Jagodzinski, Jan, ed. 2002. *Pedagogical Desire: Authority, Seduction, Transference, and the Question of Ethics.* Westport: Bergin and Garvey.

Jay, Gregory S. 1987. "The Subject of Pedagogy: Lessons in Psychoanalysis and Politics." *College English* 49.7: 785–800.

Jay, Martin. 1996. *The Dialectical Imagination: A History of the Frankfurt School and the Institute of Social Research, 1923–1950* [1973]. Berkeley: University of California Press.

Jersild, Arthur T. 1955. *When Teachers Face Themselves.* New York: Teachers College.

Johnson, T. R. 2014. *The Other Side of Pedagogy: Lacan's Four Discourses and the Development of the Student Writer*. Albany: State University of New York Press.

Jones, Edward G., and Lorne M. Mendell. 1999. "Assessing the Decade of the Brain." *Science* 284.5415: 739.

Jones, Ernest. 1910. "Psycho-Analysis and Education." *Journal of Educational Psychology* 1.9: 497–520.

Jones, Ernest. 1912. "Psycho-Analysis and Education: The Value of Sublimating Processes for Education and Re-Education." *Journal of Educational Psychology* 3.5: 241–56.

Jones, Ernest, ed. 1924. *Social Aspects of Psychoanalysis*. London: Williams and Norgate.

Jones, Ernest. 1928. *What is Psychoanalysis?* London: Allen and Unwin.

Jones, Ernest. 1957. *The Life and Work of Sigmund Freud*. 3 vols. New York: Basic Books.

Jung, Carl. 1981. *The Development of Personality*. Tr. R. F. C. Hull. Princeton: Princeton University Press.

Keats, John. 2005. *Selected Letters of John Keats*. Rev ed. Ed. Grant F. Scott. Cambridge: Harvard University Press.

Kernberg, Otto F. 2011. "Psychoanalysis and the University: A Difficult Relationship." *International Journal of Psychoanalysis* 92: 609–22.

Kernberg, Otto F. 2016. *Psychoanalytic Education at the Crossroads: Reformation, Change and the Future of Psychoanalytic Training*. London: Routledge.

Khanna, Ranjana. 2003. *Dark Continents: Psychoanalysis and Colonialism*. Durham: Duke University Press.

Kimball, Roger. 1990. *Tenured Radicals: How Politics Has Corrupted Our Higher Education*. New York: Harper and Row.

Kirsner, Douglas. 2009. *Unfree Associations: Inside Psychoanalytic Institutes: Updated Edition*. Lanham: Jason Aronson.

Klein, Melanie. 1975a. "The Development of a Child" [1921]. In *Love, Guilt and Reparation and Other Works, 1921–1945*. Ed. Roger Money-Kyrle. New York: Free Press, 1–53.

Klein, Melanie. 1975b. "The Early Development of Conscience in the Child [1933]." In *Love, Guilt and Reparation and Other Works, 1921–1945*. Ed. Roger Money-Kyrle. New York: Free Press, 248–61.

Klein, Melanie. 1975c. "Early Stages of the Oedipus Conflict [1928]." In *Love, Guilt and Reparation and Other Works, 1921–1945*. Ed. Roger Money-Kyrle. New York: Free Press, 186–98.

Kris, Ernst. 1948. "On Psychoanalysis and Education." *American Journal of Orthopsychiatry* 18.4: 622–35.

Kubie, Lawrence. 1954. "The Forgotten Man of Education." *Harvard Alumni Bulletin* (February 6, 1954): 349–53.

Kurzweil, Edith. 1989. *The Freudians: A Comparative Perspective*. New Haven: Yale University Press.

Lacan, Jacques. 1968. "De Rome 53 à Rome 67: La psychanalyse. Raison d'un échec." *Silicet* 1: 42–50.

Lacan, Jacques. 1971. "En guise de conclusion." *Lettres de l'école freudienne* 8: 205–17.

Lacan, Jacques. 1988. *The Seminar of Jacques Lacan, Book II: The Ego in Freud's Theory and in the Technique of Psychoanalysis, 1954–1955*. New York: W. W. Norton, 228–29.

Lacan, Jacques. 1990. *Television* [1974]. Tr. Denis Hollier, Rosalind Krauss, and Annette Michelson. New York: W. W. Norton.

Lacan, Jacques. 1991. *Le Séminaire, Livre XVII: L'envers de la psychanalyse*. Ed. Jacques-Alain Miller. Paris: Seuil.

Lacan, Jacques. 1992. *The Seminar of Jacques Lacan, Book VII: The Ethics of Psychoanalysis, 1959–1960* [*Le Séminaire, Livre VII: L'éthique de la psychanalyse*], 1986. Tr. Dennis Porter. New York: W. W. Norton.

Lacan, Jacques. 1997. *The Seminar of Jacques Lacan, Book III: The Psychoses, 1955–1956* [1981]. Tr. Russell Grigg. New York: W. W. Norton.

Lacan, Jacques. 1998. "Of the Subject Who Is Supposed to Know, of the First Dyad, and of the Good." In *The Seminar of Jacques Lacan, Book XI: The Four Fundamental Concepts of Psychoanalysis* [1973]. Tr. Alan Sheridan. New York: W. W. Norton, 230–43.

Lacan, Jacques. 2001a. "Allocution sur l'enseignement." In *Autres écrits*. Ed. Jacques-Alain Miller. Paris: Éditions du Seuil, 297–305.

Lacan, Jacques. 2001b. "Peut-être à Vincennes." In *Autres écrits*. Ed. Jacques-Alain Miller. Paris: Éditions du Seuil, 313–15.

Lacan, Jacques. 2004. *Séminaire livre X – L'angoisse* [*The Seminar of Jacques Lacan, Book X: Anxiety*, 2014]. Ed. Jacques-Alain Miller. Paris: Seuil.

Lacan, Jacques. 2006. *Écrits*. Tr. Bruce Fink. New York: W. W. Norton.

Lacan, Jacques. 2008. *My Teaching* [*Mon Enseignement*, 2005]. Tr. David Macey. London: Verso.

Lagache, Daniel. 1955. *La psychanalyse (Que sais-je?)*. Paris: Presses Universitaires de France.

Lagache, Daniel. 1986. "La psychologie et les sciences psychologiques [1966]." In *La folle du logis: La psychanalyse comme science exacte*. Paris: Presses Universitaires de France, 193–99.

Lampert, Magdalene. 1990. "When the Problem Is Not the Question and the Solution Is Not the Answer: Mathematical Knowing and Teaching." *American Educational Research Journal* 27.1: 29–63.

Laplanche, Jean. 1975a. "L'enseignement de la psychanalyse à l'Université." *Bulletin de Psychologie* 28.317: 653–59.

Laplanche, Jean. 1987. *Problématiques V: Le baquet: Transcendance du transfère*. Paris: Presses Universitaires de France.

Laplanche, Jean. 1989. *New Foundations for Psychoanalysis* [*Nouveaux fondements pour la psychanalyse*, 1987]. Tr. David Macey. Oxford: Basil Blackwell.

Laplanche, Jean. 2000. Interviewed by Peter Osborne and John Fletcher: "The Other Within—Rethinking Psychoanalysis." *Radical Philosophy* 102: 31–41.

Laplanche, Jean. 2004. "Pour la psychanalyse à l'Université." *Recherches en Psychanalyse* 1.1: 9–13.

Lasch, Christopher. 1974. "Freud and Women." *New York Review of Books* 21.15: 12–17.

Lay, Wilfrid. 1920. *The Child's Unconscious Mind: The Relations of Psychoanalysis to Education: A Book for Teachers and Parents*. New York: Dodd, Mead.

Lear, Jonathan. 2005. "Teaching Psychoanalysis at University and Making It Matter." *American Psychoanalyst* 39.2: 13–17.

Leary, Kimberlyn. 2000. "Racial Enactments in Dynamic Treatment." *Psychoanalytic Dialogues* 10: 639–53.

Levendosky, Alytia A., Joshua E. Turchan, Xiaochen Luo, and Evan Good. "A Re-introduction of the Psychodynamic Approach to the Standard Clinical Psychology Curriculum." *Journal of Clinical Psychology* 79.10: 2439–51.

Lieber, Emma. 2024. E-mail message to author, February 23, 2024.

Liss, Edward. 1941. "Learning Difficulties: Unresolved Anxiety and Resultant Learning Patters." *American Journal of Orthopsychiatry* 11.3: 520–23.

Long, Carol, Gillian Eagle, and Garth Stevens. 2017. "The Clinician in the University: Reflections on a South African Psychoanalytically Oriented Doctoral Program." *International Journal of Psychoanalysis* 98: 517–42.

Low, Barbara. 1924. "The Bearing of Psycho-Analysis upon Education." In *Social Aspects of Psycho-Analysis*. Ed. Ernest Jones. London: Williams & Norgate, 169–208.

Low, Barbara. 1928. *Psycho-Analysis and Education*. New York: Harcourt, Brace.

Low, Barbara. 1929. "A Note on the Influence of Psycho-Analysis upon English Education During the Last Eighteen Years. *International Journal of Psycho-Analysis* 10: 314–20.

Löwenthal, Leo. 1987. *An Unmastered Past: The Autobiographical Reflections of Leo Lowenthal*. Berkeley: University of California Press.

Luxon, Nancy. 2013. *Crisis of Authority: Politics, Trust, and Truth-Telling in Freud and Foucault*. Cambridge: Cambridge University Press.

Mannoni, Maud. 1973. *Éducation impossible*. Paris: Seuil.

Mannoni, Maud. 1999. *Separation and Creativity: Refinding the Lost Language of Childhood*. Tr. Susan Fairfield. New York: Other Press.

Marcus, Paul. 2021. *Psychoanalysis as a Spiritual Discipline: In Dialogue with Martin Buber and Gabriel Marcel*. London: Routledge.

McIvor, David W. 2015. "Pressing the Subject: Critical Theory and the Death Drive." *Constellations* 22.3: 405–19.

McWilliams, Nancy. 2000. "On Teaching Psychoanalysis in Antianalytic Times: A Polemic." *American Journal of Psychoanalysis* 60.4: 371–90.

Means, Alexander J., and Graham B. Slater. 2023. "Defending a Future University to Come." *Review of Education, Pedagogy, and Cultural Studies* 45.1: 1–3.

Medawar, Peter. 1975. "Victims of Psychiatry." *New York Review of Books* 21.21-22: 17.

Meltzer, Françoise. 1987. "Editor's Introduction: Partitive Plays, Pipe Dreams." *Critical Inquiry* 13: 215–21.

Mészáros, Judit. 2012. "Effect of Dictatorial Regimes on the Psychoanalytic Movement in Hungary before and after World War II." In *Psychoanalysis and Politics: Histories of Psychoanalysis under Conditions of Restricted Political Freedom*. Ed. Joy Damousi and Mariano Ben Plotkin. Oxford: Oxford University Press, 79–108.

Mészáros, Judit. 2014. *Ferenczi and Beyond: Exile of the Budapest School and Solidarity in the Psychoanalytic Movement during the Nazi Years* [2008]. Tr. Thomas A. Williams. London: Routledge.

Midgley, Nick. 2008. "The 'Matchbox School (1927–1932): Anna Freud and the Idea of a 'Psychoanalytically Informed Education.'" *Journal of Child Psychotherapy* 34.1: 23–42.

Midgley, Nick. 2013. *Reading Anna Freud*. London: Routledge.

Mijolla, Alain de, ed. 2005. *International Dictionary of Psychoanalysis*. Detroit: Thompson Gale.

Miles, Robert. 1993. *Racism After 'Race relations'*. London: Routledge.

Miller, Jacques-Alain. 1990. "Microscopia: An Introduction to the Reading of *Television*." In *Television* [1974], *by Jacques Lacan*. Tr. Denis Hollier, Rosalind Krauss, and Annette Michelson. New York: W. W. Norton, xi–xxxi.

Millot, Catherine. 1979. *Freud: Anti-pédagogue*. Paris: Bibliothèque d'Ornicar?

Mills, John. 2015. "Psychoanalysis and the Ideologies of Science." *Psychoanalytic Inquiry* 35: 24–44.

Mintz, Steve. 2023. "The Psychodynamics of the College Classroom." *Inside Higher Ed*, 25 July 2023, online only, https://www.insidehighered.com/opinion/blogs/higher-ed-gamma/2023/07/25/psychodynamics-college-classroom.

Mitchell, Juliet. 1974. *Psychoanalysis and Feminism*. London: Allen Lane.

Mitchell, Stephen A. 1988. *Relational Concepts in Psychoanalysis: An Integration*. Cambridge: Harvard University Press.

Mitchell, Stephen A., and Margaret J. Black. 2016. *Freud and Beyond: A History of Modern Psychoanalytic Thought* [1995]. Rev. ed. New York: Basic Books.

Murād, Yūsuf. 1943. *Shifaʾ al-Nafs* [*Healing the Psyche*]. Cairo: Dar al-Maʿarif.

Murillo, Fernando M. 2018. *A Lacanian Theory of Curriculum in Higher Education: The Unfinished Symptom*. Basingstoke: Palgrave Macmillan.

Nandy, Ashis. 1995. *The Savage Freud and Other Essays on Possible and Retrievable Selves*. Princeton: Princeton University Press.

Narly, Constantin. 1933. *Patru mari educatori: John Locke, Vasile Conta, Sigmund Freud, Georg Kerschensteiner*. Bucharest: Cultura Românească.

Neill, Alexander S. 1960. *Summerhill: A Radical Approach to Child Rearing*. New York: Hart.

Neill, Alexander S. 1993. *Summerhill School: A New View of Childhood*. Ed. Albert Lamb. New York: St. Martin's.

Nietzsche, Friedrich. 1983. "Nietzsche's Lecture Notes on Rhetoric: a Translation." Tr. Carole Blair. *Philosophy and Rhetoric* 16.2: 94–129.

Ngai, Sianne. 2005. *Ugly Feelings*. Cambridge: Harvard University Press.

Norwich, Brahm. 2013. Review of *Disavowed Knowledge: Psychoanalysis, Education and Teaching*, by Peter M. Taubman. *History of Education* 42.5: 680–84.

Obama, Barack. 2014. "Remarks by the President on Opportunity for All and Skills for America's Workers." Office of the Press Secretary, The White House. January 30, 2014. https://obamawhitehouse.archives.gov/the-press-office/2014/01/30/remarks-president-opportunity-all-and-skills-americas-workers.

Oliveira, C. Lucia M. Valladares de. 2012. "Psychoanalysis in Brazil during Vargas' Time." In *Psychoanalysis and Politics: Histories of Psychoanalysis under Conditions of Restricted Political Freedom*. Ed. Joy Damousi and Mariano Ben Plotkin. Oxford: Oxford University Press, 113–34.

Orfanos, Spyros D. 2013. "Birth of the Committee on Humanities and Psychoanalysis." *Division Review* 7: 46.

Pandolfo, Stefania. 2018. *Knot of the Soul: Madness, Psychoanalysis, Islam*. Chicago: University of Chicago Press.

Paris, Joel. 2005. *The Fall of an Icon: Psychoanalysis and Academic Psychiatry*. Toronto: University of Toronto Press.

Park, Dorothy G. 1931. "Freudian Influence on Academic Psychology." *Psychological Review* 38.1: 73–85

Park, Sandra W., and Elizabeth L. Auchincloss. 2006. "Psychoanalysis in Textbooks of Introductory Psychology: A Review." *JAPA* 54.4: 1361–80.

Paul, Robert A. 2007. "On 'The Optimal Structure for Psychoanalytic Education': Commentary on Wallerstein." *JAPA* 55.3: 991–97.

Penley, Constance. 1989. *The Future of an Illusion: Film, Feminism, and Psychoanalysis*. Minneapolis: University of Minnesota Press.

Petrin, Iulia. 2018. "Psychoanalyse in Constantin Narlys Werk *Patru Mari Educatori: John Locke, Vasile Conta, Sigmund Freud, Georg Kerschensteiner*." *Journal of Romanian Literary Studies* 15: 550–60.

Petrina, Stephen. 2004. "Luella Cole, Sidney Pressey, and Educational Psychoanalysis, 1921–1931." *History of Education Quarterly* 44.4: 524–53.

Petry, Paulo Padillo, and Fernando Hernández Hernández. 2010. "Jacques Lacan's Conception of Desire in a Course on Psychology of Art for Fine Arts Students." *Visual Arts Research* 36.2: 63–74.

Pfister, Oskar. 1915. *The Psychoanalytic Method [Die psychoanalytische Methode,* 1913]. Tr. Charles Rockwell Payne. London: Kegan Paul, Trench, Trubner and Company.

Pfister, Oskar. 1917. *Was bietet die Psychanalyse dem Erzieher?* Leipzig: Julius Klinkhardt. Reissued in 1929 as *Die Psychoanalyse im Dienste der Erziehung [Psycho-Analysis in the Service of Education].* Leipzig: Klinkhardt.

Pfister, Oskar. 1921. *Die Behandlung schwer erziehbarer und abnormer Kinder.* Bern: E. Bircher.

Pfister, Oskar. 1922. *Psycho-Analysis in the Service of Education, Being an Introduction to Psycho-Analysis.* Tr. Charles Rockwell Payne, F. Gschwind, and Barbara Low. London: Henry Kimpton.

Phillips, Adam. 1996. *Terrors and Experts.* Cambridge: Harvard University Press.

Phillips, Adam. 1998. *The Beast in the Nursery: On Curiosity and Other Thoughts.* New York: Pantheon.

Phillips, Adam. 2004. "Psychoanalysis as Education." *Psychoanalytic Review* 91.6: 779–99.

Plotkin, Mariano Ben. 2001. *Freud in the Pampas: The Emergence and Development of a Psychoanalytic Culture in Argentina.* Stanford: Stanford University Press.

Plotkin, Mariano Ben. 2022. "Freud and Latin America: An Early Relationship." *Transatlantic Cultures.* 15 April 2022.www.transatlantic-cultures.org, accessed 9 December 2023.

Powell, Dionne R. 2018. "Race, African Americans, and Psychoanalysis: Collective Silence in the Therapeutic Conversation." *JAPA* 66: 1021–49.

Pyle, Derek. 2015. "Undergraduate Psychoanalytic Studies at Hampshire College." *American Psychoanalyst* 49.4: 17–18.

Rada, Michelle. 2022. "Overdetermined: Psychoanalysis and Solidarity." *Differences* 33.2/3: 1–32.

Rank, Otto. 1932. *Modern Education: A Critique of Its Fundamental Ideas.* Tr. Mabel E. Moxon. New York: Alfred A. Knopf.

Rank, Otto, and Hanns Sachs. 1916. "The Significance of Psychoanalysis for the Mental Sciences." *Tr. Charles R. Payne. The Psychoanalytic Review* 3: 318–35.

Readings, Bill. 1997. *The University in Ruins.* Cambridge: Harvard University Press.

Redmond, Jonathan and Michael Shulman. 2008. "Access to Psychoanalytic Ideas in American Undergraduate Institutions." *JAPA* 56.2: 391–408.

Reisz, Matthew. 2008. "Off the Couch, Back on Its Feet." *Times Higher Education Supplement* 1849: 37–39.

Richards, Arnold D. 2016. "The Left and Far Left in American Psychoanalysis: Psychoanalysis as a Subversive Discipline." *Contemporary Psychoanalysis* 52.1: 111–29.

Rieff, Philip. 1959. *Freud: The Mind of the Moralist.* Chicago: University of Chicago Press.

Riker, John, Marcia Dobson, and Alexandra Wong-Appel. 2018. "Psychoanalysis and Undergraduate Education." *The American Psychoanalyst* 52.3: 27–28.

Rizzuto, Ana-María. 2003. "Psychoanalysis: The Transformation of the Subject by the Spoken Word." *Psychoanalytic Quarterly* 72.2: 287–323.

Robcis, Camille. 2013. "Fatherless Societies and Anti-Oedipal Philosophies." In *The Law of Kinship: Anthropology, Psychoanalysis, and the Family in France.* Ithaca: Cornell University Press, 168–210.

Robins, Richard W., Samuel D. Gosling, and Kenneth H. Craik. 1999. "An Empirical Analysis of Trends in Psychology." *American Psychologist* 54.2: 117–28.

Rosenberg, Brian. 2023. *"Whatever It Is, I'm Against It": Resistance to Change in Higher Education.* Cambridge: Harvard Education Press.

Roudinesco, Elisabeth. 1994. *Histoire de la psychanalyse en France, 2: 1925–1985.* Paris: Fayard.

Roudinesco, Elisabeth. 2001. *Why Psychoanalysis?* [1999]. Tr. Rachel Bowlby. New York: Columbia University Press.

Rousselle, Duane. 2022. "Psychoanalysis in India? Duane Rousselle Interviews Arka Chattopadhyay." *European Journal of Psychoanalysis* 9.2, online.

Rudberg, Monica. 1996. "The Researching Body: The Epistemophilic Project." *European Journal of Women's Studies* 3: 285–305.

Ruddick, Lisa. 2022. "Beyond the Fragmented Subject." In *The Cambridge Companion to Literature and Psychoanalysis.* Ed. Vera J. Camden. Cambridge: Cambridge University Press, 256–74.

Ruggieri, Davide. 2012. "Ein unveröffentlichter Brief von Max Horkheimer an Sigmund Freud." *Soziologie* 41.3: 289–94.

Ruitenberg, Claudia W. 2021. Review of Stella Gaon, *The Lucid Vigil: Deconstruction, Desire and the Politics of Critique. Philosophical Inquiry in Education* 28.1: 59–65.

Russo, Jane. 2007. "Psychoanalysis in Brazil—Institutionalization and Dissemination among the Lay Public." *Estudios Interdisciplinarios de América Latina y el Caribe* 18.1: 63–80.

Rustin, Michael. 2018. "Epistemic Anxiety." In *The Oxford Handbook of Philosophy and Psychoanalysis.* Ed. Richard Gipps and Michael Lacewing. Oxford: Oxford University Press, 687–708.

Saketopoulou, Avgi. 2011. "Minding the Gap: Intersections Between Gender, Race, and Class in Work with Gender Variant Children." *Psychoanalytic Dialogues* 21: 192–209.

Saketopoulou, Avgi. 2014. "Trauma Lives Us: Affective Excess, Safe Spaces and the Erasure of Subjectivity." *Bully Bloggers* (December 6, 2014), https://bullybloggers.wordpress.com/2014/12/06/trauma-lives-us-affective-excess-safe-spaces-and-the-erasure-of-subjectivity/.

Salam, Abdul, Amala Shankera, and Malika Verma. 2022. "Psychoanalysis in India: A Story of Ascent, Decline and Revival." *Psychoanalytic Psychotherapy* 36.4: 300–11.

Salvio, Paula M. 1999. "Reading Beyond Narratives of Cure in Curriculum Studies: Introductory Notes." *Journal of Curriculum Theorizing* 15.2: 185–88.

Salzberger-Wittenberg, Isca. 1993. "Learning to Understand the Nature of Relationships." In *The Emotional Experience of Learning and Teaching.* Ed. Isca Salzberger-Wittenberg, Osborne, Elsie, and Gianna Williams. London: Routledge, 21–77.

Samuels, Robert. 2020. "(Liberal) Narcissism." In *Routledge Handbook of Psychoanalytic Political Theory.* Ed. Yannis Stavrakakis. New York: Routledge, 151–61.

Santner, Eric L. 1999. "Psychoanalysis and the Enigmas of Sovereignty." *Qui Parle* 11.2: 1–19.

Santner, Eric L. 2001. *On the Psychotheology of Everyday Life: Reflections on Freud and Rosenzweig.* Chicago: University of Chicago Press.

Santner, Eric L. 2005. "Miracles Happen: Benjamin, Rosenzweig, Freud, and the Matter of the Neighbor. In Slavoj Zizek, Eric L. Santner, and Kenneth Reinhard. *The Neighbor: Three Inquiries in Political Theology.* Chicago: University of Chicago Press, 76–133.

Sarton, May. 1961. *The Small Room.* New York: W. W. Norton.

Scarfone, Dominique. 1997. *Jean Laplanche.* Paris: Presses Universitaires de France.

Schmidt, Erika S. 2018. "Educating Psychoanalysts for the Future of Psychoanalysis." In *Progress in Psychoanalysis: Envisioning the Future of the Profession.* Ed. Steven D. Axelrod, Ronald C. Naso, and Larry M. Rosenberg. London: Routledge, 181–98.

Schmidt, Vera. 1924. *Psychoanalytische Erziehung in Sowjetrussland: Bericht über das Kinderheim-Laboratorium in Moskau.* Leipzig: Internationaler Psychoanalytischer Verlag.

Schoonheten, Anna Bentinck van. 2016. *Karl Abraham: Life and Work, a Biography* [*Karl Abraham: Freuds rots in de branding,* 2013]. Tr. Liz Waters. London: Karnac.

Schowalter, John E. 2000. "Aichhorn Revisited." *Psychoanalytic Study of the Child* 55.1: 49–60.

Schwartz, Murray M. 2018. "Psychoanalysis in My Life: An Intellectual Memoir." *American Imago* 75.2: 125–52.

Scott, Joan Wallach. 2005. "Against Eclecticism." *differences: A Journal of Feminist Cultural Studies* 16.3: 114–37.

Seligman, Guy, dir. 1975. *Vivre à Bonneuil.* Institut National Audiovisual of France.

Shakry, Omnia El. 2017. *The Arabic Freud: Psychoanalysis and Islam in Modern Egypt.* Princeton: Princeton University Press.

Shakry, Omnia El. 2018a. "How Midcentury Arab Thinkers Embraced the Ideas of Freud." *Aeon* (22 January 2018), https://aeon.co/ideas/how-midcentury-arab-thinkers-embraced-the-ideas-of-freud, accessed 9 December 2023.

Shakry, Omnia El. 2018b. "Psychoanalysis and the Imaginary: Translating Freud in Postcolonial Egypt." *Psychoanalysis and History* 20.3: 313–35.

Sheehi, Lara, and Stephen Sheehi. 2022. *Psychoanalysis Under Occupation: Practicing Resistance in Palestine.* New York: Routledge.

Sheils, Merrill. 1975. "Why Johnny Can't Write." *Newsweek* 92 (December 8, 1975): 58–63.

Shulman, James L. 2023. *The Synthetic University: How Higher Education Can Benefit from Shared Solutions and Save Itself.* Princeton: Princeton University Press.

Shumway, David R., and Ellen Messer-Davidow. 1991. "Disciplinarity: An Introduction." *Poetics Today* 12.2: 201–25.

Simmons, Marlon. 2023. "Frantz Fanon and Education." In *Oxford Research Encyclopedia of Education.* Ed. George Noblit. 22 February 2023, Accessed 11 March 2024. https://oxfordre-com.proxy.library.upenn.edu/education/view/10.1093/acrefore/9780190264093.001.0001/acrefore-9780190264093-e-1770.

Snyder, Thomas D., ed. 1993. *120 Years of American Education: A Statistical Portrait.* Washington DC: Center for Education Statistics.

Sokolowsky, Laura. 2022. *Psychoanalysis under Nazi Occupation: The Origins, Impact and Influence of the Berlin Institute* [2013]. Tr. Janet Haney and John Haney. London: Routledge.

Solms, Mark. 2024. *The Revised Standard Edition of the Complete Psychological Works of Sigmund Freud.* Lanham: Rowman and Littlefield.

Sonnenberg, Stephen M. 2011. "Psychoanalysis and the United States Research University: Current Trends." *International Journal of Psychoanalysis* 92: 641–59.

Spitz, Ellen Handler. 2018. "Psychoanalysis and the Academy: Reflections on Undergraduate Teaching." *International Forum of Psychoanalysis* 27.2: 82–89.

Spivak, Gayatri Chakravorty. 2004. "Righting Wrongs." *South Atlantic Quarterly* 103.2/3: 523–81.

Srinivasan, Amia. "Sex as a Pedagogical Failure." *Yale Law Journal* 129: 1100–46.

Stamm, Karen, Meron Assefa, and Cory Page. 2023. "Will growth in psychology degrees continue?" *Monitor on Psychology* 54.8: 23.

Stein, Alexander. 2020. "Psychoanalysis in the Public Sphere: A Call for Taking Analytic Thinking, Writing and Action into the Broader World." *Psychoanalytic Perspectives* 17: 141–60.

Stepansky, Paul E. 2009. *Psychoanalysis at the Margins.* New York: Other Press.

Sterba, Editha. 1945. "Interpretation and Education." Psychoanalytic Study of the Child 1.1: 309–17.

Stern, Donnel. 2003. *Unformulated Experience: From Dissociation to Imagination in Psychoanalysis* [1997]. New York: Psychology Press.

Stock, Nick. 2023. "My Teaching. Lacanian Reflections from the Classroom." *New Associations* 40: 10.

Stolorow, Robert D. 2013. "Intersubjective-Systems Theory: A Phenomenological-Contextualist Psychoanalytic Perspective." *Psychoanalytic Dialogues* 23: 383–89.

Stone, Marc B., Zimri S. Yaseen, Brian J Miller, Kyle Richardville, Shamir N Kalaria, and Irving Kirsch. 2022. "Response to Acute Monotherapy for Major Depressive Disorder in Randomized, Placebo Controlled Trials Submitted to the US Food and Drug Administration: Individual Participant Data Analysis." *British Medical Journal* 378: e067606.

Strenger, Carlo. 2015. "Can Psychoanalysis Reclaim the Public Sphere?" *Psychoanalytic Psychology* 32.2: 293–306.

Suchet, Melanie. 2004. "A Relational Encounter with Race." *Psychoanalytic Dialogues* 14: 423–38.

Szapor, Judith. 2005. *The Hungarian Pocahontas: The Life and Times of Laura Polanyi Stricker, 1882–1959*. Boulder: East European Monographs.

Szokolszky, Ágnes. 2016. "Hungarian psychology in context. Reclaiming the past." *Hungarian Studies* 30.1: 17–56.

Tasso, Anthony F., Kevin Barrett, and Bindu Methikalam. 2022. "Who Will Teach Psychodynamics in the Future? A 10-Year Follow-Up." *The American Psychoanalyst* 56.1: 28–29.

Taubman, Peter M. 2012. *Disavowed Knowledge: Psychoanalysis, Education, and Teaching*. New York: Routledge.

Thomä, Helmut. 2004. "Psychoanalysts without a Specific Professional Identity: A Utopian Dream?" *International Forum of Psychoanalysis* 13: 213–36.

Thompson, Nellie L. 2023. "Émigré Analysts and the Transformation of Psychoanalysis in America." In *The Émigré Analysts and American Psychoanalysis: History and Contemporary Relevance*. Ed. Adrienne E. Harris. London: Routledge, 9–25.

Thornton, Clare. 2018. "Students walk out of anthropology lecture after professor uses the word 'n****r.'" *The Daily Princetonian* (February 7, 2018). https://www.dailyprincetonian.com/article/2018/02/students-walk-out-of-anthropology-lecture-after-professor-uses-the-word-nr.

Todd, Sharon. 2003. *Learning from the Other: Levinas, Psychoanalysis, and Ethical Possibilities in Education*. Albany: State University of New York Press.

Tuckett, David, ed. 2008. *Psychoanalysis Comparable and Incomparable: The Evolution of a Method to Describe and Compare Psychoanalytic Approaches*. London: Routledge.

Turkle, Sherry. 1978. *Psychoanalytic Politics: Jacques Lacan and Freud's French Revolution*. New York: Basic Books.

Tyler, Louise L. 1958. "Psychoanalysis and Curriculum Theory." *School Review* 66.4: 446–60.

Utley, Philip Lee. 1979. "Radical Youth: Generational Conflict in the Anfang Movement, 1912–January 1914." *History of Education Quarterly* 19.2: 207–28.

Vanier, Catherine, and Kareen Malone. 2017. "The Experimental School in Bonneuil-sur-Marne…with Commentary from a North American Context." *Frontiers in Psychology* 8: 1–7.

Viswanathan, Vidya B. 2007. "Courses Discount Freud's Theories." *Harvard Crimson* (30 November 2007), online.

Wallerstein. Robert S. 1998. *Lay Analysis: Life Inside the Controversy*. Hillsdale: Analytic Press.

Wallerstein, Robert S. 2007a. "The Optimal Structure for Psychoanalytic Education Today: A Feasible Proposal?" *JAPA* 55.3: 953–84.

Wallerstein, Robert S. 2007b. "A Shared Vision: Response To Commentaries." *JAPA* 55.3: 999–1005.

Wallerstein. Robert S. 2009. "Psychoanalysis in the University: A Full-Time Vision." *International Journal of Psychoanalysis* 90: 1107–21.

Wallin, Jason J. 2010. *A Deleuzian Approach to Curriculum: Essays on a Pedagogical Life*. New York: Palgrave Macmillan.

Watson, Goodwin. 1957. "Psychoanalysis and the Future of Education." *Teachers College Record* 58.5: 241–47.

Weinstein, Fred. 1990. *History and Theory After the Fall: An Essay on Interpretation*. Chicago: University of Chicago Press.

Willock, Brent. 2007. *Comparative-Integrative Psychoanalysis: A Relational Perspective for the Discipline's Second Century*. New York: Routledge.

Winnicott, D. W. 1949. "Hate in the Counter-Transference." *International Journal of Psycho-Analysis* 30: 69–74.

Winnicott, D. W. 1971. *Playing and Reality*. London: Tavistock.

Winograd, Basia, dir. 2014. *Black Psychoanalysts Speak*. PEP Video Grants.

Winograd, Basia, dir. 2016. *Psychoanalysis in El Barrio*. PEP Video Grants.

Winter, Sarah. 1999. *Freud and the Institution of Psychoanalytic Knowledge*. Stanford: Stanford University Press.

Wittels, Fritz. 1932. *Set the Children Free!* [*Die Befreiung des Kindes,* 1927]. Tr. Eden and Cedar Paul. New York: W. W. Norton.

Wołowicz, Leopold. 1914. *Jeden z problematów psychoanalizy Freuda*. Stryj: Drukarnia Augusta Olbricha.

Wordsworth, William. 1981. *The Poems, Volume One*. Ed. John O. Hayden. New Haven: Yale University Press.

Wurmser, Léon. 2006. "On Empiricism and Psychoanalysis." *JAPA* 57.1: 229–36.

Yates, Candida. 2022. "The Tensions of Teaching Psychoanalysis in the Neoliberal University." *New Associations* 38: 5.

Young-Bruehl, Elisabeth. 2008. *Anna Freud: A Biography* [1988]. 2d ed. New Haven: Yale University Press.

Zweig, Stefan. 1994. *Die Welt von Gestern: Erinnerungen eines Europäers* [1942]. Frankfurt: S. Fischer.

Zachry, Caroline. 1929. "Personality Adjustment and the School." *Personality Adjustments of School Children*. New York: Charles Scribner's Sons, 250–304.

Zaretsky, Eli. 2004. *Secrets of the Soul: A Social and Cultural History of Psychoanalysis*. New York: Knopf.

Zeavin, Hannah. 2023. "The Old Man's Back Again: What Should We Make of the Return of Sigmund Freud?" *Chronicle of Higher Education*, 26 September 2023, online only, https://www.chronicle.com/article/the-old-mans-back-again.

Zulliger, Hans. 1921. *Psychanalytische Erfahrungen aus der Volksschulpraxis*. Bern: Ernst Bircher.

Zulliger, Hans. 1940. "Psychoanalytic Experiences in Public School Practice." Part 1. Tr. Gladys V. Swackhamer. *American Journal of Orthopsychiatry* 10.3: 356–70.

Zulliger, Hans 1941. "Psychoanalytic Experiences in Public School Practice." Part 2. Tr. Gladys V. Swackhamer. *American Journal of Orthopsychiatry* 11.1: 157–71.

Zulliger, Hans. 2018. "Psychanalyse et leadership à l'école [1929]." Tr. Dominique Gelin. *Cliopsy* 1.19: 71–80.

Index

For Product Safety Concerns and Information please contact our EU
representative GPSR@taylorandfrancis.com
Taylor & Francis Verlag GmbH, Kaufingerstraße 24, 80331 München, Germany

www.ingramcontent.com/pod-product-compliance
Lightning Source LLC
Chambersburg PA
CBHW070329270326
41926CB00017B/3813